W9-BZR-673

Constructing
Grounded Theory

Constructing Grounded Theory

A Practical Guide Through Qualitative Analysis

Kathy Charmaz

Los Angeles | London | New Delhi
Singapore | Washington DC

First published 2006

Reprinted 2010 (twice)

SAGE Publications Ltd
1 Oliver's Yard
55 City Road
London EC1Y 1SP

SAGE Publications Inc.
2455 Teller Road
Thousand Oaks, California 91320

SAGE Publications India Pvt Ltd
B 1/I 1 Mohan Cooperative Industrial Area
Mathura Road, Post Bag 7
New Delhi 110044

SAGE Publications Asia-Pacific Pte Ltd
33 Pekin Street #02-01
Far East Square
Singapore 048763

British Library Cataloguing in Publication data

A catalogue record for this book is available from the British Library

ISBN13 978 0 7619 7352 2
ISBN13 978 0 7619 7353 9 (pbk)

Library of Congress Control Number 2005928035

Typeset by C&M Digitals (P) Ltd., Chennai, India
Printed on paper from sustainable resources
Printed in Great Britain by TJ International Ltd, Padstow, Cornwall

Summary of contents

Contents

Preface

This book takes you through a journey of constructing grounded theory by traversing basic grounded theory steps. The book will provide a path, expand your vistas, quicken your pace, and point out obstacles and opportunities along the way. We can share the journey but the adventure is yours. I will clarify grounded theory strategies and offer guidelines, examples, and suggestions throughout. Although some authors provide methodological maps to follow, I raise questions and outline strategies to indicate possible routes to take. At each phase of the research journey, *your* readings of your work guide your next moves. This combination of involvement and interpretation leads you to the next step. The end-point of your journey emerges from where you start, where you go, and with whom you interact, what you see and hear, and how you learn and think. In short, the finished work is a construction—yours.

Writing about methods can take unpredictable turns. In a recent issue of *Symbolic Interaction*, Howard Becker (2003) recounts why the master ethnographer Erving Goffman avoided writing about his methods. Becker tells us that Goffman believed any methodological advice would go awry and researchers would blame him for the resulting mess. Offering methodological advice invites misunderstanding—and constructive critiques. Unlike Goffman, however, I welcome entering the methodological fray and invite you to join me in it. Possibilities for methodological misunderstandings may abound but also openings for methodological clarifications and advances may occur. Bringing any method beyond a recipe into public purview inevitably invites interpretation and reconstruction—and misunderstandings. Readers and researchers' perspectives, purposes, and practices influence how they will make sense of a method. In the past, researchers have often misunderstood grounded theory methods. Published qualitative researchers add to the confusion when they cite grounded theory as their methodological approach but their work bears little resemblance to it. Numerous researchers have invoked grounded theory as a methodological rationale to justify conducting qualitative research rather than adopting its guidelines to inform their studies.

This book represents my interpretation of grounded theory and contains methodological guidelines, advice, and perspectives. The method has evolved or changed, depending on your perspective, since its originators, Barney G. Glaser and Anselm L. Strauss, set forth their classic statement of grounded theory in 1967. Each has shifted his position on certain points and added others. My version of grounded theory returns to the classic statements of the past century and reexamines them through a methodological lens of the present century. Researchers can use grounded theory methods with either quantitative or qualitative data; however, they have adopted them almost exclusively in qualitative research, which I address here. Throughout the book, I refer to the materials we work with as 'data' rather than as materials or accounts because qualitative research has a place in scientific inquiry in its own right.

In writing this book I aim to fulfil the following objectives: 1) to offer a set of guidelines for constructing grounded theory research informed by methodological developments over the past four decades; 2) to correct some common misunderstandings about grounded theory; 3) to point out different versions of the method and shifts in position within these versions; 4) to provide sufficient explanation of the guidelines that any budding scholar can follow who has a basic knowledge of research methods; and 5) to inspire beginning and seasoned researchers to embark on a grounded theory project. As consistent with the classic grounded theory statements of Glaser and Strauss, I emphasize the analytic aspects of inquiry while recognizing the importance of having a solid foundation in data. For the most part, I have used published data and excerpts so that you can seek the original sources, should you wish to see how excerpted data fit in their respective narratives.

I hope that you find my construction of grounded theory methods helpful for your construction of new grounded theories. These methods provide a valuable set of tools for developing an analytic handle on your work, and taken to their logical extension, a theory of it. Researchers who move their studies into theory construction may find Chapters 5 and 6 to be of particular interest. I realize, however, that sometimes our research objectives and audiences do not always include explicit theory construction, but providing a useful analytic framework makes a significant contribution. Grounded theory methods foster creating an analytic edge to your work. Evidence abounds that these methods can inform compelling description and telling tales. Whether you pursue ethnographic stories, biographical narratives, or qualitative analyses of interviews, grounded theory methods can help you make your work more insightful and incisive.

A long evolution precedes my traversing the grounds of this book. My ideas arose from two separate sources: an early immersion in epistemological developments in the 1960s and an innovative doctoral program that ignited my imagination. As for many graduate students of the day, Thomas Kuhn's *The Structure of Scientific Revolutions* has had a lasting effect on me, but so did the theoretical physicists who challenged conventional notions of scientific objectivity, reasoning, and truth.

As a member of the first cohort of doctoral students in sociology at the University of California, San Francisco, I had the privilege of learning grounded theory from Barney Glaser in multiple graduate seminars. Each student had a class session when all members analyzed his or her material in a free-wheeling discussion. The seminars sparkled with excitement and enthusiasm. Barney's brilliance shone as he led us away from describing our material and into conceptualizing it in analytic frameworks. I am grateful for having had the opportunity to study with him. Anselm Strauss, my dissertation chair, kept tabs on my work from the day of our first meeting until his death in 1996. He and Barney shared a commitment to raising new generations of scholars to become productive grounded theorists. When I gave Anselm a piece of writing—often just a fragment—in the morning, he would call me by evening to talk about it. Although Anselm would disagree with several points in this book, I hope that much of it might have caught his interest and have elicited the familiar chuckle that so many generations of students cherished.

A book may have long antecedents that precede its writing. My journey with grounded theory began with Barney Glaser and Anselm Strauss, whose lasting influence has not only permeated my work, but also my consciousness. So, too, in less transparent ways, my rendering of grounded theory contains lessons learned during my doctoral studies from Fred Davis, Virginia Olesen, and Leonard Schatzman about the quality of data collection and scholarship. Since then, I have developed the ideas in this book. Varied requests to articulate my version of grounded theory have enlarged my vision of it. Although none of the following people were involved in this project, responding to their earlier requests helped me to clarify my position and advance my understanding of grounded theory. I thank Paul Atkinson, Alan Bryman, Amarda Coffey, Tom Cooke, Robert Emerson, Sara Delamont, Norm Denzin, Uta Gerhardt, Jaber Gubrium, James Holstein, Yvonna Lincoln, John Lofland, Lyn Lofland, and Jonathan A. Smith.

This book could not have evolved without the support and encouragement of my editor at Sage, Patrick Brindle, and the series editor, David Silverman. I thank David Silverman for inviting me to join this series and appreciate his faith that the book would materialize. Special thanks are due to Patrick Brindle for his efforts to make it possible. I am grateful to Patrick Brindle, Antony Bryant, Adele Clarke, Virginia Olesen, and David Silverman for their astute readings of the manuscript and wonderful comments on it. Jane Hood, Devon Lanin, and Kristine Snyder each read and made useful comments on a chapter. Several times, I discussed chapters with members of the Faculty Writing Program at Sonoma State University and always enjoyed our conversations. Anita Catlin, Dolly Freidel, Jeanette Koshar, Melinda Milligan, Myrna Goodman, and Craig Winston raised sound questions. In addition to participating in stimulating discussions, Julia Allen, Noel Byrne, Diana Grant, Mary Halavais, Kim Hester-Williams, Matt James, Michelle Jolly, Scott Miller, Tom Rosen, Richard Senghas, and Thaine Stearns also wrote insightful commentaries on chapters in various stages of development. My conversations about grounded theory with Kath Melia in the early stages of the project were always stimulating.

On a more technical level, Leslie Hartman managed several nagging clerical tasks with skill and enthusiasm and Claire Reeve and Vanessa Harwood at Sage kept me apprised of details. No book comes to fruition without time to think and write. A sabbatical leave from Sonoma State University during Spring, 2004 greatly expedited my writing. Throughout the book, I draw on some excerpted or adapted material from my past publications on grounded theory with Sage Publications and I thank Patrick Brindle for permission to reprint.

Acknowledgements

The author and publisher thank the following organizations and publishers for granting permission to reproduce:

The American Occupational Therapy Foundation for excerpts from the article The self as habit: The reconstruction of self in chronic illness by Charmaz, K. (2002).

Blackwell Publishing for excerpts from Charmaz, K. (1995). The body, identity and self, *The Sociological Quarterly* 36: 657–680.

Rutgers University Press for excerpts from Charmaz, K. (1991). *Good days, bad days: The self in chronic illness and time.*

Springer Science and Business Media for an excerpt from Lempert, L.B. (1997) The other side of help: Negative effects in the help-seeking processes of abused women, *Qualitative Research*, 20, 289–309.

The Society for the Study of Symbolic Interaction, University of California Press for two figures (5.1 and 5.2) from Adele E. Clarke (2003). Situational analyses: Grounded theory mapping after the postmodern turn, *Symbolic Interaction*, 26 (4): 553–576.

1 An Invitation to Grounded Theory

A journey begins before the travellers depart. So, too, our grounded theory adventure begins as we seek information about what a grounded theory journey entails and what to expect along the way. We scope the terrain that grounded theory covers and that we expect to traverse. Before leaving we look back into the history of grounded theory in the twentieth century and look forward into its yet unrealized potential for the twenty-first century. Our last step before embarking is to lay out a map of the method and of this book.

In this book, I invite you to join a journey through a qualitative research project. You might ask, what does the journey entail? Where do I start? How do I proceed? Which obstacles might lie ahead? This book takes a short trip through data collection then follows a lengthy trail through analysis of qualitative data. Along the way, numerous guides ease your way through the analytic and writing processes. Throughout the journey we will climb up analytic levels and raise the theoretical import of your ideas while we keep a taut rope tied to your data on solid ground.

What might a path between collecting and analyzing data look like? For a moment, pretend that you have begun conducting interviews for a new research project exploring the sudden onset of a serious chronic illness. Imagine meeting Margie Arlen during her senior year in high school. Margie tells you about her troubles that accompanied a rapid onset of rheumatoid arthritis. You piece together the following sequence of events from her story:

At age 14, Margie was a star student and athlete. She was clearly slated for success in college and beyond. Her teachers saw the makings of a scholar, her coaches marveled at her athletic prowess, and her peers viewed her as in a class beyond them. Then her health rapidly deteriorated from arthritis. In a few months, she went from being lightning on the soccer field to hardly walking. The awe that other students had accorded her shifted to distance and disdain. Once, her talents and skills had set her apart from the crowd that clamored around her. Then her neck brace and belabored movements kept her apart as fellow students silently shunned her. Still, Margie learned deeper lessons. She said:

> It's [her illness and disability] taught me that the important things—like, I used to be real introverted and scared to talk with other people in a way. But now it's like I feel I can take my talents, not the sports and things like that, but I can take my talents and I go out and talk to people and become their friend, like, encouraging people and things like that, and I found that that's, like, more important and that builds more self-esteem, just being able to do things for other people, like serving missions and things like that, than, you know, being able to go out and prove that you are a good athlete. So it's changed me in that I'm a lot more outgoing now, and it's changed me in that I've realized more what's important.

Then, like her interviewer, you gently inquired, 'So what's important?' to which Margie replied,

> I think in a lot of ways it's instead of making myself look good, it's making others look good. I was always a perfectionist, and I wanted to do things fast. If I said I was going to do something, I was going to do it no matter how late I had to stay up at night … And those type of things take a toll on our body, and when I realized it's okay to say, I'm sorry I can't get this done in time or something, or I just can't do it—say 'no' in the first place—then I think that's important because otherwise you totally run yourself into the ground if you have a chronic disease, and you're going to make yourself worse. So that took a long time to learn. But I think it's really important, like setting your priorities. Concentrating on what's important and then doing that first and then letting go of whatever else. (Charmaz, 2002b: 39s)

Now think about how to study stories like Margie's. How do you make sense of the events that Margie Arlen describes? What might you see in her statements that you would like to explore further with her and others who have experienced physical losses? Imagine that you pursued these questions in a qualitative study and aimed to develop a conceptual analysis of the materials. How would you go about conducting your research and creating the analysis?

Grounded theory methods will help you get started, stay involved, and finish your project. The research process will bring surprises, spark ideas, and hone your analytic skills. Grounded theory methods foster seeing your data in fresh ways and exploring your ideas about the data through early analytic writing. By adopting grounded theory methods you can direct, manage, and streamline your data collection and, moreover, construct an original analysis of your data.

What are grounded theory methods? Stated simply, grounded theory methods consist of systematic, yet flexible guidelines for collecting and analyzing qualitative data to construct theories 'grounded' in the data themselves. The guidelines offer a set of general principles and heuristic devices rather than formulaic rules (see also Atkinson, Coffey, & Delamont, 2003). Thus, data form the foundation of our theory and our analysis of these data generates the concepts we construct. Grounded theorists collect data to develop theoretical analyses from the beginning of a project. We try to learn what occurs in the research settings we join and what our research participants' lives are like. We study how they explain their statements and actions, and ask what analytic sense we can make of them.

We begin by being open to what is happening in the studied scenes and interview statements so that we might learn about our research participants' lives. We would attend to what we hear, see, and sense during Margie Arlen's interview. Grounded theorists start with data. We construct these data through our observations, interactions, and materials that we gather about the topic or setting. We study empirical events and experiences and pursue our hunches and potential analytic ideas about them. Most qualitative methods allow researchers to follow up on interesting data in whatever way they devise. Grounded theory methods have the additional advantage of containing explicit guidelines that show us *how* we may proceed.

Margie Arlen's intriguing remarks about learning to attend to other people and to limit her activities could serve as starting points for analysis as well as for further data collection. In subsequent interviews, we would listen to the stories of other young people who have suffered recent physical losses and explore how they handled their changed lives. If possible, we would add ethnographic data by joining our research participants while at school, physical therapy, a support group, or just hanging out with friends. How do young people respond to serious illness and disability? What contributes to their different responses? We raise questions that emanate from thinking about our collected data and shape those data we wish to obtain.

As grounded theorists, we study our early data and begin to separate, sort, and synthesize these data through qualitative coding. Coding means that we attach labels to segments of data that depict what each segment is about. Coding distills data, sorts them, and gives us a handle for making comparisons with other segments of data. Grounded theorists emphasize what is happening in the scene when they code data.

Several initial codes stood out to me in Margie's interview: 'being changed,' 'concentrating on what's important,' and 'learning limits.' Such codes and our ideas about them point to areas to explore during subsequent data collection. We would compare the events and views that Margie talks about—and our codes with the next person we talk with, and the next person, and the next.

By making and coding numerous comparisons, our analytic grasp of the data begins to take form. We write preliminary analytic notes called memos about our codes and comparisons and any other ideas about our data that occur to us. Through studying data, comparing them, and writing memos, we define ideas that best fit and interpret the data as tentative analytic categories. When inevitable questions arise and gaps in our categories appear, we seek data that answer these questions and may fill the gaps. We may return to Margie and other research participants to learn more and to strengthen our analytic categories. As we proceed, our categories not only coalesce as we interpret the collected data but also the categories become more theoretical because we engage in successive levels of analysis.

Our analytic categories and the relationships we draw between them provide a conceptual handle on the studied experience. Thus, we build levels of abstraction directly from the data and, subsequently, gather additional data to check and refine our emerging analytic categories. Our work culminates in a 'grounded theory,' or an abstract theoretical understanding of the studied experience. Margie's remarks may start us on a research journey; doing comparative analysis and developing our categories advances our progress. In short, grounded theory methods demystify the conduct of qualitative inquiry—and expedite your research and enhance your excitement about it.

Emergence of Grounded Theory

The Historical Context

Grounded theory methods emerged from sociologists Barney G. Glaser and Anselm L. Strauss's (1965, 1967) successful collaboration during their studies of dying in hospitals (see Glaser & Strauss, 1965, 1968; Strauss & Glaser, 1970). In the early 1960s in the United States, hospital staff seldom talked about or even acknowledged dying and death with seriously ill patients. Glaser and Strauss's research team observed how dying occurred in a variety of hospital settings; they looked at how and when professionals and their terminal patients knew they were dying and how they handled the news. Glaser and Strauss gave their data explicit analytic treatment and produced theoretical analyses of the social organization and temporal order of dying. They explored analytic ideas in long conversations and exchanged preliminary notes analyzing observations in the field. As they constructed their analyses of dying, they developed systematic methodological strategies that social scientists could adopt for studying many other topics. Glaser and Strauss's book *The Discovery of Grounded Theory* (1967) first articulated these strategies and advocated *developing* theories from research grounded in data rather than *deducing* testable hypotheses from existing theories.

Glaser and Strauss entered the methodological scene at a propitious time. Qualitative research in sociology was losing ground. By the mid-1960s, the long tradition of qualitative research in sociology had waned as sophisticated quantitative methods gained dominance in the United States and quantitative methodologists reigned over departments, journal editorial boards, and funding agencies. Despite the awe accorded to a few qualitative stars, the presence of several strong qualitative doctoral programs, and sharp critiques of quantification from critical theorists, the discipline marched toward defining research in quantitative terms.

What kinds of methodological assumptions supported the move toward quantification? Every way of knowing rests on a theory of how people develop knowledge. Beliefs in a unitary method of systematic observation, replicable experiments, operational definitions of concepts, logically deduced hypotheses, and confirmed evidence—often taken as *the* scientific method—formed the assumptions upholding quantitative methods. These assumptions supported positivism, the dominant paradigm of inquiry in routine natural science.

Mid-century positivist conceptions of scientific method and knowledge stressed objectivity, generality, replication of research, and falsification of competing hypotheses and theories. Social researchers who adopted the positivist paradigm aimed to discover causal explanations and to make predictions about an external, knowable world. Their beliefs in scientific logic, a unitary method, objectivity, and truth legitimized reducing qualities of human experience to quantifiable variables. Thus, positivist methods assumed an unbiased and passive observer who collected facts but did not participate in creating them, the separation of facts from values, the existence of an external world separate from scientific observers and their methods, and the accumulation of generalizable knowledge about this world. Positivism led to a quest for valid instruments, technical procedures, replicable research designs, and verifiable quantitative knowledge.

Only narrowly scientific—that is, quantitative—ways of knowing held validity for positivists; they rejected other possible ways of knowing, such as through interpreting meanings or intuitive realizations. Thus, qualitative research that analyzed and interpreted research participants' meanings sparked disputes about its scientific value. Quantitative researchers of the 1960s saw qualitative research as impressionistic, anecdotal, unsystematic, and biased. The priority they gave to replication and verification resulted in ignoring human problems and research questions that did not fit positivistic research designs. If proponents of quantification acknowledged qualitative research at all, they treated it as a preliminary exercise for refining quantitative instruments. Thus, some quantitative researchers used interviews or observations to help them design more precise surveys or more effective experiments.

As positivism gained strength in mid-century, the division between theory and research simultaneously grew. Growing numbers of quantitative researchers concentrated on obtaining concrete information. Those quantitative researchers who connected theory and research tested logically deduced hypotheses from an existing theory. Although they refined extant theory, their research seldom led to new theory construction.

Glaser and Strauss's Challenge

In *The Discovery of Grounded Theory*, Glaser and Strauss countered the ruling methodological assumptions of mid-century. Their book made a cutting-edge statement because it contested notions of methodological consensus *and* offered systematic strategies for qualitative research practice. Essentially, Glaser and Strauss joined epistemological critique with practical guidelines for action. They proposed that systematic qualitative analysis had its own logic and could generate theory. In particular, Glaser and Strauss intended to construct abstract theoretical explanations of social processes.

For Glaser and Strauss (1967; Glaser, 1978; Strauss, 1987), the defining components of grounded theory practice include:

- Simultaneous involvement in data collection and analysis
- Constructing analytic codes and categories from data, not from preconceived logically deduced hypotheses
- Using the constant comparative method, which involves making comparisons during each stage of the analysis
- Advancing theory development during each step of data collection and analysis

- Memo-writing to elaborate categories, specify their properties, define relationships between categories, and identify gaps
- Sampling aimed toward theory construction, not for population representativeness
- Conducting the literature review *after* developing an independent analysis.

Engaging in these practices helps researchers to control their research process and to increase the analytic power of their work (see also Bigus, Hadden & Glaser, 1994; Charmaz, 1983, 1990, 1995b, 2003; Glaser, 1992, 1994; Glaser & Strauss, 1967; Stern, 1994b; Strauss, 1987; Strauss & Corbin, 1990, 1994). Glaser and Strauss aimed to move qualitative inquiry beyond descriptive studies into the realm of explanatory theoretical frameworks, thereby providing abstract, conceptual understandings of the studied phenomena. They urged novice grounded theorists to develop fresh theories and thus advocated delaying the literature review to avoid seeing the world through the lens of extant ideas. Glaser and Strauss's theorizing contrasted with armchair and logico-deductive theorizing because they began with data and systematically raised the conceptual level of their analyses while maintaining the strong foundation in data. Consistent with their reasoning, a completed grounded theory met the following criteria: a close fit with the data, usefulness, conceptual density, durability over time, modifiability, and explanatory power (Glaser, 1978, 1992; Glaser & Strauss, 1967).

The Discovery of Grounded Theory (1967) provided a powerful argument that legitimized qualitative research as a credible methodological approach in its own right rather than simply as a precursor for developing quantitative instruments. In the book, Glaser and Strauss (1967) challenged:

- Beliefs that qualitative methods were impressionistic and unsystematic
- Separation of data collection and analysis phases of research
- Prevailing views of qualitative research as a precursor to more 'rigorous' quantitative methods
- The arbitrary division between theory and research
- Assumptions that qualitative research could not generate theory.

Glaser and Strauss built on earlier qualitative researchers' implicit analytic procedures and research strategies and made them explicit. During the first half of the twentieth century, qualitative researchers had taught generations of students through mentoring and lengthy immersion in field research (Rock, 1979). Previous guides for conducting field research primarily dealt with data collection methods and researchers' membership roles in field settings. Authors told their readers little about how to tackle analyzing the piles of collected data. Glaser and Strauss's written guidelines for conducting qualitative research changed the oral tradition and made analytic guidelines accessible.

Merging Divergent Disciplinary Traditions

Grounded theory marries two contrasting—and competing—traditions in sociology as represented by each of its originators: Columbia University positivism and

Chicago school pragmatism and field research. The epistemological assumptions, logic, and systematic approach of grounded theory methods reflect Glaser's rigorous quantitative training at Columbia University with Paul Lazarsfeld. Glaser intended to codify qualitative research methods as Lazarsfeld had codified quantitative research (see, for example, Lazarsfeld & Rosenberg, 1955). Codifying qualitative research methods entailed specifying explicit strategies for conducting research and therefore demystified the research process.

Glaser also advocated building useful 'middle-range' theories, as the Columbia University theorist Robert K. Merton (1957) had proposed. Middle-range theories consisted of abstract renderings of specific social phenomena that were grounded in data. Such middle-range theories contrasted with the 'grand' theories of mid-century sociology that swept across societies but had no foundation in systematically analyzed data.

Glaser imbued grounded theory with dispassionate empiricism, rigorous codified methods, emphasis on emergent discoveries, and its somewhat ambiguous specialized language that echoes quantitative methods. Although *The Discovery of Grounded Theory* transformed methodological debates and inspired generations of qualitative researchers, Glaser's book *Theoretical Sensitivity* (1978) provided the most definitive early statement of the method.

Nonetheless, Strauss's Chicago school heritage also pervades the grounded theory method. Strauss viewed human beings as active agents in their lives and in their worlds rather than as passive recipients of larger social forces. He assumed that process, not structure, was fundamental to human existence; indeed, human beings created structures through engaging in processes. For Strauss, subjective and social meanings relied on our use of language and emerged through action. The construction of action was the central problem to address. In short, Strauss brought notions of human agency, emergent processes, social and subjective meanings, problem-solving practices, and the open-ended study of action to grounded theory.

All these ideas reflected the pragmatist philosophical tradition that Strauss embraced while in his doctoral program at the University of Chicago (Blumer, 1969; Mead, 1934). Pragmatism informed symbolic interactionism, a theoretical perspective that assumes society, reality, and self are constructed through interaction and thus rely on language and communication. This perspective assumes that interaction is inherently dynamic and *interpretive* and addresses how people create, enact, and change meanings and actions. Consider how Margie Arlen told of reinterpreting what had become important to her and of changing her actions accordingly. Symbolic interactionism assumes that people can and do think about their actions rather than respond mechanically to stimuli. Through the influence of Herbert Blumer and Robert Park, Strauss adopted both symbolic interactionism and the Chicago legacy of ethnographic research (Park & Burgess, 1921).

Glaser employed his analytic skills to codify qualitative analysis and thus constructed specific guidelines for doing it. Glaser and Strauss shared a keen interest in studying fundamental social or social psychological processes within a social setting or a particular experience such as having a chronic illness. Thus, for them, a finished grounded theory explains the studied process in new theoretical terms, explicates the properties of the theoretical categories, and often demonstrates the causes and conditions under which the process emerges and varies, and delineates its consequences.

Most grounded theories are substantive theories because they address delimited problems in specific substantive areas such as a study of how newly disabled young people reconstruct their identities. The logic of grounded theory can reach across substantive areas and into the realm of formal theory, which means generating abstract concepts and specifying relationships between them to understand problems in multiple substantive areas (see Kearney, 1998). For example, if we developed a theory of identity loss and reconstruction among young people with new disabilities, we could examine our theoretical categories in other areas of life in which people have experienced a sudden major loss, such as occurs with a partner's sudden death, lay-off from work, or loss of place due to a natural disaster. Each exploration within a new substantive area can help us to refine the formal theory. Glaser and Strauss's logic led them to formal theorizing when they took the theoretical categories that they had developed about status passage during their studies of dying and examined it as a generic process that cut across varied substantive areas (see Glaser & Strauss, 1971).

The *Discovery* book found receptive audiences and became a major force in igniting the 'qualitative revolution' (Denzin & Lincoln, 1994: ix) that gained momentum throughout the latter part of the twentieth century. Glaser and Strauss's explicit strategies and call for developing theories from qualitative data spread throughout disciplines and professions. Their book inspired new generations of social scientists and professionals, especially nurses, to pursue qualitative research. Many doctoral students in nursing at the University of California, San Francisco learned grounded theory methods from Glaser or Strauss and later became leaders in their profession and experts in qualitative inquiry (see Chenitz & Swanson, 1986; Schreiber & Stern, 2001).

Developments in Grounded Theory

Since Glaser and Strauss's classic statements in 1967 (Glaser & Strauss) and 1978 (Glaser), they have taken grounded theory in somewhat divergent directions (Charmaz, 2000). For years, Glaser remained consistent with his earlier exegesis of the method and thus defined grounded theory as a method of discovery, treated categories as emergent from the data, relied on direct and, often, narrow empiricism, and analyzed a basic social process. Strauss (1987) moved the method toward verification and his co-authored works with Juliet M. Corbin (Corbin & Strauss, 1990; Strauss & Corbin, 1990, 1998) furthered this direction.

Strauss and Corbin's version of grounded theory also favors their new technical procedures rather than emphasizing the comparative methods that distinguished earlier grounded theory strategies. Glaser (1992) contends that Strauss and Corbin's procedures force data and analysis into preconceived categories and, thus, contradict fundamental tenets of grounded theory. Despite Glaser's numerous objections to Strauss and Corbin's version of grounded theory, their book serves as a powerful statement of the method and has instructed graduate students throughout the world.

In the 1960s, Glaser and Strauss fought the dominance of positivistic quantitative research. Ironically, by 1990 grounded theory not only became known for its rigor and usefulness, but also for *its* positivistic assumptions. It has gained acceptance from quantitative researchers who sometimes adopt it in projects that use mixed methods. The flexibility and legitimacy of grounded theory methods continues to appeal to qualitative researchers with varied theoretical and substantive interests.

Meanwhile, a growing number of scholars have moved grounded theory away from the positivism in both Glaser's and Strauss and Corbin's versions of the method (see Bryant, 2002, 2003; Charmaz, 2000, 2002a, 2006a; Clarke, 2003, 2005; Seale, 1999). Like any container into which different content can be poured, researchers can use basic grounded theory guidelines such as coding, memo-writing, and sampling for theory development, and comparative methods are, in many ways, neutral.

Grounded theory guidelines describe the steps of the research process and provide a path through it. Researchers can adopt and adapt them to conduct diverse studies. *How* researchers use these guidelines is not neutral; nor are the assumptions they bring to their research and enact during the process. Antony Bryant (2002) and Adele Clarke (2003, 2005) join me in contending that we can use basic grounded theory guidelines with twenty-first century methodological assumptions and approaches. This book takes on the challenge of how to do that.

Constructing Grounded Theory

In their original statement of the method, Glaser and Strauss (1967) invited their readers to use grounded theory strategies flexibly in their own way. I accept their invitation and return to past grounded theory emphases on examining processes, making the study of action central, and creating abstract interpretive understandings of the data. This book provides *a* way of doing grounded theory that takes into account the theoretical and methodological developments of the past four decades.

I view grounded theory methods as a set of principles and practices, not as prescriptions or packages. In the following chapters, I emphasize flexible guidelines, not methodological rules, recipes, and requirements. During our journey through the research process, I aim to clarify what grounded theorists do and to show you how we do it. Hence, I discuss the guidelines throughout subsequent chapters with sufficient detail so that you can use them on your own and give them a sound appraisal.

Grounded theory methods can complement other approaches to qualitative data analysis, rather than stand in opposition to them. I occasionally draw on excellent examples from qualitative studies whose authors do not claim grounded theory allegiance or whose writing only acknowledges specific aspects of the approach. These authors bring an imaginative eye and an incisive voice to their studies—and inspire good work. Their works transcend their immediate circles.

The classic grounded theory texts of Glaser and Strauss (1967) and Glaser (1978) provide an explicit method for analyzing processes. I have talked about the research process and studying process, but what is a process?[1] A process consists of unfolding temporal sequences that may have identifiable markers with clear beginnings and endings and benchmarks in between. The temporal sequences are linked in a process and lead to change. Thus, single events become linked as part of a larger whole. Even the most regimented process may contain surprises because the present arises from the past but is never quite the same. The present emerges with new characteristics (Mead, 1932). Thus the experience and outcome of a specific process has some degree of indeterminacy, however small it might be.

Throughout the book, I build on my earlier discussions of the grounded theory method (see esp. Charmaz, 1990, 2000, 2002a, 2003, 2005) and on a symbolic interactionist theoretical perspective. Grounded theory serves as a way to learn about the worlds we study and a method for developing theories to understand them. In the classic grounded theory works, Glaser and Strauss talk about discovering theory as emerging from data separate from the scientific observer. Unlike their position, I assume that neither data nor theories are discovered. Rather, we are part of the world we study and the data we collect. We *construct* our grounded theories through our past and present involvements and interactions with people, perspectives, and research practices.

My approach explicitly assumes that any theoretical rendering offers an *interpretive* portrayal of the studied world, not an exact picture of it. (Charmaz, 1995b, 2000; Guba & Lincoln, 1994; Schwandt, 1994). Research participants' implicit meanings, experiential views–and researchers' finished grounded theories–are constructions of reality. In keeping with its Chicago school antecedents, I argue for building on the pragmatist underpinnings in grounded theory and advancing interpretive analyses that acknowledge these constructions.

Constructing Grounded Theory at a Glance

The organization of this book reproduces the logic of grounded theory in linear form. We start with gathering data and end by writing our analysis and reflecting on the entire process. In practice, however, the research process is not so linear. Grounded theorists stop and write whenever ideas occur to them. Some of our best ideas may occur to us late in the process and may lure us back to the field to gain a deeper view. Quite often, we discover that our work suggests pursuing more than one analytic direction. Thus, we may focus on certain ideas first and finish one paper or project about them but later return to our data and unfinished analysis in another area. Throughout this book, I treat grounded theory methods as constituting a craft that researchers practice. Like any craft, practitioners vary in their emphasis on one or another aspect but taken together share commonalities, which I address in the book (see Figure 1.1).

Chapter 2, 'Gathering Rich Data,' considers decisions about getting started and choosing approaches to data-gathering. Researchers can use grounded theory strategies with a variety of data collection methods. I treat these methods as tools to use rather than as recipes to follow. I advocate gathering

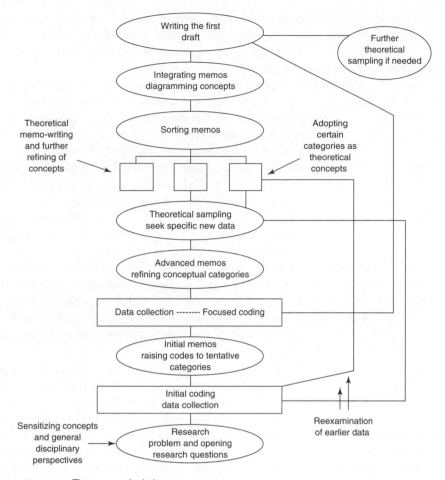

FIGURE 1.1 The grounded theory process

rich—detailed and full—data and placing them in their relevant situational and social contexts. This chapter introduces several major approaches to data-gathering and gives guidelines for using data to learn how people make sense of their situations and act on them.

As we learn how our research participants make sense of their experiences, we begin to make analytic sense of their meanings and actions. Chapter 3, 'Coding in Grounded Theory Practice,' shows how to do coding and thus label bits of data according to what they indicate. The chapter focuses on two main types of grounded theory coding: 1) initial line-by-line coding, a strategy which prompts you to study your data closely—line-by-line—and to begin conceptualizing your ideas, and 2) focused coding, which permits you to separate, sort, and synthesize large amounts of data.

Certain codes crystallize meanings and actions in the data. Writing extended notes called memos on telling codes helps you to develop your ideas. In Chapter 4, 'Memo-writing,' I show how grounded theorists take these codes apart and analyze them in memos. You write memos throughout your research.

Memos provide ways to compare data, to explore ideas about the codes, and to direct further data-gathering. As you work with your data and codes, you become progressively more analytic in how you treat them and thus you raise certain codes to conceptual categories.

Chapter 5, 'Theoretical Sampling, Saturation, and Sorting,' explains theoretical sampling, the grounded theory strategy of obtaining further selective data to refine and fill out your major categories. In this chapter, I also question the meaning of theoretical saturation as indicating that no new properties of the category emerge during data collection. I next discuss sorting memos to fit the theoretical categories and show relationships that integrate the work. I introduce diagramming because increasing numbers of grounded theorists use it as an alternative way to integrate their ideas and to establish the logic of their ordering.

Chapter 6, 'Reconstructing Theory in Grounded Theory Studies,' asks you to reassess what theory means. I explore meanings of theory in the social sciences and conceptions of theorizing in grounded theory. I juxtapose positivist and interpretive kinds of grounded theory to clarify how contrasting forms of analysis flow from different starting points. The chapter ends with a discussion of three examples of theorizing in grounded theory and a reconstruction of their respective theoretical logic. Each example differs in theoretical emphasis, scope, and reach but taken together they show the versatility and usefulness of grounded theory methods.

Chapter 7, 'Writing the Draft,' explains differences between writing to develop an analysis and writing for an audience. Grounded theory strategies lead you to concentrate on your analysis rather than on arguments about it, to delay the literature review, and to construct an original theory that interprets your data. These strategies contradict traditional requirements for reporting research. The chapter reconciles tensions between grounded theory methods and traditional forms of social scientific reportage by offering guidelines for constructing arguments, writing the literature review, and developing a theoretical framework. The chapter ends by addressing ways to render our ideas through writing.

Last, Chapter 8, 'Reflecting on the Process,' discusses criteria for assessing grounded theories as products of research and ends the book with questions about our quest for knowledge and a call for action.

And now our journey through the research process begins …

NOTE

1 My definition of process draws heavily on pragmatist conceptions of emergence and partly concurs with aspects of varied views expressed by Russell Kelley, Dan E. Miller, Dennis Waskul, Angus Vail, and Phillip Vannini during a listserv discussion on SSSITalk, January 25, 2005. (www.soci.niu.edu/~archives/SSSITALK)

2 Gathering Rich Data

Our grounded theory adventure starts as we enter the field where we gather data. We step forward from our disciplinary perspectives with a few tools and provisional concepts. A grounded theory journey may take several varied routes, depending on where we want to go and where our analysis takes us. Ethnographic methods, intensive interviewing, and textual analysis provide tools for gathering data as we traverse these routes. A brief excursion in this chapter explores the benefits each tool promises and the limits it imposes.

What do you want to study? Which research problem might you pursue? Which tools will help you proceed? How do you use methods to gather rich data? Rich data get beneath the surface of social and subjective life. An inquiring mind, persistence, and innovative data-gathering approaches can bring a researcher into new worlds and in touch with rich data. Consider how Patrick L. Biernacki (1986) began his grounded theory research for his book *Pathways from Heroin Addiction: Recovery without Treatment*:

> The idea for this research originated several years ago during a study I was conducting of people who had stopped smoking marijuana (Biernacki & Davis, 1970). Although the reasons some people gave for finding it necessary to stop using marijuana might today seem insignificant, it was of interest at that time. Regardless of the relative importance of the research, it did bring me into contact with people who had been addicted to opiates along with marijuana, and who had stopped using the opiate drugs. This chance discovery of a few 'naturally' recovered addicts opened the door to a slew of questions about the ultimate fate of opiate addicts. Were the cases I found unusual? Were most addicts destined to remain addicted for their entire lives? Was some form of therapeutic intervention always necessary to break an opiate addiction? Or was it possible, at least for some people, to break the addiction and recover through their own resolve and effort? (p. 200)

The intriguing topic piqued Biernacki's curiosity. But how could he find data to study it? He states:

> Locating and interviewing ex-addicts who had undergone some form of treatment would have presented few difficulties. ... Ferreting out respondents

who met the research criteria for *natural recovery* was another matter. ... In fact, because of the widely held belief that 'once an addict, always an addict,' many clinicians and researchers in the field thought that naturally recovering addicts, the focus of the proposed study, did not exist or if they did, it was not with any great frequency. (p. 203)

Like Biernacki's quest to find suitable study participants, your research adventure begins with finding data.[1] Discover how exciting empirical research can be through gathering rich data. Let the world appear anew through your data. Gathering rich data will give you solid material for building a significant analysis. Rich data are detailed, focused, and full. They reveal participants' views, feelings, intentions, and actions as well as the contexts and structures of their lives. Obtaining rich data means seeking 'thick' description (Geertz, 1973), such as writing extensive fieldnotes of observations, collecting respondents' written personal accounts, and/or compiling detailed narratives (such as from transcribed tapes of interviews).

Researchers generate strong grounded theories with rich data. Grounded theories may be built with diverse kinds of data—fieldnotes, interviews, and information in records and reports. The kind of data the researcher pursues depends on the topic and access. Often, researchers gather several types of data in grounded theory studies and may invoke varied data-gathering strategies. What do we need to think about to gain rich data for an emerging grounded theory? How might we construct rich data with our methodological tools?

Thinking about Methods

Seeing through Methods

Methods extend and magnify our view of studied life and, thus, broaden and deepen what we learn of it and know about it. Through our methods, we first aim to see this world as our research participants do—from the inside. Although we cannot claim to replicate their views, we can try to enter their settings and situations to the extent possible. Seeing research participants' lives from the inside often gives a researcher otherwise unobtainable views. You might learn that what outsiders assume about the world you study may be limited, imprecise, mistaken, or egregiously wrong.

Qualitative researchers have one great advantage over our quantitative colleagues. We can add new pieces to the research puzzle or conjure entire new puzzles—*while we gather data*—and that can even occur late in the analysis. The flexibility of qualitative research permits you to follow leads that emerge. Grounded theory methods increase this flexibility and simultaneously give you more focus than many methods. Used well, grounded theory quickens the speed of gaining a clear focus on what is happening in your data without sacrificing the detail of enacted scenes. Like a camera with many lenses, first you view a broad sweep of the landscape. Subsequently, you change your lens several times to bring scenes closer and closer into view.

With grounded theory methods, you shape and reshape your data collection and, therefore, refine your collected data. Nonetheless, methods wield no magic. A method provides *a* tool to enhance seeing but does not provide automatic insight. We must *see through* the armament of methodological techniques and the reliance on mechanical procedures. Methods alone–whatever they might be–do not generate good research or astute analyses. How researchers use methods matters. Mechanistic applications of methods yield mundane data and routine reports. A keen eye, open mind, discerning ear, and steady hand can bring you close to what you study and are more important than developing methodological tools (Charmaz & Mitchell, 1996).

Methods *are* merely tools. However, some tools are more useful than others. When combined with insight and industry, grounded theory methods offer sharp tools for generating, mining, and making sense of data. Grounded theory can give you flexible guidelines rather than rigid prescriptions. With flexible guidelines, you direct your study but let your imagination flow.

Although methods are merely tools, they do have consequences. Choose methods that help you answer your research questions with ingenuity and incisiveness. *How* you collect data affects *which* phenomena you will see, *how*, *where*, and *when* you will view them, and *what* sense you will make of them.

Just as the methods we choose influence what we see, what we bring to the study also influences what we *can* see. Qualitative research of all sorts relies on those who conduct it. We are not passive receptacles into which data are poured (Charmaz, 1990, 1998; cf. Glaser & Strauss, 1967; Glaser, 1978). We are not scientific observers who can dismiss scrutiny of our values by claiming scientific neutrality and authority. Neither observer nor observed come to a scene untouched by the world. Researchers and research participants make assumptions about what is real, possess stocks of knowledge, occupy social statuses, and pursue purposes that influence their respective views and actions in the presence of each other. Nevertheless, researchers, not participants, are obligated to be reflexive about what we bring to the scene, what we see, and how we see it.

Let your research problem shape the methods you choose. Your research problem may point to one method of data collection. If, for example, you wanted to learn how people conceal a history of illegal drug use, then you need to think of ways you can reach these individuals, gain their trust, and obtain solid data from them. If they want to keep their pasts secret, they may refuse to fill out questionnaires or to participate in focus groups. However, people who define themselves as recovering addicts might agree to talk with you. Once you have established trust, someone who uses drugs might invite you to hang out in the scene.

Certain research problems indicate using several combined or sequential approaches. If you aim to explore experiences of living with cancer, you might be able to join a local support or volunteer group, conduct interviews, engage in Internet discussion groups, and distribute questionnaires. In any study, questions may occur to you during the research that lead you to construct new data-gathering methods and to revise earlier ones. Once you begin collecting data, your research participants may give you materials that you had not anticipated collecting but help to further your ideas. Some participants might invite you to read their personal journals; others might tell you about organizational records that would give you information.

The logic of grounded theory guides your *methods of data-gathering* as well as of theoretical development. Aim to create or adopt methods that hold a promise of advancing your emerging ideas. Such innovation can occur at any point during the research. You will learn things during your research that you would have liked to have explored earlier. Think about what kind of approach would enable you to gain this needed data and in which type of setting you will find it. For one project, it might mean framing certain questions to allow participants to make disclosures, such as this question, 'Some people have mentioned having — experience. Have you experienced something like that?' Ethnographers and interviewers might return to research participants with whom they have already talked and ask this type of question. Numerous interviewers, however, face constraints of time, funding, or institutional access that permit only one interview per participant. These interviewers might ask subsequent participants such questions toward the end of the conversation in their interviews. For other projects and purposes, the researcher might find constructing an open-ended questionnaire helpful.

Barney G. Glaser (2002) says that 'All is data.' Yes, everything you learn in the research setting(s) or about your research topic can serve as data. However, data vary in quality, relevance for your emerging interests, and usefulness for interpretation. Researchers also vary in their ability to discern useful data and in their skill and thoroughness in recording them. Moreover, *people* construct data—whether researchers construct first-hand data through interviews or field-notes or gather texts and information from other sources such as historical documents, government records, or organizational information compiled for private discussion or public dissemination. We may treat such documents, records, and census data as facts; however, individuals constructed them. Whatever stands as data flows from some purpose to realize a particular objective. In turn, purposes and objectives arise under particular historical, social, and situational conditions.

Grounded theorists' background assumptions and disciplinary perspectives alert them to look for certain possibilities and processes in their data. These assumptions and perspectives often differ among disciplines but nonetheless shape research topics and conceptual emphases. Blumer's (1969) notion of sensitizing concepts is useful at this juncture. These concepts give you initial ideas to pursue and sensitize you to ask particular kinds of questions about your topic. Grounded theorists often begin their studies with certain guiding empirical interests to study and, consistent with Blumer, general concepts that give a loose frame to these interests. For

> Consistent with Blumer's (1969) depiction of sensitizing concepts, grounded theorists often begin their studies with certain research interests and a set of general concepts. These concepts give you ideas to pursue and sensitize you to ask particular kinds of questions about your topic.

example, I began my studies of people with chronic illnesses with an interest in how they experienced time and how their experiences of illness affected them.

My guiding interests led to bringing concepts such as self-concept, identity, and duration into the study. But that was only the start. I used those concepts as *points of departure* to form interview questions, to look at data, to listen to interviewees, and to think analytically about the data. Guiding interests, sensitizing concepts, and disciplinary perspectives often provide us with such points of departure for developing, rather than limiting, our ideas. Then we develop specific concepts by studying the data and examining our ideas through successive levels of analysis.

Professional researchers and many graduate students already have a sound footing in their disciplines before they begin a research project and often have an intimate familiarity with the research topic and the literature about it. All provide vantage points that can intensify looking at certain aspects of the empirical world but may ignore others. We may begin our studies from these vantage points but need to remain as open as possible to whatever we see and sense in the early stages of the research.

In short, sensitizing concepts and disciplinary perspectives provide a place to *start*, not to *end*. Grounded theorists use sensitizing concepts as tentative tools for developing their ideas about processes that they define in their data. If particular sensitizing concepts prove to be irrelevant, then we dispense with them. In contrast, the logico-deductive model of traditional quantitative research necessitates operationalizing established concepts in a theory as accurately as possible and deducing testable hypotheses about the relationships between these concepts. In this model, the research is locked into the original concepts.

What happens if your qualitative data do not illuminate your initial research interests? Pertti Alasuutari (1995) shows how his research team tackled this problem:

> This process, in which we chewed over the main problems of our project and made false starts and rethought it all over again, is hardly an exceptional beginning for a research project. It's just that researchers rarely report on all of this. However, an early failure to choose the right road does not have to mean you are ultimately trapped in a dead-end. ... Revise your strategy on the basis of that result and you might be able to move on to another result.
>
> In our case the false starts we made and the research ideas we had to discard as unrealistic in view of existing resources led to a better plan and clearer view of how the project should be carried out. (p. 161)

Grounded theorists evaluate the fit between their initial research interests and their emerging data. We do not force preconceived ideas and theories directly upon our data. Rather, we follow leads that we *define* in the data, or design another way of collecting data to pursue our initial interests. Thus, I started with research interests in time and self-concept but also pursued other topics that my respondents defined as crucial. For example, I felt compelled to explore their concerns about disclosing illness, something I had not anticipated. Their dilemmas about disclosing and feelings about doing so emerged as a recurrent theme.[2] Subsequently, I studied how, when, why, and with whom ill people talk about their conditions. More recently, I began to explore when and why chronically ill people remain silent about their illnesses (Charmaz, 2002b).

Tensions between data collection strategies and what constitutes 'forcing' are unresolved in grounded theory. What might stand as a viable means of gathering data to one grounded theorist could be defined as forcing the data into a preconceived framework by another. Glaser (1998) cautions against preconceiving 'interview guides, units for data collection, samples, received codes, following diagrams, rules for proper memoing and so forth' (p. 94). However, an open-ended interview guide to explore a topic is hardly of the same order as imposing received codes on collected data. Simply thinking through how to word open-ended questions helps novices to avoid blurting out loaded questions and to avert forcing responses into narrow categories. Researchers' inattention to methods of data collection results in forcing data in unwitting ways and likely is repeated over and over.

Reaching for Quality

The quality—and credibility—of your study starts with the data. The depth and scope of the data make a difference. A study based upon rich, substantial, and relevant data stands out. Thus, in addition to their usefulness for developing core categories, two other criteria for data are their suitability and sufficiency for depicting empirical events.

Whatever methods you choose, plan to gather sufficient data to fit your task and to give you as full a picture of the topic as possible within the parameters of this task. Readers and reviewers will see your study as a serious effort and you will have a strong foundation from which to speak. A novice may mistake good, but limited, data for an adequate study. Consider the design of the study as a whole. For example, an ethnographer who engages in detailed sustained observation and concludes the study with ten intensive interviews of key informants has far more to draw on than someone who has simply conducted ten rich interviews. What fits the requirements for an undergraduate project seldom suffices for a doctoral dissertation. Skimpy data may give you a wonderful start but do not add up to a detailed study or a nuanced grounded theory. A researcher can rarely make persuasive, much less definitive, statements from limited data.

Some grounded theorists (Glaser, 1998; Stern, 1994a) argue against attending to the amount of data. Numerous other researchers have embraced a similar stance to legitimize small studies with skimpy data. For both Glaser and Stern, small samples and limited data do not pose problems because grounded theory methods aim to develop conceptual categories and thus data collection is directed to illuminate properties of a category and relations between categories. Their reasoning can help you streamline data collection. It can also lead to what Dey (1999: 119) calls a 'smash and grab' data collection strategy and to superficial analyses.

What kind of data stands as rich and sufficient? Asking yourself the following questions may help you evaluate your data:

- Have I collected enough background data about persons, processes, and settings to have ready recall and to understand and portray the full range of contexts of the study?

- Have I gained detailed descriptions of a range of participants' views and actions?
- Do the data reveal what lies beneath the surface?
- Are the data sufficient to reveal changes over time?
- Have I gained multiple views of the participants' range of actions?
- Have I gathered data that enable me to develop analytic categories?
- What kinds of comparisons can I make between data? How do these comparisons generate and inform my ideas?

Interpretive qualitative methods mean entering research participants' worlds. Blumer's (1969) dictum to 'Respect your subjects' reminds us to preserve our participants' human dignity even if we question their perspectives or practices. One way of respecting our research participants is through trying to establish rapport with them. Dey (1999) points out that Glaser and Strauss's (1967) smash and grab data collection strategy dispenses with rapport, which for many projects is a prerequisite to gaining solid data. If researchers do not establish rapport, they risk losing access to conduct subsequent interviews or observations.

Our respect for our research participants pervades how we collect data and shapes the content of our data. We demonstrate our respect by making concerted efforts to learn about their views and actions and to try to understand their lives from their perspectives. This approach means we must test our assumptions about the worlds we study, not unwittingly reproduce these assumptions. It means discovering what our research participants take for granted or do not state as well as what they say and do. As we try to look at their world through their eyes, we offer our participants respect and, to our best ability, understanding, although we may not agree with them. We try to understand but do not necessarily adopt or reproduce their views as our own; rather we interpret them. We attempt to learn but we cannot know what occurs in people's heads (see also Murphy & Dingwall, 2003). Nonetheless, a careful interpretive understanding often marks classic qualitative studies and represents a stunning achievement (see, for example, Clark, 1997; Fine, 1986, 1998; Mitchell, 2002). Kristin Luker's (1984) book *Abortion and the Politics of Motherhood* exemplifies this type of interpretive understanding. She studied the views of pro-life and pro-choice women and offered respect and interest to members of both groups. She portrayed their contrasting views and provided an even-handed analysis of both groups' positions. See how Luker presents the logic of pro-life activists:

> Because they were not on the whole exposed during childhood and youth to the idea that embryos belong to a different moral category than persons already born, the abortion reform movement strikes them as a sudden and capricious rejection of centuries of 'respect for unborn life.' ... For people who really do believe that embryos have always been treated with respect—and our data suggest that most all pro-life people believe this— the wide acceptance of abortion in American society is truly frightening because it seems to represent a willingness of society to strip the rights of personhood from 'persons' who have always enjoyed them. If the rights of personhood can be so easily taken away from babies (embryos), who among us will be next? (p. 156)

Gathering Grounded Theory Data

Classic grounded theory (Glaser & Strauss, 1967; Glaser, 1978) emphasizes creating analyses of action and process. The grounded theory approach of simultaneous data collection and analysis helps us to keep pursuing these emphases as we shape our data collection to inform our emerging analysis. Thus, the first grounded theory question to ask follows:

- What's happening here? (Glaser, 1978)

This question spawns looking at what is happening at either of two levels:

- What are the basic social processes?
- What are the basic social psychological processes?

Such questions get you started. The answers may not be as straightforward as the questions suggest. What you define as basic is always an interpretation, even when major participants concur. Glaser and Strauss (1967; Glaser, 1978) emphasize *the* basic social process that the researcher discovers in the field. Although the classic texts present the analysis of basic social processes as fundamental to the grounded theory method, Glaser's (2002) revision disavows the pursuit of a basic social process, stating that doing so forces the data.

You may find many things happening in the setting. Everything may seem significant—or trivial. Reflect on what you are seeing and hearing. Depending on your assessment, such questions as the following may help.

- From whose point of view is a given process fundamental? From whose view is it marginal?
- How do the observed social processes emerge? How do participants' actions construct them?
- Who exerts control over these processes? Under what conditions?
- What meanings do different participants attribute to the process? How do they talk about it? What do they emphasize? What do they leave out?
- How and when do their meanings and actions concerning the process change?

These questions may be deceptive. The easy answer may slice no deeper than a paper cut—and not pierce fundamental social processes. These processes may remain unseen and unstated but shape participants' actions and understandings within the setting. Might definitions of 'the' basic social process in the setting differ according to various participants' positions and resulting vantage points? On which information and experiences do participants define the processes in which they are engaged? Do they provide an idealized picture wrapped in public relations rhetoric rather than one reflecting the realities people struggle with? When does a basic social process become visible or change? A community agency, for example, may purport to do good works for clients. Yet a close examination may reveal that the most basic process is keeping the agency solvent. Consider the following ways to construct data:

- Attending to actions and processes as well as to words
- Delineating the context, scenes, and situations of action carefully
- Recording who did what, when it occurred, why it happened (if you can ascertain the reasons), and *how* it occurred
- Identifying the *conditions* under which specific actions, intentions, and processes emerge or are muted
- Looking for ways to interpret these data
- Focusing on specific words and phrases to which participants seem to attribute particular meaning
- Finding taken-for-granted and hidden assumptions of various participants; showing how they are revealed through and affect actions.

Grounded Theory in Ethnography

Ethnography means recording the life of a particular group and thus entails sustained participation and observation in their milieu, community, or social world. It means more than participant observation alone because an ethnographic study covers the round of life occurring within the given milieu(x) and often includes supplementary data from documents, diagrams, maps, photographs, and, occasionally, formal interviews and questionnaires.

Participant observers may limit their focus to one aspect of daily life. In contrast, ethnographers seek detailed knowledge of the multiple dimensions of life within the studied milieu and aim to understand members' taken-for-granted assumptions and rules (Ashworth, 1995; Charmaz & Olesen, 1997).

What should an ethnographer study in the field? Whatever is happening there. By remaining open to the setting and the actions and people in it, ethnographers have the opportunity to work from the ground up and to pursue whatever they find to be of the greatest interest.

Research participants allow ethnographers to see their worlds and their actions within them. The goal of much ethnography is to gain an insider's depiction of the studied world. Nonetheless, like other researchers, ethnographers bring their theoretical training and methodological tools to their work. From the research participants' standpoint, the ironic outcome may be an outsider's report (Pollner & Emerson, 2001).

Although standard textbooks call for an open mind and accepting demeanor in the field, ethnographers bring divergent styles to their studies. The research problems they address, the participants they meet, and the constraints they encounter all shape their involvement. In one setting, an ethnographer may find participants eager to tell their personal and collective stories. In another, the ethnographer may remain welcome only if he or she provides a novel presence in the setting. The extent to which ethnographers move from passive observation to full participation depends on the specific study, including its objectives, agreements about access, involvement, reciprocities, and emergent relationships with members. Quite possibly, an ethnographer may become more involved in the scene than anticipated. Similarly, he or she may find this involvement to be of a different order than expected. As a naïve ethnographer in an institutional care facility, I thought I would be able to slip back to my room and write notes at times during the day. The administrator who had given me permission to live there held quite a different view: institutional life trumped research roles. He insisted that I spend the days—and most evenings—participating in the residents' activities. He informed me, 'Everyone is a therapist here.'

What's basic in a setting depends on participants' positions, actions, and intentions. Actions may defy stated intentions. Different participants have different vantage points—and, sometimes, competing agendas. Do they realize when they hold competing agendas? How do they act on them? When, if ever, does conflict emerge?

If you happened to read fieldnotes of observations in a grounded theory project, you might find that these notes:

- Record individual and collective actions
- Contain full, detailed notes with anecdotes and observations
- Emphasize significant processes occurring in the setting
- Address what participants define as interesting and/or problematic
- Attend to participants' language use
- Place actors and actions in scenes and contexts
- Become progressively focused on key analytic ideas.

From the start, a grounded theory study takes a different form than other types of ethnographies. Grounded theory ethnography gives priority to the studied *phenomenon* or *process*—rather than to a description of a setting. Thus, from the beginnings of their fieldwork, grounded theory ethnographers study what is happening in the setting and make a *conceptual* rendering of these actions. A grounded theory ethnographer likely moves across settings to gain more knowledge of the studied process. Other ethnographic approaches often focus on topics such as kinship networks, religious practices, and the organization of work in a specific community. Subsequently, these ethnographers provide full descriptions of these topics in the studied setting and usually take a more structural than processual approach.

> Grounded theory ethnography gives priority to the studied *phenomenon* or *process*—rather than the setting itself.

To the extent that ethnographers treat their topics as separate segments of the studied world or as structures but not processes, completing a grounded theory analysis poses difficulties. Their fieldnotes may describe the topic as a thing, an object, without showing the actions and process that construct it. The ethnographer as well as the participants may take the processes for granted that construct the studied topic or structure.

On another level, consider the relative congruence between your overall research goals and the data you gather and record. Be open to what you have and where it takes you (Atkinson, 1990). Exciting new horizons may appear. Sometimes, however, you may need to expand your access within a setting. If you wish to write about how an organization processes people, you will need to show how people move through the organization—or are moved through it. Organizational spatial allocations and arrangements may provide telling data. For example, if you want to know when, how, and why staff in a retirement facility assign and reassign residents to spatial areas with different levels of care, you need to do more than discover how residents use social areas such as the television lounge. Certainly residents' use of the lounge may yield telling observations about certain constraints due to the physical setting but provides no information on staff decisions about levels of care.

A potential problem with ethnographic studies is seeing data everywhere and nowhere, gathering everything and nothing. The studied world seems so interesting (and probably is) that the ethnographer tries to master knowing it all. Mountains of unconnected data grow (see also Coffey & Atkinson, 1996) but they do not say much. What follows? Low level description and, if a bit more sophisticated, lists of unintegrated categories. Ethnographers who leave data undigested seldom produce fresh insights and, sometimes, may not even complete their projects, despite years of toil.

Enter grounded theory. Paradoxically, concentrating on a basic social process can help you to gain a more complete picture of the *whole* setting than the former approach common in earlier ethnographic work. Ethnographers can make connections between events by using grounded theory to study processes. A grounded theory emphasis on comparative method leads ethnographers 1) to compare data with data from the *beginning* of the research, not after all the data are collected, 2) to compare data with emerging categories, and 3) to demonstrate relations between concepts and categories. Grounded theory strategies can increase ethnographers' involvement in their *research inquiry*, despite pressures they might face to be full participants in their research settings. In this sense, grounded theory dispels the positivist notion of passive observers who merely absorb their surrounding scenes. Grounded theorists select the scenes they observe and direct their gaze within them. If used with care and thoroughness, grounded theory methods provide systematic guidelines for probing beneath the surface and digging into the scene. These methods help in maintaining control over the research process because they assist the ethnographer in focusing, structuring, and organizing it.

Grounded theory methods move ethnographic research toward theoretical development by raising description to abstract categories and theoretical interpretation. In the past, ethnography suffered from a rigid and artificial separation of data collection and analysis. Grounded theory methods preserve an open-ended approach to studying the empirical world yet add rigor to ethnographic research by building systematic checks into both data collection and analysis. The logic of grounded theory entails going back to data and forward into analysis. Subsequently you return to the field to gather further data and to refine the emerging theoretical framework. This logic aids you in overcoming several ethnographic problems: 1) accusations of uncritically adopting research participants' views, 2) lengthy unfocused forays into the field setting, 3) superficial, random data collection, and 4) reliance on stock disciplinary categories.

Thin, unfocused data may tempt ethnographers to fall back on lifting stock concepts from their disciplinary shelves. Grounded theory prompts taking a fresh look and creating novel categories and concepts. That is the strength and the core of the method. Moving back and forth between data and analysis also helps you from feeling overwhelmed and to avoid procrastinating (see also, Coffey & Atkinson, 1996). Both can happen when researchers collect data without direction.

Current trends toward limited data and 'instant' theorizing[3] have long been associated with grounded theory and now permeate other methods, including ethnography. A competent ethnographic study demands time and commitment. Grounded theory can help you trim excess work but the core tasks still need to be done. Gathering rich ethnographic data means starting by engaging the studied phenomena–get involved!

You can make the most of what you bring to the setting. Novices often bring energy and openness. Some experienced ethnographers may be so imbued with disciplinary ideas and procedures that they have difficulty moving beyond them. Other experienced ethnographers sense areas to pursue without articulating them and, moreover, without being wedded to them. Novices may flounder. A few guidelines can turn floundering into flourishing. Mitchell (in Charmaz & Mitchell, 2001) has found that student ethnographers flourish with a little help. He asks students to study actions and actors and provides the questions below to spark their thinking. You may find several questions that help you to view the events in your research setting. If so, adopt them, but follow what you observe in the setting first. We can use Mitchell's questions to initiate inquiry, not to substitute a formula for it.

- What is the setting of action? When and how does action take place?
- What is going on? What is the overall activity being studied, the relatively long-term behavior about which participants organize themselves? What specific acts comprise this activity?
- What is the distribution of participants over space and time in these locales?
- How are actors [research participants] organized? What organizations effect, oversee, regulate or promote this activity?
- How are members stratified? Who is ostensibly in charge? Does being in charge vary by activity? How is membership achieved and maintained?
- What do actors pay attention to? What is important, preoccupying, critical?
- What do they pointedly ignore that other persons might pay attention to?
- What symbols do actors invoke to understand their worlds, the participants and processes within them, and the objects and events they encounter? What names do they attach to objects, events, persons, roles, settings, equipment?
- What practices, skills, strategems, methods of operation do actors employ?
- Which theories, motives, excuses, justifications or other explanations do actors use in accounting for their participation? How do they explain to each other, not to outside investigators, what they do and why they do it?
- What goals do actors seek? When, from their perspective, is an act well or poorly done? How do they judge action–by what standards, developed and applied by whom?
- What rewards do various actors gain from their participation?[4] (Charmaz & Mitchell, 2001, p. 163)

An ethnographer may invoke such questions when learning about context and content, meaning and action, structures and actors. Grounded theory can expedite ethnographers' delving into problematic topics that emerge in the field. A grounded theory strategy: Seek data, describe observed events, answer fundamental questions about what is happening, then develop theoretical categories to understand it. This approach also remedies weaknesses in grounded theory studies, especially those that rely on single accounts given to field investigators. How people explain their actions to each other may not resemble their statements to an interviewer. Moreover, participants' most important explanations may consist of tacit understandings. If so, then participants seldom articulate them out loud among themselves, let alone to non-members.

Understanding derives most directly from the immediacy of our participation in social actors' shared worlds (Prus, 1996). In practical terms, this means the researcher needs to share some experiences, but not necessarily all viewpoints, with those being studied. Bergson states, 'Philosophers agree in making a deep distinction between two ways of knowing a thing. The first implies going all around it, the second entering into it' (Bergson, 1903: 1). The ethnographer's job is to explore the second way. Grounded theory studies often move around an object; these methods generate a map of the object of study from the outside, but may not enter it. Such studies may look at phenomena from a variety of locations and standpoints (see, for example, Glaser & Strauss, 1965, 1968). Yet grounded theory ethnographers can go deep into experience to make an interpretive rendering (see, for example, Baszanger, 1998; Casper, 1998; Timmermans, 1999).

Intensive Interviewing

The Interview Conversation

Intensive interviewing has long been a useful data-gathering method in various types of qualitative research. Most essentially, an interview is a directed conversation (Lofland & Lofland, 1984, 1995); intensive interviewing permits an in-depth exploration of a particular topic or experience and, thus, is a useful method for interpretive inquiry. Other forms of interviewing, such as informational interviewing, might be indicated for certain grounded theory projects, particularly those with an objectivist cast (but see Hermes, 1995).

The in-depth nature of an intensive interview fosters eliciting each participant's interpretation of his or her experience. The interviewer seeks to understand the topic and the interview participant has the relevant experiences to shed light on it (see Fontana & Frey, 1994; Seidman, 1997). Thus, the interviewer's questions ask the participant to describe and reflect upon his or her experiences in ways that seldom occur in everyday life. The interviewer is there to listen, to observe with sensitivity, and to encourage

> An interview is a directed conversation (Lofland & Lofland, 1984, 1995); an intensive interview permits an in-depth exploration of a particular topic with a person who has had the relevant experiences.

the person to respond. Hence, in this conversation, the participant does most of the talking.

For a grounded theory study, devise a few broad, open-ended questions. Then you can focus your interview questions to invite detailed discussion of topic. By creating open-ended, non-judgmental questions, you encourage unanticipated statements and stories to emerge. The combination of how you construct the questions and conduct the interview shapes how well you achieve a balance between making the interview open-ended and focusing on significant statements.

The structure of an intensive interview may range from a loosely guided exploration of topics to semi-structured focused questions. Although the intensive interview may be conversational, it follows a different etiquette. The researcher should express interest and want to know more. What might be rude to ask or be glossed over in friendly agreement in ordinary conversation—even with intimates—becomes grist for exploration. Research participants often expect their interviewers to ask questions that invite reflections about the topic. Rather than uttering 'uh huhs' or just nodding as if meanings are automatically shared, an interviewer might say, 'That's interesting, tell me more about it.' In your role as an interviewer, your comments and questions help the research participant to articulate his or her intentions and meanings. As the interview proceeds, you may request clarifying details to obtain accurate information and to learn about the research participant's experiences and reflections. Unlike ordinary conversation, an interviewer can shift the conversation and follow hunches. An interview goes beneath the surface of ordinary conversation and examines earlier events, views, and feelings afresh.

Intensive interviews allow an interviewer to:

- Go beneath the surface of the described experience(s)
- Stop to explore a statement or topic
- Request more detail or explanation
- Ask about the participant's thoughts, feelings, and actions
- Keep the participant on the subject
- Come back to an earlier point
- Restate the participant's point to check for accuracy
- Slow or quicken the pace
- Shift the immediate topic
- Validate the participant's humanity, perspective, or action
- Use observational and social skills to further the discussion
- Respect the participant and express appreciation for participating.

Now compare these interviewing entitlements to disclosures in ordinary life. Conversational rules may dictate that you listen, not ask for clarification, agree with the speaker—at least tacitly-but not question, let the speaker direct conversational flow, rather than stop it to explore an earlier point, and hear a story but not repeat it in your words to recapture the other person's. Think about what ensues after a friend has shared a long story with you. Can you imagine saying to her, 'Let's see if I have grasped these events correctly,' followed by your portrayal of each twist and turn in her story.

A research participant also has conversational prerogatives in the interview. Intensive interviews allow research participants to:

- Break silences and express their views
- Tell their stories and to give them a coherent frame
- Reflect on earlier events
- Be experts
- Choose what to tell and how to tell it
- Share significant experiences and teach the interviewer how to interpret them
- Express thoughts and feelings disallowed in other relationships and settings
- Receive affirmation and understanding.

Negotiations During the Interview

An interview is contextual and negotiated. Whether participants recount their concerns without interruption or researchers request specific information, the result is a construction–or reconstruction–of a reality. Interview stories do not reproduce prior realities (Murphy & Dingwall, 2003; Silverman, 2000). Rather these stories provide accounts from particular points of view that serve specific purposes, including assumptions that one should follow tacit conversational rules during the interview.

Neutral questions do not mean a neutral interview. Instead an interview reflects what interviewers and participants bring to the interview, impressions during it, and the relationship constructed through it. Interviewers must remain attuned to how participants perceive them, and how both participants' and interviewers' past and immediate identities may influence the character and content of interaction. The past as well as the present informs participants' tacit questions and negotiations about the interview process and discussion during it. Research participants appraise the interviewer, assess the situation, and act on their present assessments and prior knowledge, often in taken-for-granted ways. People who have experienced crises may seek direction from their interviewer about what to say and how deep to go. Interviewers learn how deep to go and when to explore a point further with probes as they become sensitive to their participants' concerns and vulnerabilities.

Relative differences in power and status may be acted on and played out during an interview. Powerful people may take charge, turn the interview questions to address topics on their own terms, and control the timing, pacing and length of the interview. Both powerful and disempowered individuals may distrust their interviewers, the sponsoring institutions, and the stated purpose of the research, as well as how the findings might be used. During interviews, professionals may recite public relations rhetoric rather than reveal personal views, much less a full account of their experiences. Clients may raise silent or overt questions about whether the interviewer represents officials or advocates–and test his or her loyalties.

In addition to the dynamics of power and professional status, gender, race, and age may affect the direction and content of interviews. Men may view intensive interviews as threatening because they occur within a one-to one relationship, render control of interaction ambiguous, foster self-disclosure and, therefore, risk loss of public persona (Schwalbe & Wolkomir, 2002). Men's potential discomfort may heighten, should the topic of the interview such as disability or divorce challenge their masculinity claims. While studying divorced fathers, Terry Arendell (1997) observed a subtle shift in emphasis from the focus on divorce during certain interviews. When these fathers revealed a major concern with their identities as men, their interview statements took on a meta-discourse about masculinity. Men who hide their emotions behind a thick wall of impression management may not agree to be interviewed; others may weave around questions rather than address them directly. As Arendell discovered, some men enact and dramatize gendered relations during the interview.

Interviewing women poses other dilemmas. When the interviewer is a man, gender dynamics may enter the interview. When the interviewer and participant are both women, class, age, and/or race and ethnic differences may still influence how the interview proceeds. Nonetheless, women from diverse backgrounds often volunteer to be interviewed for a variety of sensitive topics. The quality of women's responses may range widely when other people had silenced them about the interview topic. Their responses to the interview may range from illuminating, cathartic, or revelatory to uncomfortable, painful, or overwhelming. The topic, its meaning, and the circumstances of the participant's life, as well as the interviewer's skills, affect how women experience their respective interviews (see also Reinharz & Chase, 2001).

As implied above, differences between interviewer and research respondent in race, class, gender, age, and ideologies may affect what happens during the interview. These status attributes should be seen in relation to the interview topic. Male participants often prefer to talk with a woman about private experiences but may enjoy teaching a younger male interviewer about their work lives. Similarly, elderly participants might be quite willing to discuss sexuality in late life with a middle-aged or older interviewer but not with a young person.

Consider how you can best use the flexibility of interviewing. Grounded theory methods encourage using both ethnographic and interviewing approaches. You may start observing to study a topic and as your analysis proceeds return to participants with more focused queries.

Fitting Intensive Interviewing with Grounded Theory

Intensive qualitative interviewing fits grounded theory methods particularly well. Both grounded theory methods and intensive interviewing are open-ended yet directed, shaped yet emergent, and paced yet unrestricted. Although researchers often choose intensive interviewing as a single method, it complements other methods such as observations, surveys, and research participants' written accounts.

> Both grounded theory methods and intensive interviewing are open-ended but directed, shaped yet emergent, and paced yet flexible approaches.

An interviewer assumes more direct control over the construction of data than most other methods such as ethnography or textual analysis. Grounded theory methods require that researchers take control of their data collection and analysis, and in turn these methods give researchers more analytic control over their material. Qualitative interviewing provides an open-ended, in-depth exploration of an aspect of life about which the interviewee has substantial experience, often combined with considerable insight. The interview can elicit views of this person's subjective world. Interviewers sketch the outline of these views by delineating the topics and drafting the questions. Interviewing is a flexible, emergent technique; ideas and issues emerge during the interview and interviewers can immediately pursue these leads.

Grounded theory methods depend upon a similar type of flexibility as in-depth interviewing. As grounded theorists we aim to learn what is happening from the beginning of our research. Our attempts to learn help us to correct tendencies to follow preconceived notions about what is happening in the field. In addition to picking up and pursuing themes in interviews, we look for ideas through studying our data and then return to the field and gather focused data to answer analytic questions and to fill conceptual gaps. Thus, the combination of flexibility and control inherent in in-depth interviewing techniques fit grounded theory strategies for increasing the analytic incisiveness of the resultant analysis. Grounded theory interviewing differs from much in-depth interviewing because we narrow the range of interview topics to gather specific data for developing our theoretical frameworks as we proceed with conducting the interviews.

Conducting Interviews

How might you go about doing an interview for a grounded theory study? Your first question may suffice for the whole interview if stories tumble out. Receptive 'uh huhs,' a few clarifying questions or comments may keep a story coming when a participant can and wants to tell it. I choose questions carefully and ask them slowly to foster the participant's reflections. Interviewers use in-depth interviewing to explore, not to interrogate (Charmaz, 1991b). Framing questions takes skill and practice. Questions must explore the interviewer's topic and fit the participant's experience. As evident below, these kinds of questions are sufficiently general to cover a wide range of experiences and narrow enough to elicit and elaborate the participant's specific experience.

I include sample questions below to give you ideas about how to frame questions to study process. These questions also reflect a symbolic interactionist emphasis on learning about participants' views, experienced events, and actions. The sample questions are intended to study individual experience. For a project concerning organizational or social processes, I direct questions to the collective practices first and, later, attend to the individual's participation in them and views of them.

These sample questions are merely examples to consider. Think about them and write some open-ended questions. Trim your list of questions to as few as possible. I have never asked all the questions below and often don't get beyond an initial set of questions in one session. I seldom take an interview guide with me into the interview. I prefer to keep the interview informal and conversational; however, novices need more structure. Having an interview guide with well-planned open-ended questions and ready probes can increase your confidence and permit you to concentrate on what the person is saying. Otherwise you may miss obvious points to explore because you become distracted by what to ask next and how to ask it. Subsequently, you may ask a series of 'do you' questions that cut off exploring the topic. At worst, your line of questioning can slip into an interrogation. Both defeat the purpose of conducting an intensive interview. Interviewing takes skill, but you can learn how to do it.

Just as you may need to give special consideration to interviewing certain participants, many topics require special attention. Studying life disruptions or stigmatized behaviors may raise questions of being intrusive. Participants sometimes tell painful stories during the interview that they never imagined telling that may or may not pertain to your study. I follow several principles in such cases that may help you. First, I assume that participants' comfort level has higher priority than obtaining juicy data. Second, I pay close attention as to when to probe. Often, I just listen, particularly when the participant appears to be reexperiencing feelings in the described incident. Third, I try to understand the experience from the participant's view and to validate its significance to this person. Fourth, I slant ending questions toward positive responses to bring the interview to closure at a positive level. No interview should end abruptly after an interviewer has asked the most searching questions or when the participant is distressed. The rhythm and pace of the interview should bring the participant back to a normal conversational level before ending. The following sample interview questions illustrate the above points.

Increasingly, institutional review boards (IRBs) and human subjects committees demand that researchers submit detailed descriptions of their research plans and complete instruments for review. Such detail is inconsistent with the emergent nature of qualitative research in general and grounded theory methods in particular. Interview questions pose special problems in seeking approval from IRBs and human subjects committees. Proposed interview questions must be sufficiently detailed to convince evaluators that no harm will befall research participants yet open enough to allow unanticipated material to emerge during the interview. A well-thought-out list of open-ended questions helps.

BOX 2.1   A SAMPLE OF GROUNDED THEORY INTERVIEW QUESTIONS ABOUT A LIFE CHANGE

Initial Open-ended Questions

1. Tell me about what happened [or how you came to ——].
2. When, if at all, did you first experience —— [or notice ——]?
3. [If so,] what was it like? What did you think then? How did you happen to ——? Who, if anyone, influenced your actions? Tell me about how he/she or they influenced you.
4. Could you describe the events that led up to —— [or preceded ——]?
5. What contributed to ——?
6. What was going on in your life then? How would you describe how you viewed —— before —— happened? How, if at all, has your view of —— changed?
7. How would you describe the person you were then?

(Continued)

(Continued)

Intermediate Questions
1. What, if anything, did you know about ——?
2. Tell me about your thoughts and feelings when you learned about ——.
3. What happened next?
4. Who, if anyone, was involved? When was that? How were they involved?
5. Tell me about how you learned to handle ——.
6. How, if at all, have your thoughts and feelings about —— changed since ——?
7. What positive changes have occurred in your life [or ——] since ——?
8. What negative changes, if any, have occurred in your life [or ——] since ——?
9. Tell me how you go about ——. What do you do?
10. Could you describe a typical day for you when you are ——? [Probe for different times.] Now tell me about a typical day when you are ——.
11. Tell me how you would describe the person you are now. What most contributed to this change [or continuity]?
12. As you look back on ——, are there any other events that stand out in your mind? Could you describe [each one] it? How did this event affect what happened? How did you respond to —— [the event; the resulting situations]?
13. Could you describe the most important lessons you learned through experiencing ——?
14. Where do you see yourself in two years [five years, ten years as appropriate]? Describe the person you hope to be then. How would you compare the person you hope to be and the person you see yourself as now?
15. What helps you to manage ——? What problems might you encounter? Tell me the sources of these problems.
16. Who has been the most helpful to you during this time? How has he/she been helpful?
17. Has any organization been helpful? What did —— help you with? How has it been helpful?

Ending Questions
1. What do you think are the most important ways to ——? How did you discover [or create] them? How has your experience before —— affected how you handled ——?
2. Tell me about how your views [and/or actions depending on topic and preceding responses] may have changed since you have ——.
3. How have you grown as a person since ——? Tell me about your strengths that you discovered or developed through ——. [If appropriate] What do you most value about yourself now? What do others most value in you?
4. After having these experiences, what advice would you give to someone who has just discovered that he or she ——?
5. Is there anything that you might not have thought about before that occurred to you during this interview?
6. Is there anything else you think I should know to understand —— better?
7. Is there anything you would like to ask me?

The questions in Box 2.1 overlap—intentionally so. They permit you to go back to an earlier thread to gain more information, or to winnow unnecessary or potentially uncomfortable questions. Using a tape recorder allows you to give full attention to your research participant with steady eye contact and gives you detailed data. Taking notes on key points during the interview helps as long as jotting notes does not distract you or your participant. Your notes remind you to return to earlier points and suggest how to frame your follow-up questions.

We must guard against forcing interview data into preconceived categories (Glaser, 1978). Interviewing challenges us to create a balance between asking significant questions and forcing responses—more so than other forms of qualitative data collection. An interviewer's questions and interviewing style shape the context, frame, and content of the study. Subsequently, a naïve researcher may inadvertently force interview data into preconceived categories. Not only can asking the wrong questions result in forcing the data, but also how interviewers pose, emphasize, and pace their questions can force the data. The wrong questions fail to explore pivotal issues or to elicit participants' experiences in their own language. Such questions may also impose the researcher's concepts, concerns, and discourse upon the research participant's reality—from the start. Transcribed, tape-recorded interviews make it easy to see when your questions don't work or force the data. When irrelevant, superficial, or forced questions shape the data collection, the subsequent analysis suffers. Thus, researchers need to be constantly reflexive about the nature of their questions and whether they work for the specific participants and the nascent grounded theory.

The focus of the interview and the specific questions asked likely differs depending on whether the interviewer adopts a more constructivist, or more objectivist approach. A constructivist would emphasize eliciting the participant's definitions of terms, situations, and events and try to tap his or her assumptions, implicit meanings, and tacit rules. An objectivist would be concerned with obtaining information about chronology, events, settings, and behaviors. Then, too, Glaser's (1978) version of grounded theory would produce different questions than Strauss and Corbin's (1990, 1998) approach.

On a more general level, we all need to be aware of the assumptions and perspectives that we import into our interview questions. Consider the following questions:

- 'Tell me about the stressors in your situation.'
- 'What coping techniques do you use to handle these stressors?'

These questions might work with a sample of research participants, such as nurses, for whom the terms 'stressors' and 'coping techniques' are common parlance, as long as the interviewer asked participants to define these terms at some point. However, the term 'stressors' might be alien to other participants, such as elderly nursing home patients, much less the thought of identifying sources of stress and having explicit techniques for dealing with them. Paying attention to participants' language, meanings, and lives is crucial here.

Like other skilled interviewers, grounded theory interviewers must remain active in the interview and alert to interesting leads (see Gorden, 1987;

Gubrium & Holstein, 2001; Holstein & Gubrium, 1995; Rubin & Rubin, 1995; Seidman, 1998 for suggestions). Sound interview strategies help the researcher go beyond common sense tales and subsequent obvious, low-level categories that add nothing new. Any competent interviewer shapes questions to obtain rich material and, simultaneously, avoids imposing preconceived concepts on it. Keeping the questions open-ended helps enormously. When participants use terms from the lexicon of their experience, such as 'good days' and 'bad days,' the interviewer can ask for more detail. Contrast the difference between these questions:

- 'Tell me what a good day is like for you.'
- 'Do you feel better about yourself on a good day?'

The first question leaves the response open to the participant's experience and conceptions. This question invites the participant to frame and explore his or her views of a good day. The second closes down the discussion and relegates the answer to a 'yes' or 'no.' This question also assumes both the definitional frame and that participant and interviewer share it.

Interview questions that allow the participant to reflect anew on phenomena elicit rich data. 'Tell me about,' 'how,' 'what,' and 'when' questions yield rich data, particularly when you buttress them with queries to elaborate or to specify such as 'Could you describe—further' (see Charmaz, 2002a). Look for the 'ums' and 'you know's' and then explore what they indicate. What do long pauses indicate? How might they reflect a struggle to find words? When might a 'you know' signal taken-for-granted meanings? When might 'you know' seek the interviewer's concurrence or suggest that the respondent is struggling to articulate an experience? In my research, however, respondents' stories about illness often spilled out non-stop. For example, one participant who had multiple sclerosis said,

> There's always the bladder infection. It seems like, you know, there for— in the nursing home there wasn't [a bladder infection]. There were two or three years [without them]. When I came out [from the nursing home] it seems like that's all I deal with—bladder infections ... So I just cleared bladder infection. It was stressful and it's been a year of that bladder infection, and I probably have another one and this has just been a week and a half. So I could always tell with my back pain and the way I sleep and—and with every bladder infection, the medicines, they kill the good bacteria too. So you get a yeast infection and it's like you just live round-the-clock [with illness and care] and it's—and that's—if all I have to deal with that's one thing, but I have the stress of my—my family. And that's taken a real toll. And then my bowels don't work. This bladder medicine gives you diarrhea. (Charmaz, 1991a: 73)

A researcher has topics to pursue. Research participants have problems to solve, goals to pursue, and actions to perform, and they hold assumptions, ideas, and feelings about all these concerns. Your research questions and mode of inquiry shape your subsequent data and analysis. Thus, becoming self-aware about why and how you gather data enables you to assess your effectiveness. You learn to sense when you are gathering rich, useful data that do not undermine or demean your respondent(s). Not surprisingly then, grounded theory methods work best when the grounded theorist engages in data collection as well as data analysis. This way, you can explore nuances of meaning and process that hired hands might easily miss.

Respondents' stories may tumble out or the major process in which people are engaged may jump out at you. However, respondents may not be so forthcoming nor may major processes be so obvious. Even if they are, it usually takes considerable work to discover the subtlety and complexity of respondents' intentions and actions. The researcher may have entered the implicit world of meaning, but not of explicit words. For example, some of my participants spoke of incidents in which they told other people about their illnesses. They described these people as being initially sympathetic, but later they sensed that they were being treated with insincerity, and felt their social and personal worth was undermined. Often the meaning of such incidents showed in the emotions they expressed when retelling the events, more than in the words they chose.

> The researcher may have entered the implicit world of meaning, but not of explicit words.

For some topics, closer study and direct questioning may suffice. For other topics, you may need to redirect inquiry. For example, our language contains few words with which to talk about time. Thus, many of my research participants' attitudes toward and actions concerning time remained unspoken and taken for granted. Yet their stories about illness often depended on conceptions of time and referred to implicit qualities of experienced time. For example, the woman's statement above about bladder infections referred to the speed and unevenness of her days. When you plan to explore such areas, then you try to devise ways to make relevant observations or to construct questions that will foster pertinent responses. To illustrate, I asked my respondents questions like, 'As you look back on your illness, which events stand out in your mind?' 'What is a typical weekday like for you?' Glaser (1992) might say I force the data here by asking preconceived questions of it. Instead, I *generate* data by investigating taken-for-granted aspects of life. At whatever level you attend to your participants' meanings, intentions, and actions, you can create a coherent analysis by using grounded theory methods. Hence, the method is useful for fact-finding descriptive studies as well as more conceptually developed theoretical statements.

> Studying your data prompts you to learn nuances of your research participants' language and meanings.

Studying your data prompts you to learn nuances of your research participants' language and meanings. Subsequently, you learn to define the directions where your data can take you. Through studying interview audiotapes, for example, you attend closely to your respondents' feelings and views. They will live in your mind as you listen carefully over and over to what they were saying. For example, one student in my class remarked:

> What an impact the words had on me when I sat home alone transcribing the tapes. I was more able to hear and feel what these women were

saying to me. I realized how, at times, I was preoccupied with thoughts of what my next question was, how my eye contact was, or hoping we were speaking loud enough for the tape-recorder. (Charmaz, 1991b: 393)

If you attend to respondents' language, you can bridge their experience with your research questions. Then you can learn about their meanings rather than make assumptions about what they mean. For example, when my respondents with chronic illnesses talked about having 'good days' and 'bad days,' I probed further and asked more questions around their taken-for-granted meanings of good and bad days. I asked questions such as: 'What is a good day like?' 'Could you describe what a bad day is?' 'What kinds of things do you do on a good day?' 'How do these activities compare with those on a bad day?' I discovered that good days mean 'minimal intrusiveness of illness, maximal control over mind, body, and actions, and greater choice of activities' (Charmaz, 1991a: 50). The meaning of good days also extends to increased temporal and spatial horizons, to the quality of the day and to realizing the self one wishes to be. But had I not followed up and asked respondents about the meanings of these terms, their specific properties would have remained implicit. Thus, I gained a more textured, dense understanding of how time and self were related.

Textual Analysis

All qualitative research entails analyzing texts; however, some researchers study texts that they only partially shape or that they obtain from other sources. Elicited texts involve research participants in producing written data in response to a researcher's request and thus offer a means of generating data. Extant texts consist of varied documents that the researcher had no hand in shaping. Researchers treat extant texts *as* data to address their research questions although these texts were produced for other—often very different—purposes. Archival data such as letters from a historical figure or era are a major source of extant texts. We may use elicited and extant texts as either primary or supplementary sources of data.

Texts do not stand as objective facts although they often represent what their authors assumed were objective facts (Prior, 2003). People construct texts for specific purposes and they do so within social, economic, historical, cultural, and situational contexts. Texts draw on particular discourses and provide accounts that record, explore, explain, justify, or foretell actions, whether the specific texts are elicited or extant. For example, police officers may record and give traffic tickets for certain violations but not those that they deem to be trivial. Their recordings are aimed to fulfill their official roles, not to serve as research data. As a discourse, a text follows certain conventions and assumes embedded meanings. Researchers can compare the style, contents, direction, and presentation of material to a larger discourse of which the text is a part. As accounts, texts tell something of intent and have intended—and perhaps unintended—audiences.

Elicited Texts

Elicited texts involve research participants in writing the data. A mailed questionnaire or, increasingly, Internet surveys containing open-ended questions are common sources of these texts. In addition, ethnographers and interviewers may ask their participants to write texts. Asking participants to record family or work histories, keep personal diaries, write daily logs, or answer written questions all generate elicited texts. These texts, like published autobiographies, may elicit thoughts, feelings, and concerns of the thinking, acting subject as well as give researchers ideas about what structures and cultural values influence the person. Researchers' guidelines for elicited texts may range from detailed instructions to minimal suggestions.

On a social psychological level, contrasts between elicited written documents and direct observations may tell a poignant tale. For example, when conducting an ethnographic study of a residential care setting, I asked members to log what they did on a Wednesday and on a Sunday to gain more knowledge of their views of typical days in the institution. After I collected the residents' logs of their typical days, I discovered that one woman had recorded a packed schedule of her reading and writing pursuits. Yet I had seen that she had slept during most of these periods. While engaged in a conversation with a staff nurse, I discovered that this woman had recorded her typical day of three years before (Calkins, 1970). Once a published writer, she wished to be identified by her past, not her present. If I had not collected the logs, I might have missed learning how some elders and ill people construct fictional identities in the present that they reconstruct from actual identities in the past. These identities reflect meanings and preferred images of self, not outright lies. In a similar way, interview respondents may wish to appear affable, intelligent, or politically correct and thus shape their responses accordingly. However, interviews pose possibilities for checking a story that a text does not.

In the example above, my sustained presence in the setting allowed me to search for reasons for disparities between observed realities and written responses. When elicited texts are written by anonymous authors, the researcher has no means of comparing them with other data about the same people.

Elicited texts such as logs, journals, diaries or written responses to specific questions share some of the advantages and disadvantages of conventional surveys and interviews. Like questionnaires, anonymous elicited texts can foster frank disclosures that a person might not wish to make to an interviewer. Revealing secrets that risk shame, disgrace, or failure are among these disclosures. Research participants may not wish to discuss their genetic histories, sex lives, financial situations, troubles at work, personal failures, feelings, or unfulfilled hopes and dreams but might be willing to write about them anonymously. Participants can tell as much or little about themselves as they wish. Still, this approach relies on participants' prior writing skills and practices. Not all participants possess the skill, comfort, and confidence to write full accounts. Murphy and Dingwall (2003) state that elicited texts generate data that resemble interview data. True—they do when the questions posed resemble interview questions and the participants respond to them as such, rather than as bureaucratic forms, quick surveys, management ploys, or trivial inquiries. Thus, elicited texts work best when participants have a stake in the addressed topics, experience in the relevant areas, and view the questions as significant.

As in questionnaire construction, researchers who use elicited texts cannot modify or reword a question once they ask it. Nor do they have any immediate possibility of following up on a statement, encouraging a response, or raising a question even when they may be able to interview research participants later. If consistent with earlier entry and access agreements, researchers might talk with known participants further about their written responses. Although having access to multiple forms of data strengthens a study, qualitative researchers increasingly use personal accounts, letters, responses to open-ended questionnaires, and media resources without other forms of data collection and without the possibility of pursuing such data collection.

Extant Texts

Extant texts contrast with elicited texts in that the researcher does not affect their construction. Among those we might use are public records, government reports, organizational documents, mass media, literature, autobiographies, personal correspondence, Internet discussions, and earlier qualitative materials from data banks. In the past, researchers have valued extant texts because of their relative availability, typically unobtrusive method of data collection, and seeming objectivity.[5]

When researchers use extant texts, their readers may believe such texts mirror reality. A corporate annual report, data on the distribution of homelessness in your hometown, US census data on race may all look like reports of 'facts.' Yet they reflect shared definitions concerning each topic and the power to enforce these definitions. Report writers may adopt definitions that alter or contradict their readers' meanings of seemingly concrete categories such as profits and losses.

Extant texts such as medical charts, police records, or school policy statements may all provide useful information and all have serious limitations. For example, health care workers who foresee possible litigation may limit their notes in medical charts. While working as a nursing assistant during his ethnographic study of a nursing home, Timothy Diamond (1992) examined patients' medical charts. He discovered that staff notes not only erased prior uncharted events but also that the caring work of nursing assistants remained invisible. Through his field research, Diamond learned what staff charted, how they used charts, and what they left out.

Exploring the purposes and objectives of records allows placing them into perspective and perhaps seeking more data from other sources. Extant texts can complement ethnographic and interview methods. Answering questions about information in these texts can serve as valuable data:

- What are the parameters of the information?
- On what and whose facts does this information rest?
- What does the information mean to various participants or actors in the scene?
- What does the information leave out?

- Who has access to the facts, records, or sources of the information?
- Who is the intended audience for the information?
- Who benefits from shaping and/or interpreting this information in a particular way?
- How, if at all, does the information affect actions?

Pretend that you had collected all the reports in an organization you were studying. You might find sharp differences between organizational reports and the field observations that you made. For example, you might discover that managers redefine their failed projects and tout them as successes in their yearly reports. Such important data could direct your analysis in pivotal ways.

For some projects, extant texts provide an independent source of data from the researcher's collected first-hand materials (Reinharz, 1992). Many qualitative researchers make use of demographic data as a backdrop for their topics. Some explore the weaknesses of such data to frame their arguments. Others look for earlier materials that can inform their research questions. I drew upon written personal accounts, primarily published autobiographies, of their respective authors' experience with chronic illness. Rather than assuming such texts are objective sources of data, uncontaminated by the researcher, you can treat them analytically as another source of data. These texts may also spark your ideas and provide evidence for your hunches. Occasionally, you may come across a text that provides strong evidence for an analytic point long after you have drafted it. After I had developed my category 'recapturing the past' I happened to read Kathleen Lewis's (1985) poignant account of having lupus erythematosus. Her statement supported my category:

> My family and I kept taking the 'old me' off the shelf, hoping one day she might return and we could go back to our past lives. We'd sigh and put her back on the shelf, but she lingered in our memories and hopes, thwarting any attempts of accepting and living in the present as it was. It was always, 'Tomorrow we'll …' or 'Remember yesterday, when …?' (p. 45)

Qualitative researchers often use texts as supplementary sources of data. Ethnographers rely most heavily on their fieldnotes but make use of newsletters, records, and reports when they can obtain them. Comparisons between fieldnotes and written documents can spark insights about the relative congruence–or lack of it–between words and deeds. Ethnographers observe what is happening in the setting and learn about the local culture. Both organizational rhetoric and reports may pale in the face of observed worlds. These texts may fulfill intriguing organizational purposes, but researchers cannot assume that they mirror organizational processes. Thus, such texts may provide useful statements about an organization's professed images and claimed objectives–the front stage view aimed to shape its public reputation. When significant audiences accept these statements, the organization can shield backstage realities and often more fundamental objectives from scrutiny, such as recruitment of new members or organizational survival or dominance.

Studying Texts

To the extent possible, we need to situate texts in their contexts. Now Internet research offers endless opportunities for textual analysis–and poses enormous methodological issues. Texts without contexts are major among them. Where do the data come from? Who participated in shaping them? What did the authors intend? Have participants provided sufficient information for us to make a plausible interpretation? And do we have sufficient knowledge of the relevant worlds to read their words with any understanding? On the Internet, participants may alter what we define as basic information–age, gender, race, ethnicity, and social class origins–as well as the specific content of their responses.

Much textual analysis is without context, or worse, out of context. How do you place texts into context? Providing description of the times, actors, and issues gives you a start. Multiple methods help, such as interviewing key participants, and using several types of documents also helps. Texts that tell the story behind other texts at least suggest the social context for the analysis. Both the detail of the texts themselves and the thoroughness of the analysis figure here. Cynthia Bogard (2001) drew upon the *New York Times* and the *Washington Post* stories about local homelessness as well as archival data, television reports, and scholarly publications to reconstruct a view of the context surrounding homelessness in New York and Washington and the kind of claims-making about homelessness that occurred in each city. Rather than treating newspaper reports as objective historical records, she viewed them as 'dominant and elite voices in the public conversation about a social problem … [and thus] important sites of reality construction' (2001: 431). Bogard not only emphasized advocates and adversaries' claims but also developed an analysis of the emergent contexts in which these claims occurred. The depth and comprehensiveness of Bogard's scrutiny of these texts furthers our understanding of homelessness and of how people make claims about reality.

A major way of using texts is as objects for analytic scrutiny themselves rather than for corroborating evidence. Archival records and written narratives, video and photographic images, Internet posts and graphics may give you insights into perspectives, practices, and events not easily obtained through other qualitative methods. Nonetheless, all these texts are products. The processes that shape them may be ambiguous, invisible, and, perhaps, unknowable. A close investigation of the text helps you to study it. Among the possible ways to approach a text, these questions may arise:

- How was the text produced? By whom?
- What is the ostensible purpose of the text? Might the text serve other unstated or assumed purposes? Which ones?
- How does the text represent what its author(s) assumed to exist? Which meanings are embedded within it? How do those meanings reflect a particular social, historical, and perhaps organizational context?
- What is the structure of the text?
- How does its structure shape what is said? Which categories can you discern in its structure? What can you glean from these categories? Do the categories change in sequential texts over time? How so?

- Which contextual meanings does the text imply?
- How does its content construct images of reality?
- Which realities does the text claim to represent? How does it represent them?
- What, if any, unintended information and meanings might you see in the text?
- How is language used?
- Which rules govern the construction of the text? How can you discern them in the narrative? How do these rules reflect both tacit assumptions and explicit meanings? How might they be related to other data on the same topic?
- When and how do telling points emerge in the text?
- What kinds of comparisons can you make between texts? Between different texts on the same topic? Similar texts at different times such as organizational annual reports? Between different authors who address the same questions?
- Who benefits from the text? Why?

Most grounded theorists would start with the content of the texts. I also address their structure and relationships between structure and content. Grounded theories of textual material can address form as well as content, audiences as well as authors, and production of the text as well as presentation of it.

Concluding Thoughts

With any data-gathering approach, consider how participants invoke ideas, practices, and accounts from both the larger and local cultures of which they are a part. Keep in mind that they may not simply borrow from these cultures or reproduce them; rather, they may make innovations as they adapt them to serve their immediate purposes. Similarly, as researchers, we adapt language and meanings as we record data; data are never entirely raw. Recording data alone confers interpretations of them because we place a conceptual frame on them through our use of language and understandings about the world.

Scrutinizing how you collect data and which data you obtain helps to locate them. Such scrutiny also helps you when coding and categorizing because you will be able to place your emerging analysis in its social context. Then you can make more precise comparisons when coding data. By studying your methods, you will improve both your methodological skills and the quality of your data. Subsequently, your scrutiny may lead you to realize later that collecting another kind of data with a different method may answer questions in your emerging analysis. For large projects such as theses, you might use two or more data-gathering approaches. For a major funded research project, multi-method and multi-site approaches often prove to be useful. If you construct a research proposal that builds in possibilities for pursuing data in several settings, you have the flexibility later on to use or develop methods that address emergent questions.

In the interim, we next move on to begin the analytic phase of our grounded theory journey, through coding our early data.

NOTES

1 Biernacki (1986) devised a sophisticated form of snowball sampling with referral chains to find his sample of naturally recovered addicts. His project was eventually funded and he and his staff conducted 101 lengthy interviews with these former addicts as well as comparative interviews with recovered addicts who had undergone treatment.

2 Matthew J. James reminded me that all research has emergent themes (Personal communication, September 17, 2004). True, but the degree to which various methodological approaches encourage or inhibit them differs. Grounded theory methods are founded on facilitating emergence.

3 Grounded theory studies have long been accused of building analyses on haphazard, skimpy data (Lofland & Lofland, 1984). Creswell (1998) views grounded theory as primarily based upon a limited number of interviews (20–30), but he does not challenge using a small sample. Depending on the purpose and the quality of data and analysis, a limited sample might be sufficient. A dissertation or major study requires more interviews when they are the sole source of data.

   Now the tendency to shortcut data collection permeates all kinds of methods, including ethnography. As Schneider (1997) argues, the rush to theorizing reflects political and career decisions beyond specific research problems to the detriment of both theory and research.

4 These ethnographic questions are adapted from Mitchell's (1991) longer list.

5 Not all telling texts may be so straightforward. The most significant extant texts may be relatively unavailable and require obtrusive methods to find. Obtaining these texts may contradict informed consent rules and institutional review board policies that serve to protect the powerful. Dalton's *Men Who Manage* (1959) offers a classic example. Dalton received the confidential documents confirming the status characteristics of managers from a secretary who believed in the value of Dalton's project.

3 Coding in Grounded Theory Practice

The first analytic turn in our grounded theory journey brings us to coding. Grounded theory coding requires us to stop and ask analytic questions of the data we have gathered. These questions not only further our understanding of studied life but also help us direct subsequent data-gathering toward the analytic issues we are defining. Grounded theory coding consists of at least two phases: initial and focused coding. During initial coding we study fragments of data—words, lines, segments, and incidents—closely for their analytic import. From time to time, we may adopt our participants' telling terms as *in vivo* codes. While engaging in focused coding, we select what seem to be the most useful initial codes and test them against extensive data. Throughout the process, we compare data with data and then data with codes. We may follow special procedures to elaborate our codes or move to extant theoretical codes but only if indicated by our emerging analysis. Signposts and guides make our sojourn with coding accessible and ease our way around obstacles.

Consider the following interview excerpt from Bonnie Presley, who had long known she had systemic lupus erythematosus and had recently learned that she also had discoid lupus erythematosus. At the time of this interview, Bonnie was 48 years old and divorced from her second husband. After leaving a partner with whom she had lived for several years, she lived alone with her three cats. During the past year, she had had several immobilizing episodes of illness; the first one had been life-threatening. Currently, she was attempting to regain her strength after being ill for almost three months. Bonnie's good friend and neighbor, Linda, was keeping a watchful eye on her. Linda was bringing Bonnie food and made her tea since Bonnie felt too weak to care for herself.

Although Bonnie's adult daughter, Amy, now lived in the area, their calls and Amy's visits remained sporadic. Years before, Amy could not understand how the mother she had known as a fitness buff could have become so sedentary. Bonnie's youthful physical appearance belied her health status because her symptoms remained invisible to an untrained eye. In the early years of her illness, Bonnie had found it difficult to tell Amy about her illness and its seriousness.[1] Amy had moved away before Bonnie first became ill and Bonnie had either understated what was happening or avoided telling Amy. Bonnie recounted her realization about how she had told Amy the news about her recent crisis:

> She found out from Linda that I was, had been in bed for days and she called me up, 'You never tell me, and I have to find out from Linda,' and 'Why don't you tell me who you are and what's going on and ...' Well, I don't know how long after that, but that Saturday the pain started right here and it, throughout the day it got worse and worse and worse. And she–I kept thinking that, well, I can deal with this, so I took some kind of a pain pill and nothing helped. And that was about one in the afternoon. Well, it got worse and worse so that every time I took a breath the pain was horrible, so by seven, eight o'clock that night, I was scared because I knew that if it got any worse I wasn't going to be able to breathe. So I called her and then I told her what was going on, that I was going to be driven to the doctor because they were going to try giving me shots of zylocain or something to try to locate a point to where maybe it would go in there and numb the pain for me so that I could breathe. Well, I called her and told her this. And I have a car phone. She says, 'Well, Mom I'll call you later or you call me.' Well, I didn't call her; she didn't call me. That was Saturday night. She didn't call me until—she called me about noon on Monday, and I finally said, 'Well look, this is why I don't tell you, because when I told you Saturday night, you never called, you didn't care or anything and it really hurt my feelings. So that's why I don't tell you when I have this going on.' And she said to me, 'Well, Mom, you sounded perfectly fine.' And I said, 'Well, what do you expect me to do, become an emotional wreck or something?' I said, 'I have to keep everything still and quiet in me in order to control, because if I went into emotional frenzy, I would have not been able to breathe,' you know. So she started really trying to understand that just because I was scared to death, I was in horrible pain, but when I called her, I guess I was just a normal mom.

What sense might we make of stories like Bonnie's? How do we synthesize hundreds of pages of interviews, fieldnotes, documents, and other texts to develop a grounded theory? Whether we have collected stories, scenes, or written statements, we study and define these materials to analyze what happened and what they might mean.

Qualitative coding, the process of defining what the data are about, is our first analytic step. Coding means naming segments of data with a label that simultaneously categorizes, summarizes, and accounts for each piece of data.[2] Coding is the first step in moving beyond concrete statements in the data to making analytic interpretations. We aim to make an interpretative rendering that begins with coding and illuminates studied life.

> Coding means categorizing segments of data with a short name that simultaneously summarizes and accounts for each piece of data. Your codes show how you select, separate, and sort data to begin an analytic accounting of them.

BOX 3.1   GROUNDED THEORY CODING EXAMPLE

Receiving second-hand news
Being left out; Accusing mother of
   repeated not telling; (questioning
   ethical stance?) Being confronted
Facing self and identity questions;
   Demanding self-disclosure and
   information
Experiencing escalating pain
Expecting to manage pain
Inability to control pain

Rapid worsening of pain
Having excruciating pain
Becoming frightened; Foreseeing
   breathing crisis
Breaking the news; Informing
   daughter of plan

Explaining projected treatment

Having access for making contact
Leaving follow-up contact
   open-ended
No follow-up
Ascertaining the time between
   contacts
Explaining lack of disclosure
Accusing daughter of not caring
Expressing hurt; Assuming lack of
   caring; Making negative
   inferences (of a moral lapse?)
Accounting for not telling
Sounding fine
Questioning daughter's expectations
Explaining need for emotional control
Seeing life-threatening risk of
   losing control
Teaching that mode of telling
   does not reflect state of being

Sounding like a 'normal' mom

She found out from Linda that I was, had been in bed for days and she called me up, 'You never tell me, and I have to find out from Linda,' and 'Why don't you tell me who you are and what's going on and ...' Well, I don't know how long after that, but that Saturday the pain started right here and it, throughout the day it got worse and worse and worse. And she–I kept thinking that, well, I can deal with this, so I took some kind of a pain pill and nothing helped. And that was about one in the afternoon. Well, it got worse and worse so that every time I took a breath the pain was horrible, so by seven, eight o'clock that night, I was scared because I knew that if it got any worse I wasn't going to be able to breathe. So I called her and then I told her what was going on, that I was going to be driven to the doctor because they were going to try giving me shots of zylocain or something to try to locate a point to where maybe it would go in there and numb the pain for me so that I could breathe. Well, I called her and told her this. And I have a car phone. She says, 'Well, Mom I'll call you later or you call me.' Well, I didn't call her; she didn't call me. That was Saturday night. She didn't call me until—she called me about noon on Monday, and I finally said, 'Well look, this is why I don't tell you, because when I told you Saturday night, you never called, you didn't care or anything and it really hurt my feelings. So that's why I don't tell you when I have this going on.' And she said to me, 'Well, Mom, you sounded perfectly fine.' And I said, 'Well, what do you expect me to do, become an emotional wreck or something?' I said, 'I have to keep everything still and quiet in me in order to control, because if I went into emotional frenzy, I would have not been able to breathe,' you know. So she started really trying to understand that just because I was scared to death, I was in horrible pain, but when I called her, I guess I was just a normal mom.

Our codes show how we select, separate, and sort data to begin an analytic accounting of them. Qualitative codes take segments of data apart, name them in concise terms, and propose an analytic handle to develop abstract ideas for interpreting each segment of data. As we code, we ask: which theoretical categories might these statements indicate?

You might have wondered what qualitative codes look like and how researchers construct them. A quick look at my codes of Bonnie Presley's story will give you an idea (see Box 3.1).

The codes in Box 3.1 attempt to portray meanings and actions in Bonnie's story. We gain a sense of both Bonnie's and Amy's concerns, as Bonnie presents them. Her story shows how telling news can be fraught with problems. Misunderstandings and dilemmas arise. Hesitancies occur. Accusations ensue. Explanations follow. Telling the news can open the self to view, risk emotional costs, and force questions about relationships. Not telling or delayed telling can also rent or rupture bonds. Familial failures, ethical slights, and moral claims accrue, from one or another person's view. Rhetorical styles may be meant—or misunderstood—as delivering fundamental judgments. For both Bonnie and Amy, disclosing illness became a contested area in which charged questions ignited about whom each was to the other. Events may force disclosure, as Bonnie's story indicates. What people tell, when they tell it, and how they tell it all matter. How Bonnie told her daughter affected how her daughter understood and acted on the news. Bonnie had concentrated on not risking loss of emotional control but later realized that her straightforward way of informing Amy may have understated the seriousness of the episode and fueled misunderstandings. By maintaining emotional control when informing her daughter, Bonnie's daughter thought she 'sounded perfectly fine,' like 'just a normal mom.'

Note that the codes stick closely to the data, show actions, and indicate how dilemmas surrounding disclosure arise. Certain codes, such as 'being left out,' 'facing self and identity questions,' 'demanding self-disclosure and information,' are central to analyzing Bonnie's story, as are those about accounting, explaining, and providing reasons. Other codes preserve events, suggest contexts, and portray viewpoints, such as 'receiving second-hand news,' 'expecting to manage pain,' and 'sounding like a "normal" mom.' Many of the codes are short. They also imply crucial relationships between telling and self, as defined by both self and other. Hence, the codes suggest building categories concerned with telling, disclosing, self, and identity. I placed two codes in parentheses because they are less firmly apparent here than others and represent ideas to look for in further data. Consistent with a grounded theory emphasis on emergence, questions about these codes arise from my reading of the data rather than emanating from an earlier frame applied to them.

Grounded Theory Coding

Grounded theory coding generates the bones of your analysis. Theoretical integration will assemble these bones into a working skeleton. Thus, coding is more than a beginning; it shapes an analytic frame from which you build the analysis.

I lay out coding strategies for developing the frame. Try them. See how they work for you. Grounded theory coding fosters studying action and processes, as you can see in the codes of Bonnie Presley's story.

Coding is the pivotal link between collecting data and developing an emergent theory to explain these data. Through coding, you *define* what is happening in the data and begin to grapple with what it means. The codes take form together as elements of a nascent theory that explains these data and directs further data-gathering. By careful attending to coding, you begin weaving two major threads in the fabric of grounded theory: generalizable theoretical statements that transcend specific times and places and contextual analyses of actions and events.

> Coding is the pivotal link between collecting data and developing an emergent theory to explain these data. Through coding, you *define* what is happening in the data and begin to grapple with what it means.

Grounded theory coding consists of at least two main phases: 1) an initial phase involving naming each word, line, or segment of data followed by 2) a focused, selective phase that uses the most significant or frequent initial codes to sort, synthesize, integrate, and organize large amounts of data. While engaged in initial coding, you mine early data for analytic ideas to pursue in further data collection and analysis. Initial coding entails a close reading of the data as indicated by my codes of Bonnie Presley's story. During initial coding, the goal is to remain open to all possible theoretical directions indicated by your readings of the data. Later, you use focused coding to pinpoint and develop the most salient categories in large batches of data. Theoretical integration begins with focused coding and proceeds through all your subsequent analytic steps.

The actual research you conduct through analyzing your data likely differs—at least somewhat—from what you may have planned earlier in a research or grant proposal. We learn through studying our data. Qualitative coding guides our learning. Through it, we begin to make sense of our data. How we make sense of it shapes the ensuing analysis. Careful attention to coding furthers our attempts to understand acts and accounts, scenes and sentiments, stories and silences from our research participants' view. We want to know what is happening in the setting, in people's lives, and in lines of our recorded data. Hence, we try to understand our participants' standpoints and situations, as well as their actions within the setting.

The logic of grounded theory coding differs from quantitative logic that applies *preconceived* categories or codes to the data. As the example above illustrates, we *create* our codes by defining what we see in the data. Codes emerge as you scrutinize your data and define meanings within it. Through this active coding, you interact with your data again and again and ask many different questions of them. As a result, coding may take you into unforeseen areas and new research questions.

Language plays a crucial role in how and what we code. Most fundamentally, the empirical world does not appear to us in some natural state apart from human experience. Rather we know the empirical world through language and the actions we take toward it. In this sense, no researcher is neutral because language confers form and meaning on observed realities. Specific use of language reflects views and values. We share one language with colleagues and perhaps another with friends; we attribute meanings to specific terms and hold perspectives. Our codes arise from the languages, meanings, and perspectives through which we learn about the empirical world, including those of our participants as well as our own. Coding impels us to make our participants' language problematic to render an analysis of it. Coding should inspire us to examine hidden assumptions in our own use of language as well as that of our participants.

We *construct* our codes because we are actively naming data—even when we believe our codes form a perfect fit with actions and events in the studied world. We may think our codes capture the empirical reality. Yet it is *our* view: we choose the words that constitute our codes. Thus we define what we see as significant in the data and describe what we think is happening. Coding consists of this initial, shorthand defining and labeling; it results from a grounded theorist's actions and understandings. Nonetheless, the process is interactive. We interact with our participants and subsequently interact with them again many times over through studying their statements and observed actions and re-envisioning the scenes in which we know them. As we define our codes and perhaps later refine them, we try to understand participants' views and actions from their perspectives. These perspectives usually assume much more than what is immediately apparent. We must dig into our data to interpret participants' tacit meanings. Close attention to coding helps us to do that.

Close attention to coding follows the first grounded theory mandate: *Study your emerging data* (Glaser, 1978).

From the beginning, you may sense that the process of coding produces certain tensions—between analytic insights and described events, whether spoken accounts or written observations, between static topics and dynamic processes, and between participants' worlds and professionals' meanings.

Initial Coding

The Logic of Initial Coding

When grounded theorists conduct initial coding, we remain open to exploring whatever theoretical possibilities we can discern in the data. This initial step in coding moves us toward later decisions about defining our core conceptual categories. Through comparing data with data, we learn what our research participants view as problematic and begin to treat it analytically. During initial coding, we ask:

- 'What is this data a study of?' (Glaser, 1978: 57; Glaser & Strauss, 1967)
- What does the data suggest? Pronounce?
- From whose point of view?
- What theoretical category does this specific datum indicate? (Glaser, 1978)

Initial coding should stick closely to the data. Try to see actions in each segment of data rather than applying preexisting categories to the data. Attempt to code with words that reflect action. At first, invoking a language of action rather than of topics may feel strange. Look closely at actions and, to the degree possible, code data *as* actions. This method of coding curbs our tendencies to make conceptual leaps and to adopt extant theories *before* we have done the necessary analytic work.

Students often believe that they must rely on earlier concepts and invoke them before they begin coding to make their qualitative research legitimate. They make statements like, 'I'm going to use Max Weber's concept of routinization,' or 'My advisor wants me to use Anselm Strauss's concept of "negotiations".' Such approaches preclude ideas from emerging as you code events. The openness of initial coding should spark your thinking and allow new ideas to emerge. Earlier grounded theory rules prescribed conducting initial coding without having preconceived concepts in mind (Glaser, 1978, 1992). I agree with Glaser's approach of keeping initial coding open-ended yet acknowledge that researchers hold prior ideas and skills. As Dey (1999: 251) states, 'There is a difference between an open mind and an empty head.' Try to remain open to seeing what you can learn while coding and where it can take you. In team research, several individuals may code data separately and then compare and combine their different codings.

Initial codes are provisional, comparative, and grounded in the data. They are provisional because you aim to remain open to other analytic possibilities and create codes that best fit the data you have. You progressively follow up on codes that indicate that they fit the data. Then you gather data to explore and fill out these codes.

Initial grounded theory coding can prompt you to see areas in which you lack needed data. Realizing that your data have gaps—or holes—is part of the analytic process. It is inevitable when you adopt an emergent method of conducting research.[3] After all, making 'discoveries' about the worlds you study and pursuing these discoveries to construct an analysis is what grounded theory is about. Such discoveries reflect what you learn and how you conceptualize it. The advantage of grounded theory strategies is that you may learn about gaps and holes in your data from the earliest stages of research. Then you can locate sources of needed data and gather them. Hence, simultaneous data collection and analysis can help you go further and deeper into the research problem as well as engage in developing categories.

Codes are also provisional in the sense that you may reword them to improve the fit. Part of the fit is the degree to which they capture and condense meanings and actions. Compelling codes capture the phenomenon and grab the reader.

Initial Coding Practices

Speed and spontaneity help in initial coding. Working quickly can spark your thinking and spawn a fresh view of the data. Some codes fit the data and grab the reader immediately. You can revise others to improve the fit. My original code of the first line of Bonnie Presley's story above was 'receiving news indirectly.' It condensed the statement but the neutral wording drained the incident of its intensity and importance. Changing the code to 'receiving second-hand news' suggested the reduced value of the news, implied the receiver's diminished status, and alluded to her angry response.

Comparing incidents of the same order between data spurs you to think analytically about them. Bonnie Presley revealed a reluctance to tell her daughter, delayed in telling her, and imparted difficult news in a matter-of-fact manner. Yet, from time to time, she and Amy talked about their problems in giving and getting news about Bonnie's illness. Because Bonnie no longer had much contact with her own mother, dilemmas of disclosure did not arise with her. No disclosures occurred. Bonnie's grandmother, of whom she was very fond, had partly raised her. Bonnie protected her grandmother from worry by treating her situation lightly and by minimizing the implications of her symptoms. My data included other cases of inter-generational tensions. Several other single women I studied who had no children and few close family ties had conflicted relationships with their aging mothers. As geographical and emotional distance increased, these women correspondingly curtailed sharing their news. From the data and brief descriptions above, avoiding disclosure, delaying disclosure, and controlling information all emerged as salient codes.

Glaser (1978) shows how coding with gerunds helps you detect processes and stick to the data. Think of the difference in imagery between the following gerunds and their noun forms: describing versus description, stating versus statement, and leading versus leader. We gain a strong sense of action and sequence with gerunds. The nouns turn these actions into topics. Staying close to the data and, when possible, starting from the words and actions of your respondents, preserves the fluidity of their experience and gives you new ways of looking at it. These steps encourage you to begin analysis from their perspective. That is the point. If you ignore, gloss over, or leap beyond participants' meanings and actions, your grounded theory will likely reflect an outsider's, rather than an insider's view. Outsiders often import an alien professional language to describe the phenomenon. If your data are thin and if you don't push hard in coding, you may mistake routine rationales for analytic insights. Thus, accepting participants' orchestrated impressions at face value can lead to outsider analyses.

Picking up general terms from an interview such as 'experience' or 'event' and calling them codes tells you little about the participant's meaning or action. If general terms seem significant, qualify them. Make your codes fit the data you have rather than forcing the data to fit them.

A code for coding:

- Remain open
- Stay close to the data
- Keep your codes simple and precise
- Construct short codes
- Preserve actions
- Compare data with data
- Move quickly through the data.

In short, remain open to what the material suggests and stay close to it. Keep your codes short, simple, active and analytic. The first two guidelines above reflect your stance toward coding. The remaining guidelines suggest how to do coding.

Word-by-Word Coding

The size of the unit of data to code matters. Some grounded theorists conduct nuanced coding and move through their data word by word. This approach may be particularly helpful when working with documents or certain types of ephemera, such as Internet data. Word-by-word analysis forces you to attend to images and meanings. You may attend to the structure and flow of words, and how both affect the sense you make of them, as well as their specific content.

Line-by-Line Coding

For many grounded theorists, line-by-line coding is the first step in coding (see Box 3.2). Line-by-line coding means naming each line of your written data (Glaser, 1978). Coding every line may seem like an arbitrary exercise because not every line contains a complete sentence and not every sentence may appear to be important.[4] Nevertheless, it can be an enormously useful tool. Ideas will occur to you that had escaped your attention when reading data for a general thematic analysis.[5]

Line-by-line coding works particularly well with detailed data about fundamental empirical problems or processes whether these data consist of interviews, observations, documents, or ethnographies and autobiographies. For example, if you plan to study how older women who have been full-time homemakers handle divorce, you have identified an area to explore about which you may hear stories in interviews, support groups, and job training programs that take on vivid meanings when studied line by line.

Detailed observations of people, actions, and settings that reveal visibly *telling* and *consequential* scenes and actions lend themselves to line-by-line coding. Generalized observations such as 'the meeting droned on' give you little substance to code.

Fresh data and line-by-line coding prompt you to remain open to the data and to see nuances in it. When you code early in-depth interview data, you gain a close look at what participants say and, likely, struggle with. This type of coding can help you to identify implicit concerns as well as explicit statements. Engaging in line-by-line coding helps you to refocus later interviews. The following flexible strategies help you code:

- Breaking the data up into their component parts or properties
- Defining the actions on which they rest
- Looking for tacit assumptions
- Explicating implicit actions and meanings
- Crystallizing the significance of the points
- Comparing data with data
- Identifying gaps in the data.

By using these strategies flexibly and following leads in your data, coding leads to developing theoretical categories, some of which you may define in your initial codes. Stick with what you define in your data. Build your analysis step-by-step from the ground up without taking off on theoretical flights of fancy. Having a credible amount of data that speaks to your research topic further strengthens the foundation of your study.

Your research participants' actions and statements teach you about their worlds, albeit sometimes in ways they may not anticipate. Studying your data through line-by-line coding sparks new ideas for you to pursue. Hence, the grounded theory method itself contains correctives that reduce the likelihood that researchers merely superimpose their preconceived notions on the data. Line-by-line coding provides an early corrective of this type.

In the examples of line-by-line coding in Box 3.2, my interest in time and self-concept comes through in the first two codes in Excerpt 1. Note how I kept the codes active and close to the data. Initial codes often range widely across a variety of topics. Because even a short statement or excerpt may address several points, it could illustrate several different categories. I could use the excerpt in Box 3.2 to show how avoiding disclosure serves to control identity. I could also use it either to show how a respondent learns that other people see his or her illness as inexplicable or how each day is unpredictable. Having multiple interviews of the same individuals allows me to see how social and emotional isolation begins and progresses.

The logic of 'discovery' becomes evident as you begin to code data. Line-by-line coding forces you to look at the data anew. Compare what you see when you read a set of fieldnotes or an interview as an entire narrative with what you gain when you do word-by-word, line-by-line, or incident-by-incident coding on the same document. Entire narratives may net several major themes. Word-by-word, line-by-line, segment-by-segment, and incident-by-incident coding may generate a range of ideas and information. Therefore, you 'discover' ideas on which you can build.

Initial codes help you to separate data into categories and to see processes. Line-by-line coding frees you from becoming so immersed in your respondents' worldviews that you accept them without question. Then you fail to look at your data critically and analytically. Being critical about your data does not necessarily mean being critical of your research participants. Instead, being critical forces asking *yourself* questions about your data. These questions help you to see actions and to identify significant processes. Such questions include:

- What process(es) is at issue here? How can I define it?
- How does this process develop?
- How does the research participant(s) act while involved in this process?
- What does the research participant(s) profess to think and feel while involved in this process? What might his or her observed behavior indicate?
- When, why, and how does the process change?
- What are the consequences of the process?

Through coding each line of data, you gain insights about what kinds of data to collect next. Thus, you distill data and direct further inquiry early in the

BOX 3.2   INITIAL CODING: LINE-BY-LINE CODING

Excerpt 1   *Christine Danforth, age 37, lupus erythematosus, Sjögren's syndrome, back injuries*

Lupus erythematosus is a systemic, inflammatory autoimmune disease of the connective tissue that affects vital organs as well as joints, muscles, and nerves. Sjögren's syndrome is a related autoimmune inflammatory disease characterized by dry mucous membranes of the eyes and mouth.

Shifting symptoms, having inconsistent days
Interpreting images of self given by others
Avoiding disclosure
Predicting rejection

Keeping others unaware
Seeing symptoms as connected
Having others unaware
Anticipating disbelief
Controlling others' views
Avoiding stigma
Assessing potential losses and risks of disclosing

If you have lupus, I mean one day it's my liver; one day it's my joints; one day it's my head, and it's like people really think you're a hypochondriac if you keep complaining about different ailments ... It's like you don't want to say anything because people are going to start thinking, you know, 'God, don't go near her, all she is–is complaining about this.' And I think that's why I never say anything because I feel like everything I have is related one way or another to the lupus but most of the people don't know I have lupus, and even those that do are not going to believe that ten different ailments are the same thing. And I don't want anybody saying, you know, [that] they don't want to come around me because I complain.

Excerpt 2   *Joyce Marshall, age 60, minor heart condition, recent small CVA (stroke)*

In her case, the stroke left her with weakness, fatigue, and slowed responses when tired.

Meaning of the CVA

Feeling forced to live one day at a time

I have to see it [her CVA] as a warning. I can't let myself get so anxious. I have to live one day at a time.

Having a worried past

Earlier losses
Difficulty in living one day at a time; concentrating on today
Giving up future orientation
Managing emotions through living one day at a time
Reducing life-threatening risk

I've been so worried about John [her husband who had had life-threatening heart attacks and lost his job three years before retirement] and preparing to get a job [her first in 38 years] ... It's just so hard with all this stress ... to concentrate on what I can do today. I always used to look to the future. I can't now; it upsets me too much. I have to live one day at a time now or else there may not be any me.

data collection. Line-by-line coding gives you leads to pursue. If, for example, you identify an important process in your fifteenth interview, then you can return to earlier respondents and see if that process explains events and experiences in their lives. If not, you can seek new respondents who can illuminate this process. Hence, your data collection becomes more focused, as does your coding.

Coding Incident to Incident

Whether or not you conduct line-by-line coding depends on the type of data you have collected, their level of abstraction, the stage of the research process, and your purpose for collecting these data. Grounded theorists often conduct a close cousin of line-by-line coding through a comparative study of incidents. Here you compare incident with incident, then as your ideas take hold, compare incidents to your conceptualization of incidents coded earlier. That way you can identify properties of your emerging concept.

A similar logic applies to observational data. Making comparisons between incidents likely works better than word-by-word or line-by-line coding, in part because the fieldnotes already consist of your own words (see, for example, Charmaz & Mitchell, 2001). Compare incident to incident. Concrete, behavioristic descriptions of people's mundane actions may not be amenable to line-by-line coding, particularly when you observed a scene but do not have a sense of its context, its participants, and did not interact with them. Students often think observing behavior in public places is the easiest type of qualitative research to conduct. Not so. Both the researcher's data and analytic approach make a difference. Few novices have the eye and ear to record nuances of action and interaction. More likely, they record concrete behaviors in a general way and gradually learn to make more acute observations.

Still, detailed observations alone do not guarantee creating an insightful theoretical analysis although they may generate excellent description. The mode of analysis matters. Comparative methods help you to see and make sense of observations in new, analytic ways. Conducting a line-by-line coding of one observation after another of people's actions in a public place may not spark fresh ideas. Instead, making comparisons between observations gives you clues to follow if not immediate ideas. If the people you study bring you into their world, for example, you may record all kinds of incidents in anecdotes, conversations, and observations in your fieldnotes that abound with meaning. You may see first-hand how your participants manage daily life without them telling you—and you may learn much more.

The more unproblematic—that is, routine, familiar, and ordinary—observed events seem to you, the more problematic creating an original conceptual analysis of them will be. Breaking through the ordinariness of routine events takes effort. To gain analytic insights from observations of routine actions in ordinary settings, first compare and code similar events. Then you may define subtle patterns and significant processes. Later, comparing *dissimilar* events may give you further insights.

Using Comparative Methods

Whatever unit of data you begin coding in grounded theory, you use *'constant comparative methods'* (Glaser & Strauss, 1967) to establish analytic distinctions–and thus make comparisons at each level of analytic work. At first, you compare data with data to find similarities and differences. For example, compare interview statements and incidents within the same interview and compare statements and incidents in different interviews. Making sequential comparisons helps. Compare data in earlier and later interviews of the same individual(s) or compare observations of events at different times and places. When you conduct observations of a routine activity, compare what happens on one day with the same activity on subsequent days.

If your codes define another view of a process, action or belief than your respondent(s) hold, note that. Your observations and ideas do matter. Do not dismiss your own ideas if they do not mirror the data. Your ideas may rest on covert meanings and actions that have not entirely surfaced yet. Such intuitions form another set of ideas to check. Our task is to make analytic sense of the material, which may challenge taken-for-granted understandings.

What you see in your data relies in part upon your prior perspectives. Rather than seeing your perspectives as truth, try to see them as representing one view among many. That way, you may gain more awareness of the concepts that you employ and might impose on your data. To illustrate, you might already possess a repertoire of psychological concepts that you ordinarily invoke to understand behavior. Invoking these concepts in your codes can lead you to prejudge what is happening. Try to avoid assuming that respondents, for example, repress or deny significant 'facts' about their lives. Instead, look for how they understand their situations before you judge their attitudes and actions through your own assumptions. Seeing the world through their eyes and understanding the logic of their experience brings you fresh insights. Afterwards, if you still enlist disciplinary terms as codes, you will use them more consciously rather than automatically. Thus, you can elect to use only those terms that fit your data.

Advantages of Initial Coding

From the start, careful word-by-word, line-by-line, incident-by-incident coding moves you toward fulfilling two criteria for completing a grounded theory analysis: fit and relevance. Your study fits the empirical world when you have constructed codes and developed them into categories that crystallize participants' experience. It has relevance when you offer an incisive analytic framework that interprets what is happening and makes relationships between implicit processes and structures visible.

Careful coding also helps you to refrain from imputing your motives, fears, or unresolved personal issues to your respondents and to your collected data. Some years ago, a young man in my seminar conducted research on adaptation to disability. He had become paraplegic himself when he was hit by a car while bicycling. Stories of courage, hope, and innovation filled his ten in-depth interviews. Narratives of grief, anger, and loss permeated his analysis of them. After I noted that his analysis did not reflect his collected material, he realized how his feelings had colored his perceptions of other people's disabilities. His was an important realization. However, he might have arrived at it before he handed in his paper had he done more assiduous coding. Line-by-line coding might have changed his ideas about his date early in the analysis.

Coding forces you to think about the material in new ways that may differ from your research participants' interpretations. Your analytic eye and disciplinary background lead you to look at their statements and actions in ways that may not have occurred to them. By studying the data, you may make fundamental processes explicit, render hidden assumptions visible, and give participants new insights. Thomas (1993) says that a researcher must take the familiar, routine, and mundane and make it unfamiliar and new. Think of seeing a once-familiar landscape with a fresh eye after a long absence. You see familiar landmarks with acuity unlike days past when they blurred together. Word-by-word and line-by-line coding help you to see the familiar in new light. Incident coding aids you in discovering patterns and contrasts. You may gain surprising insights about how people's actions fit together or come into conflict. You also gain distance from your preconceptions and your participants' taken-for-granted assumptions about the material so that you *can* see it in new light.

In Vivo Codes

Grounded theorists generally refer to codes of participants' special terms as *in vivo* codes. Their specialized terms provide a useful analytic point of departure. *In vivo* codes help us to preserve participants' meanings of their views and actions in the coding itself. *Pay attention to language while you are coding. In vivo* codes serve as symbolic markers of participants' speech and meanings. Whether or not they provide useful codes in the later more integrated analysis depends on how you treat them analytically. Like any other code, they need to be subjected to comparative and analytic treatment. Although the terms may be catchy, *in vivo* codes do not stand on their own in a robust grounded theory; these codes need to be integrated into the theory. When you scrutinize them carefully, three kinds of *in vivo* codes prove to be useful:

- Those general terms everyone 'knows' that flag condensed but significant meanings
- A participant's innovative term that captures meanings or experience
- Insider shorthand terms specific to a particular group that reflect their perspective.

In vivo codes that condense meanings consist of widely used terms that participants assume everyone shares. In contrast, take participants' usage as problematic rather than reproducing it. Hence, we look for their implicit meanings and attend to how they construct and act upon these meanings. In doing so, we can ask, what analytic category(ies) does this code suggest? Unpacking such terms not only gives you a great opportunity to understand implicit meanings and actions but also to make comparisons between data and with your emerging categories.

Today, everyone knows what the general term 'battered woman' means; however, certain groups assume specific meanings when they use the term. Donileen Loseke (1992) discovered that claims-makers' use of the term depicted a particular set of characteristics that did not fit all women who suffered physical abuse. For claims-makers, a battered woman meant an economically and emotionally dependent mother who suffered repeated, escalating physical abuse, had low self-esteem and poor coping skills, could not rely on informal help or formal services, and had no place to go. These claims-makers then acted on their meanings when deciding who would receive services and what these services should include. An older, affluent woman without children would not fit their definition, despite having been beaten.

Some *in vivo* codes simultaneously reflect condensed meanings of a general term and reveal an individual's fresh perspective. After suffering a sudden onset of a serious chronic condition, one man said he intended to pursue 'making a comeback' (Charmaz, 1973). By borrowing a term from once-successful celebrities, he defined his stance toward dealing with chronic illness. Other participants' actions and statements indicated that they shared this stance, although they did not invoke this vivid term.

In vivo codes are characteristic of social worlds and organizational settings. For example, Calvin Morrill's (1995: 263–268) glossary of executives' terms in one corporation included both general terms and specific labels that no doubt furthered his understanding of how they dealt with conflict. Executives imbued some terms, such as 'bozo,' 'roadblock,' or 'jumping ship,' with meanings that echoed ordinary parlance, although many terms assumed specific meanings within the organization and evoked metaphors of combat, violence, and violation. Morrill includes among them:

BLACK KNIGHT	An executive who often engages in covert action against opponents, does not support his intra-departmental colleagues in disputes … ; (in take-over imagery, *black knight* refers to an unfriendly acquirer from the perspective of an acquired firm). (p. 263)
FLYING LOW	Not confronting an offender with longstanding grievances against their behavior. (p. 265)
RAPE	An executive's allowing himself or herself to be publicly criticized by another without *calling out* the challenger. (p. 266)
SMALL BURSTS OF FIRE	Short public criticisms of a colleague delivered in rapid succession. (p. 267)
VAPORIZING	Terminating an executive from the company or creating the conditions under which an executive resigns from the corporation. (p. 267)

At organizational or collective levels of analysis, *in vivo* codes reflect assumptions, actions, and imperatives that frame action. Studying these codes and exploring leads in them allows you to develop a deeper understanding of what is happening and what it means. Such codes anchor your analysis in your research participants' worlds. They offer clues about the relative congruence between your interpretation of participants' meanings and actions and their overt statements and actions. *In vivo* codes can provide a crucial check on whether you have grasped what is significant. Elijah Anderson (2003) speaks to this point in his ethnographic memoir of his study (1976) of African-American men who hung out on a Chicago street corner. Anderson discovered three groups: 'respectables,' 'non-respectables,' and 'near-respectables.' He related these categories to his teacher, Howard Becker, who asked him what the men called themselves. Anderson reviewed his data and realized that the men's terms of 'regular,' 'hoodlum,' and 'winehead,' stood out. After invoking their terms and clarifying what the men meant by them, Anderson stated that he experienced a dramatic increase in his understanding of their worlds. From a grounded theory standpoint, for example, it would be fascinating to explicate the process of how men become defined as belonging to one category or another, who designates and enforces the categories, and how these categories make actions predictable.

In each study you conduct, participants will word or write things in ways that crystallize and condense meanings. Hearing and seeing their words anew allows you to explore their meanings and to understand their actions through coding and subsequent data collection. Pursue telling terms. One young doctor with severe diabetes explained himself as being 'supernormal' (Charmaz, 1973, 1987). As our conversation unfolded, his meaning of supernormal became clear. Not only did he intend to manage being a physician without his condition deterring him, he also aimed to excel beyond his peers. His hopes and plans symbolized identity goals in social life that transcended psychological predilections. Once I grasped the idea of pursuing supernormal identity goals, I saw this process reflected in other participants' actions and stated intentions. Similarly, other *in vivo* codes emerged as I heard many people advocate 'taking one day at a time,' and listened to their stories of having 'good days' and 'bad days.' Subsequently, I sought the condensed meanings and actions that these terms covered and coded for them.

Focused Coding

Focused coding is the second major phase in coding. These codes are more directed, selective, and conceptual than word-by-word, line-by-line, and incident-by-incident coding (Glaser, 1978). After you have established some strong analytic directions through your initial line-by-line coding, you can begin focused coding to synthesize and explain larger segments of data. Focused coding means using the most significant and/or frequent earlier codes to sift through large amounts of data. One goal is to determine the adequacy of those codes. Focused coding requires decisions

> Focused coding means using the most significant and/or frequent earlier codes to sift through large amounts of data. Focused coding requires decisions about which initial codes make the most analytic sense to categorize your data incisively and completely.

about which initial codes make the most analytic sense to categorize your data incisively and completely.

But moving to focused coding is not entirely a linear process. Some respondents or events will make explicit what was implicit in earlier statements or events. An 'Aha! Now I understand,' experience may prompt you to study your earlier data afresh. Then you may return to earlier respondents and explore topics that had been glossed over, or that may have been too implicit to discern initially or unstated.

BOX 3.3   FOCUSED CODING

	Excerpt 1 *Christine Danforth, age 37, lupus erythematosus, Sjögren's syndrome, back injuries*
	If you have lupus, I mean one day it's my liver; one day it's my joints; one day it's my head, and it's like people really think you're a hypochondriac if you keep complaining about different ailments … It's like you don't want to say anything because people are going to start thinking, you
Avoiding disclosure	know, 'God, don't go near her, all she is–is complaining about this.' And I think that's why I never say anything because I feel like everything I have is related one way or another to the lupus but most of the people don't know I have lupus, and even those that do are not going to believe that ten different ailments are the same thing. And I don't want anybody saying, you know, [that]
Assessing potential losses and risks of disclosing	they don't want to come around me because I complain.
	Excerpt 2 *Joyce Marshall, age 60, minor heart condition, recent small CVA (stroke)*
Feeling forced to live one day at a time	I have to see it [her CVA] as a warning. I can't let myself get so anxious. I have to live one day at a time.
	I've been so worried about John [her husband who had had life-threatening heart attacks and lost his job three years before retirement] and preparing to get a job [her first in 38 years] … It's
Concentrating on today	just so hard with all this stress … to concentrate
Giving up future orientation	on what I can do today. I always used to look to the future. I can't now; it upsets me too much.
Managing emotions	I have to live one day at a time now or else there
Reducing life-threatening risk	may not be any me.

The strength of grounded theory coding derives from this concentrated, active involvement in the process. You act upon your data rather than passively read them. Through your actions, new threads for analysis become apparent. Events, interactions, and perspectives come into analytic purview that you had not thought of before. Focused coding checks your preconceptions about the topic.

In the first excerpt in Box 3.3, I selected the codes 'avoiding disclosure' and 'assessing potential losses and risks of disclosing' to capture, synthesize, and understand the main themes in the statement. In the second, the following codes were most useful: 'feeling forced to live one day at a time,' 'concentrating on today,' 'giving up future orientation,' 'managing emotions,' and 'reducing life-threatening risk.' Again, I tried to keep the codes active and close to the data. Through focused coding, you can move across interviews and observations and compare people's experiences, actions, and interpretations. Note how the codes condense data and provide a handle on them.

Consistent with the logic of grounded theory, coding is an emergent process. Unexpected ideas emerge. They can keep emerging. After you code a body of data, compare your codes and data with each other. A telling code that you constructed to fit one incident or statement might illuminate another. An earlier incident may alert you to see a subsequent one with incisiveness. I had witnessed several tense moments with couples during which spouses declared that their partner's disabilities robbed him or her of former competencies.

Consider the following fieldnotes from an early interview with Andrei, a retired college professor, and his wife, Natasha, both of whom had chronic illnesses:

> I asked [Andrei], 'Did you keep up with professional work after you retired?' He said: 'I used to teach extension courses but due to the budget and that governor, there isn't any money for extension courses.' She [Natasha] cut in [to me], 'Andrei used to be an extremely successful speaker; partly his enthusiasm, partly his articulateness, but with the speech problems, he can't do it ...' [He said, slowly and painfully] 'The schools don't have any money ... I can't speak very well.'
>
> I felt desperately sorry for him at this point. Whether or not both factors were at play at the point when they stopped calling him for extension teaching, this was a terrible moment for him when she said it. Regardless of the real reason, at this precise moment knowing *what* she thought of his deteriorating competence was critical to him. Participating in this short sequence was like watching someone who was observing his own identity crumbling away – it was painful both for him and for me, although I got the impression that she was so caught up in her perceptions of accuracy that she didn't actually see how it defaced him. ... Acknowledging that he can't speak very well was said like an admission of guilt or inferiority that was previously hidden from view. (Charmaz, 1983: 119–120)

From such early observations, I developed the code of 'identifying moment.' In each case, the judgment imparted a shocking image of whom the ill person had become. Such disquieting views proclaimed negative changes and underscored their permanence. The code 'identifying moment' alerted me to other brief interactions in which someone conferred a significant identity on a person with chronic illness. One example occurred some years later when I entered a care home that primarily served impoverished elders. The assistant at the desk said that her supervisor had not informed her that I was coming to talk with residents (as had been arranged). Six elders in wheelchairs were lined up against the wall and one middle-aged woman was walking toward the desk. The people in wheelchairs perked up and regarded me with interest, as is common in institutions where few residents have visitors. Without looking up, the assistant nodded toward the middle-aged woman and said, 'You can talk to Mary there; she's one of the smart ones and there aren't many of them.' At this pronouncement, six heads in wheelchairs drooped in unison. Mary looked proud to be chosen. I realized that I had just witnessed another identifying moment– a positive one for Mary but a negative one for the other residents.

Through comparing data to data, we develop the focused code. Then we compare data to these codes, which helps to refine them. In the first example, I compared situations in which participants had freely discussed the disability in question before, with those in which they had not. Before the incident when Andrei acknowledged his speech difficulties, his physician had told me that Andrei's impaired speech was never openly discussed. I also compared these incidents for their intensity and impact. At first, the code only represented negative identifying moments. As I obtained more data, I found and defined positive identifying moments. 'Identifying moments' began as a code, which I developed as a category (Charmaz, 1991a). Because the notion of identifying moments resonates with many experiences, Will van den Hoonaard (1997) treats it as a sensitizing concept for other researchers to use as a starting point.

Axial Coding

Strauss and Corbin (1990, 1998; Strauss, 1987) present a third type of coding, axial coding, to relate categories to subcategories. Axial coding specifies the properties and dimensions of a category.

Strauss (1987: 64) views axial coding as building 'a dense texture of relationships around the "axis" of a category.' Thus, axial coding follows the development of a major category, although it may be in an early stage of development. The purposes of axial coding are to sort, synthesize, and organize large amounts of data and reassemble them in new ways after open coding (Creswell, 1998).

> Axial coding relates categories to subcategories, specifies the properties and dimensions of a category, and reassembles the data you have fractured during initial coding to give coherence to the emerging analysis.

Initial coding fractures data into separate prices and distinct codes. Axial coding is Strauss and Corbin's (1998) strategy for bringing data back together again in a coherent whole. According to Strauss and Corbin (p. 125), axial coding answers questions such as 'when, where, why, who, how, and with what consequences.' With these questions, a researcher can describe the studied experience more fully, although Corbin and Strauss contend that linking relationships between categories occurs on a conceptual rather than descriptive level. For them, analyzing data means converting text into concepts, which seems to be the intent of Strauss's and Corbin's use of axial coding. These concepts specify the dimensions of a larger category. Axial coding aims to link categories with subcategories, and asks how they are related. Clarke views axial coding as elaborating a category and uses diagramming to integrate relevant categories.[6] For her, an integrative diagram aims to link categories with categories to form a substantive theory of action.

While engaged in axial coding, Strauss and Corbin apply a set of scientific terms to make links between categories visible. They group participants' statements into components of an organizing scheme to answer their questions above. In one such organizing scheme, Strauss and Corbin include: 1) *conditions*, the circumstances or situations that form the structure of the studied phenomena; 2) *actions/interactions*, participants' routine or strategic responses to issues, events, or problems; and 3) *consequences*, outcomes of actions/interactions. Strauss and Corbin use conditions to answer the why, where, how come, and when questions (p. 128). Actions/interactions answer by whom and how questions. Consequences answer questions of 'what happens' because of these actions/interactions.

Axial coding provides a frame for researchers to apply. The frame may extend or limit your vision, depending on your subject matter and ability to tolerate ambiguity. Students who prefer to work with a preset structure will welcome having a frame. Those who prefer simple, flexible guidelines—and can tolerate ambiguity—do not need to do axial coding. They can follow the leads that they define in their empirical materials.

Although I have not used axial coding according to Strauss and Corbin's formal procedures, I have developed subcategories of a category and showed the links between them as I learned about the experiences the categories represent. The subsequent categories, subcategories, and links reflect how I made sense of the data.

The earlier coding examples of Bonnie Presley and Christine Danforth's interviews indicate that telling other people about having a chronic illness poses emotional and interactional dilemmas. Such dilemmas arose in many interviews; I had not planned to study them. Not surprisingly, the first two categories that I saw in early interviews were disclosing illness and avoiding disclosure. I outlined their respective properties through comparing data with data of the same kind of experience or event. The apparent pain in participants' stories led me to view 'disclosing' as revealing and often risky. Bonnie Presley's risks included exacerbating a medical crisis. Many other people risked making themselves emotionally vulnerable and having uncontrollable feelings. Disclosing was not a neutral form of talking.

Next, I reexamined the data I had coded during initial coding. Participants dealt with information about themselves both by avoiding disclosure of illness and by telling people about it; however, some forms of telling lacked control and sometimes not telling at all occurred when participants felt overwhelmed. When participants' lacked control in telling, they exposed themselves by blurting out their concerns instead of managing and metering self-revelations.

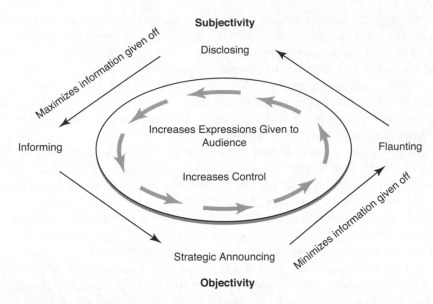

FIGURE 3.1   Forms of telling

Subsequently, I coded for the range between spontaneous statements and staged pronouncements. I linked forms of telling explicitly to the relative absence or presence of participants' control in relaying information and the extent to which they invoked explicit strategies. After discovering that people invoked different forms of telling, I then looked more closely at the following:

- Biographical and interactional contexts of their telling
- Social and experiential conditions affecting whom various participants told
- Participants' stated intentions for telling
- What participants told these individuals
- How participants told them.

I coded for if, when, how, and why participants changed their earlier forms of telling. These strategies may lead to charting causes and conditions of the observed phenomenon. In my analysis of forms of telling (see Figure 3.1), studying these data led to seeing that the participant's subjective stake in telling exceeded what a researcher could plot along a simple continuum. Rather, subjectivity and objectivity meet when participants flaunt illness. It became apparent that some individuals flaunt illness when it has caused them unresolved problems of self-acceptance and acceptance by others.

No explicit frame guided my analytic constructions of participants' accounts and experiences or elicited the emphasis. Although axial coding may help researchers to explore their data, it encourages them to *apply* an analytic frame to the data. In that sense, relying on axial coding may limit what and how researchers learn about their studied worlds and, thus, restricts the codes they construct.

Whether axial coding helps or hinders remains a question (see Kelle, 2005). Whether and to what extent it offers a more effective technique than careful comparisons remains debatable. At best, axial coding helps to clarify and to extend the analytic power of your emerging ideas. At worst, it casts a technological overlay on the data–and perhaps on your final analysis. Although intended to obtain a more complete grasp of the studied phenomena, axial coding can make grounded theory cumbersome (Robrecht, 1995).

Theoretical Coding

Theoretical coding is a sophisticated level of coding that follows the codes you have selected during focused coding. Glaser (1978: 72) introduced theoretical codes as conceptualizing 'how the substantive codes may relate to each other as hypotheses to be integrated into a theory.' In short, theoretical codes specify possible relationships between categories you have developed in your focused coding. Glaser (1992) argues that these codes preclude a need for axial coding because they 'weave the fractured story back together' (Glaser, 1978: 72). Theoretical codes are integrative; they lend form to the focused codes you have collected. These codes may help you tell an analytic story that has coherence. Hence, these codes not only conceptualize how your substantive codes are related, but also move your analytic story in a theoretical direction.

Glaser (1978) presents a series of 18 theoretical coding families that include analytic categories such as his 'Six Cs: Causes, Contexts, Contingencies, Consequences, Covariances, and Conditions' (p. 74), 'degree,' 'dimension,' 'interactive,' 'theoretical,' and 'type' coding families as well as ones that derive from major concepts such as 'identity–self,' 'means–goals,' 'cultural,' and 'consensus' families. Several of Glaser's coding families indicate a specific analytic category but merge conceptual distinctions. For example, the 'unit' family includes the following structural units: group, family organizational, aggregate, territorial, societal, status and role units. Glaser also includes situations, social worlds and social contexts, which certainly may serve as units of analysis but connote emergent, rather than structural properties. In *Doing Grounded Theory* (1998), Glaser enlarges on several earlier coding families and extends the list to include more coding families such as: the 'paired opposite,' 'representation,' 'scale,' 'random walk,' 'structural-functional,' and 'unit identity' families.

If you use them skillfully, theoretical codes may hone your work with a sharp analytic edge. They can add precision and clarity–as long as they fit your data and substantive analysis. They can aid in making your analysis coherent and comprehensible. Depending on the data you have and on what you learn about them, you may find that your analysis takes into account several coding families. For example, you may clarify the general context and specific conditions in which a particular phenomenon is evident. You may be able to specify the conditions under which it changes and to outline its consequences. You might learn its temporal and structural orderings and discover participants' strategies for dealing with them. If you understand the temporal ordering, you likely include an analysis of process. Thus, despite not delving into substance, this short example alone brings in the following analytic coding families: the 'Six Cs,' 'temporal ordering,' 'ordering' (Glaser includes structural ordering here, see

p. 78), 'strategy,' and 'process.' The links provided by the codes may also point to areas that you can strengthen.

Strauss's (1978a, 1993) work on social worlds and social arenas influenced Adele E. Clarke (1998), who subsequently developed the concepts. In the following passage, she offers an explicit rationale for the theoretical concepts that emerged early in her research as an integrating coding family:

> Social worlds and arenas analysis offers a number of analytic advantages in studies of disciplinary formation. First, and of special import in historical research, social worlds analysis bridges internal and external concerns by encompassing the involvement and contributions of all the salient social worlds. Both internal and external topics may be relevant. Social worlds are genuinely social units of analysis, elastic and plastic enough to allow very diverse applications. One can avoid misrepresenting collective social actors as monolithic by examining diversity within worlds, while still tracking and tracing their overall collective perspectives, ideologies, thrusts, and goals. One can comfortably analyze the work of particular individuals as important to the arena, without being limited to an individual approach. Perhaps most important, in the very framing of an arena, one is analytically led to examine the negotiations within and between worlds that are most consequential for the development of the arena over time. (p. 265)

Your earlier substantive analysis should indicate the kind of theoretical codes that you invoke. In short, like any other extant concept, theoretical codes must earn their way into your grounded theory (Glaser, 1978). When we look at how analytic styles and conceptual toolkits take hold in a discipline, we discover fads and trends among them. Such fads and trends limit ways of seeing as well as perhaps forcing data into old boxes. Glaser points out that over-reliance on the strategy coding family leads scholars to impute conscious intentions when participants may not hold them (p. 76). Similar problems arise with other theoretical codes. Glaser proposes, 'Perhaps the most frequent implicit rubric in studies is a problem of social order [usually disorder]' (p. 78). Yet counter-arguments proclaim that enlisting the concept of 'disorder' prevents researchers from seeing alternative social structural forms. Marxists have long argued that the consensus model precludes seeing conflict and domination. Some symbolic interactionists have applied such concepts as 'career,' 'work,' 'negotiation,' and 'strategy' wholesale to their studies (Charmaz, 2005).

For example, Goffman's (1959, 1967, 1969) analyses assume a strategic model of interaction and a social actor who strategizes about how to control encounters:

> Regardless of the particular [interactional] objective which the individual has in mind and of his motive for having this objective, it will be in his interests to control the conduct of the others, especially their responsive treatment of him. This control is achieved largely by influencing the definition of the situation which the others come to formulate, and he can influence this definition by expressing himself in such a way as to give them the kind of impression that will lead them to act voluntarily in accordance with his

own plan. Thus, when an individual appears in the presence of others, there will usually be some reasons for him to mobilize his activity so that it will convey an impression to others which it is in his interests to convey. (1959: 3–4)

In the passage above, you see Goffman's explicit concern with strategy and control.

Often the theoretical integration provided by theoretical codes remains implicit in the analysis. For example, symbolic interactionism informs my study of people with chronic illness, *Good Days, Bad Days: The Self in Chronic Illness and Time* (1991a), but remains in the background. The substantive analysis of how people experience illness takes the foreground in the book and, thus, comes across most strongly. The codes that arose from symbolic interactionist sensibilities give a theoretical foundation or conceptual infrastructure that integrates the narrative. Readers from other disciplines may remain unaware of the implicit theoretical frame that organizes a given piece of work. For example, the connections between time and self are clear in the following example although not every reader will see their links to symbolic interactionism.

> A desire to recapture the past reflects yearning for a lost self. That yearning results from grieving for accumulated losses from illness. Here, the person defines losses and acknowledges illness. Though she writes that she learned to live moment by moment after her stroke, poet May Sarton simultaneously longed for her past self: 'Now I am frightfully lonely because I am *not* my self. I can't see a friend for over a half-hour without feeling as though my mind were draining away like air rushing from a balloon'. (1988, p. 18)
>
> The sorrow for a past self increases when people believe that they might not reclaim it. Even after trying to wait out illness or treatment, regaining the past self and recapturing the past may remain elusive. Sarton suggests this elusiveness when she writes that 'to manage such a passive *waiting* life for so many months I have had to bury my real self— and now realize that bringing back that real self is going to be even more difficult than it was to bury it'. (1988, p. 78) (Charmaz, 1991a: 194)

Sarton's lament reflects the idea that one's self-concept has boundaries and content, as a symbolic interactionist would argue. Our self-concepts provide a way of knowing ourselves, a way of separating what is ours and what is distinct from us. Sarton shows us that her self-concept remains in the past and now is at odds with the images of self given in her current predicament.

What stands as a theoretical coding family? Glaser (1978) offers no criteria for establishing what we should accept as a coding family or reasons why we should accept his depiction of them. He states that his list of coding families contains overlapping categories and points out that a new coding family can arise from a preexisting one. Social scientists often draw from several coding families simultaneously. As Glaser acknowledges, the coding families are neither exhaustive nor mutually exclusive. Nor are they reflective of the same level and type of abstraction. Some coding families refer to recognizable analytic terms and some draw on sociological concepts. The names of several coding families, such as 'interactive,' 'reading,' 'mainline,' seem arbitrary and vague. Their meanings as well as those of others remain embedded in the narrative (see p. 76–81). 'Interactive' refers to 'mutual effects,' 'reciprocity,' 'mutual dependency,' and the like rather than to interaction, *per se.* The 'reading family' includes 'concepts,' 'problems,' and 'hypotheses.' The 'mainline family' includes a sweeping array of structural concepts and concerns such as 'social institutions,' and 'social order,' along with 'socialization,' 'social interaction,' and 'social worlds,' which Glaser also lists in the unit family.

Several conceptual families are noticeably absent in Glaser's list, including those that focus on agency and action, power, networks, and narrative and biography. Others such as inequality remain buried in a larger unit. Conflict is relegated to the larger family of consensus, indicating a subordination that conflict theorists would rightfully and vigorously contest.[7] More recently, theoretical currents such as feminist theory and postmodern concepts form other families. Glaser acknowledges that new coding families may emerge from earlier ones. Many of his (1998) recent additions hearken back to positivist concepts.

How might ordinary grounded theory coding compare with axial coding and using theoretical codes? Think about the preceding discussion and diagram titled 'Forms of Telling.' (Figure 3.1) The types of telling themselves might be seen as dimensions of the larger category of telling. Each type has particular properties and reflects views of self and identity as well as immediate interactional circumstances. In one sense, the types reflect a range from subjectivity to objectivity along a continuum. The types differed by degrees in the following areas: felt emotional intensity, difficulty in telling, emotional and informational control in the telling, amount and kind of planning, and intended audience effect. A number of participants found that their forms of telling differed at various points in their illness. When people felt shocked by a diagnosis or first episode of illness, they blurted the news without control. If they felt demeaned or devalued for having told their news, then they became more measured in their telling and may move from spontaneous disclosing to strategized informing. When episodes accrue and people discover costs of telling, they may resort to occasional strategic announcing. Although many people may become strategic about how, when, where, and to whom they disclose, relatively few engage in flaunting. From this brief discussion, you can see how studying processes can shape an analysis. Note that a consequence of one type of telling can set the conditions for a person to engage in another.

The kinds of links in the preceding example emerged as I studied my data about imparting illness news. Quite possibly further in-depth data or additional comprehensive data about forms of telling would lead to more links. Now a word of caution. These theoretical codes may lend an aura of objectivity to an analysis, but the codes themselves do not stand as some objective criteria about which scholars would agree or that they could uncritically apply. When your analysis indicates, use theoretical codes to help you clarify and sharpen your analysis but avoid imposing a forced framework on it with them. It helps to interrogate yourself about whether these theoretical codes interpret all the data.

Reducing Problems in Coding

Wrestling with Preconceptions

Throughout the grounded theory literature, researchers are enjoined to avoid forcing their data into preconceived codes and categories. Foremost among these are extant theories. We also must guard against forcing our preconceptions on the data we code. The student above who forced his own view of disability on his interview data, imposed what sociologists call 'common sense theorizing' on his analysis (Schutz, 1967). His reasoning arose from his notions of how the world works and from his own experience as a disabled man. Grounded theorists, like other researchers, may unwittingly start from their own preconceptions about what a particular experience means and entails.

Preconceptions that emanate from such standpoints as class, race, gender, age, embodiment, and historical era may permeate an analysis without the researcher's awareness. If so, these invisible standpoints linger outside the frame for discussing the analysis and remain fundamentally unproblematic for researchers who hold them. These researchers may deny their existence.[8]

Every researcher holds preconceptions that influence, but may not determine, what we attend to and how we make sense of it. Shadows of capitalism, competition, and individualism may enter Western social scientists' analyses without our realizing it because they frame the way we know the world. Erving Goffman's detailed fieldwork, keen observations, and compelling categories made him one of the most astute social scientists of the twentieth century. Nonetheless, particularly in his early works, Goffman invoked an individualistic, competitive, strategic, and hierarchical model of human nature that fits 1950s North American cultural conceptions of white, upwardly mobile, middle-class men (Charmaz, 2004). Such taken-for-granted assumptions influence what we attend to and how we make sense of it. In the statement below, Goffman provides trenchant advice for conducting excellent ethnographic work. As incisive as his advice is, we also gain a glimpse of his preconceptions.

> As graduate students, we're only interested in being smart, and raising our hands, and being defensive—as people usually are—and forming the right associations, and all that. And if you're going to do good fieldwork it seems to me that's got to go by the board. ...
> You have to open yourself up in ways you're not in ordinary life. You have to open yourself up to being snubbed. You have to stop making points to show how 'smart-assed' you are. And that is extremely difficult for graduate students (especially on the East Coast). Then you have to be willing to be a horse's ass. (Goffman, 2004: 127–128)

Our preconceptions may only become apparent when our taken-for-granted standpoints are challenged. Rosanna Hertz (2003) faced such challenges long after her ethnographic study of a kibbutz, conducted 20 years before. Recently, the son of a couple in the kibbutz asked to live with her. Through his presence, she discovered that this family had defined her relationship to them as 'family' and she had seen it as a 'transaction' bounded by her now long-past stay in the kibbutz. Hertz states that she realized 'how tricky perception is and how deeply rooted assumptions and ideological preferences can challenge even the most ardent efforts at openness' (p. 474).

Several strategies foster revealing such preconceptions. Achieving intimate familiarity with the *studied phenomenon* is a prerequisite. Such familiarity not only includes an in-depth knowledge of people who contend with the phenomenon, but also a level of understanding that pierces their experience. This level moves you beyond taking the same things for granted that your respondents assume. Initial coding can move you in this direction by inducing you to wrestle with your participants' interpretive frames of reference, which may not be your own. Taking a reflexive stance toward challenges, as Hertz does above, may result in questioning one's perspectives and practices.

From the standpoint of grounded theory, each preconceived idea should *earn* its way into your analysis—including your own ideas from previous studies (Glaser, 1978). That means you do fresh heavy analytic work first. I have argued that preconceived theoretical concepts may provide starting points for looking *at* your data but they do not offer automatic codes *for* analyzing these data. Ask, for example, have class, race, gender, or age issues emerged that need analytic attention? If you apply theoretical concepts from your discipline at all, you must ensure that these concepts work. Several safeguards against imposing them may help. Consider these questions:

- Do these concepts help you understand what the data indicate?
- If so, how do they help?
- Can you explicate what is happening in this line or segment of data with these concepts?
- Can you adequately interpret this segment of data without these concepts? What do they add?

If extant concepts are not integral for understanding your data, they do not have a place in your codes or your later analysis. The best approach is for you to define what is happening in your data first.

Preconceptions work their way into how we think and write. Researchers who believe themselves to be objective social scientists often assume that their judgments of participants are correct. This stance can lead to treating one's unexamined assumptions as fact. Be careful about applying a language of intention, motivation, or strategies *unless the data support your assertions.* You cannot assume what is in someone's mind—particularly if he or she does not tell you.[9] If people tell you what they 'think,' remember that they provide enacted accounts reflecting social context, time, place, biography, and audience. Participants' unstated purposes in telling you what they 'think' may be more significant than their stated thoughts. If you reframe participants' statements to fit a language of intention, you are forcing the data into preconceived categories—yours, not theirs. Making comparisons between data about what people say and do, however, strengthens your assertions about implicit meanings.

A fine line exists between interpreting data and imposing a preexisting frame on it.

While coding, problems may arise by:

- Coding at too general a level
- Identifying topics instead of actions and processes
- Overlooking how people construct actions and processes
- Attending to disciplinary or personal concerns rather than participants' concerns
- Coding out of context
- Using codes to summarize but not to analyze.

During a grounded theory workshop, the participants engaged in a coding exercise with the same data about professionals in a clinical setting. One participant coded almost every statement and described incident in the data as 'stress'—undifferentiated, unexamined stress, at that. Her reasons for seeing stress as significant were understandable; however, she was coding at too general a level with a topic that consumed her but did not take into account actions and processes in the fieldnotes. Other workshop participants whose codes stuck more closely to the data created a nuanced set of codes that synthesized what they saw happening in the data.

Take an examined stance about whose point of view your codes reflect, which categories they indicate, and when you bring in abstract ideas. Such a stance toward coding fosters treating your ideas as problematic as well as those of your research participants. Consider using the following questions to check how you code:

- How does my coding reflect the incident or described experience?
- Do my analytic constructions begin from this point?
- Have I created clear, evident connections between the data and my codes?
- Have I guarded against rewriting—and therefore recasting—the studied experience into a lifeless language that better fits *our* academic and bureaucratic worlds than those of our participants?

Granted, we bring different views to the data we witness. We see things that our participants may not. As our codes become more abstract, we couch them in analytic terms that our participants do not share but may resonate with such as the idea of an 'identifying moment' discussed above. Through illuminating experience, codes forge a bridge between described data and our emerging analysis.

Transforming Data into Codes

Coding relies on having solid data. How and what you record affects what you have to code. Increasingly, qualitative research draws on in-depth and focus group interviews. A few qualitative researchers advocate coding from notes rather than transcribed interviews. Presumably, you grasp the important points and eliminate clutter. This approach assumes an objective transparency of what participants say and do. It also assumes that any keen interviewer will record the most telling material and record it well. This approach may further assume that researchers' notes and codes have 'captured' their participants' views and actions. None of these assumptions may be true—even for experienced researchers.

Coding full interview transcriptions gives you ideas and understandings that you otherwise miss. Thus, the method of data collection not only forms your materials, but also frames your codes. Coding full transcriptions can bring you to a deeper level of understanding. In contrast, coding from and across notes might give you a wider view. It also can, however, contribute to grounded theorists going around the studied phenomenon rather than into it. An emphasis on plausibility rather than thoroughness and systematic study risks constructing superficial analyses.

Transcribing entire interviews and fieldnotes also has some hidden benefits. Your first reading and coding of the data need not be the final one. Rich, thorough data can generate many research questions. Such data contain the makings of several analyses, whether or not you realize it early in your research. You can save a set of related codes to develop later. You can return and recode a set of old data. In both cases, your codes spark new ideas. In the meantime, the full recordings preserve details for these ideas to ignite later. You may be amazed at the diverse ideas you can gain from the data for one project. Thus, coding and recoding not only leads you in new directions but also directly to theoretical sampling of your new categories as well. The early theoretical sampling gives you the added bonus of being able to move across substantive fields with greater ease.[10]

Any method of data collection frames what you can code. Ethnographers rely more on what they hear than what they see and interviewers often rely on only what they hear. Record what you see as well as what you hear. An interviewer sees a scene and at least one person. Notes about these observations are data to code. In one of Abdi Kusow's (2003) interviews of Somali immigrants, his observations constituted most of his data. Kusow had already found that many potential participants declined to be interviewed because of the volatile political climate in Somalia. One participant referred him to a young woman who consented to the interview. When Kusow arrived, the TV was blaring and she and several small children were watching it. She did not suggest leaving the room, kept the TV on, and answered his questions in monosyllables. Kusow saw her responses as 'basically her way of giving me no information at all' (p. 596). Kusow's anecdote suggests a dictum for interviewers: Code your observations of the setting, scene, and participant as well as your interviews. Revealing data resides in such observations.

Concluding Thoughts

Coding routes your work in an analytic direction while you are in the early stages of research. You can make grounded theory coding familiar through practice, then evaluate how it works for you. By remaining open to the data as you had been open to statements and events in the research setting, you will discover subtle meanings and have new insights. I recommend completing a close initial coding at the level that best fits your data and task.

Coding is part work but it is also part play. We play with the ideas we gain from the data. We become involved with our data and learn from them. Coding gives us a focused way of viewing data. Through coding we make discoveries and gain a deeper understanding of the empirical world.

Theoretical playfulness allows us to try out ideas and to see where they may lead. Coding gives us a preliminary set of ideas that we can explore and examine analytically by writing about them. Grounded theory coding is flexible; if we wish, we can return to the data and make a fresh coding. We can go forward to writing about our codes and weighing their significance.

Coding is that first part of the adventure that enables you to make the leap from concrete events and descriptions of them to theoretical insight and theoretical possibilities. Grounded theory coding is more than a way of sifting, sorting, and synthesizing data, as is the usual purpose of qualitative coding. Instead grounded theory coding begins to unify ideas analytically because you kept in mind what the possible theoretical meanings of your data and codes might be. Now that you have some codes, it's time to proceed to memo-writing to develop them. The next chapter offers ideas for writing your memos.

NOTES

1 For earlier stories of Bonnie Presley's dilemmas in telling her daughter, see Charmaz (1991a: 132–133).

2 For an innovative discussion on categorizing see Bowker & Star, 1999.

3 Discovering that the data have holes is not limited to qualitative research. Survey researchers who conduct standardized interviews sometimes discover when conversing with respondents afterwards that their questions do not tap significant areas. Quantitative researchers must stick to the same instrument but qualitative researchers can remedy such problems while gathering data.

4 By 1992, Glaser seems to disavow line-by-line coding as he advises against taking apart a single incident. He states that line-by-line coding produces a 'helter skelter' of over-conceptualizing the incident and generates too many categories and properties (p. 40) without yielding an analysis. Nonetheless, a researcher can select the most telling codes gained through line-by-line coding of an incident and make comparisons between incidents.

5 Take a set of data and test the value of line-by-line coding by comparing the general type of thematic analysis that most qualitative researchers conduct with grounded theory coding. First, read the data and then identify and record themes in them. Next conduct line-by-line coding. List the most significant codes and compare them with your list of themes.

6 Personal communication, September 20, 2004.

7 This point pertains to the 1970s, when Glaser wrote *Theoretical Sensitivity*, as well as today. For almost forty years, most sociological theorists have treated conflict as an oppositional concept to consensus, not as a subcategory of it.

8 Feminist standpoint theorists such as Dorothy Smith (1987), Nancy Hartsock (1998), and Patricia Hill Collins (1990) have made powerful arguments about hidden assumptions.

9 The relative truth of an account is situated and constructed. Our renderings of these accounts are further constructions.

10 Increasingly institutional review committees cause stumbling blocks and losses of time. The logic of moving across settings—and getting the permissions to access each setting—can thwart a researcher's plans to conduct theoretical sampling. Thus, beginning with a collected set of re-coded data and proposing to engage in further study in another setting is an efficient way to limit and pace proposals to move through these committees.

4 Memo-writing

Our journey through the research process takes an analytic break at this point as we stop and write informal analytic notes, commonly called memos. Memos chart, record, and detail a major analytic phase of our journey. We start by writing about our codes and data and move upward to theoretical categories and keep writing memos throughout the research process. Writing memos expedites your analytic work and accelerates your productivity. I offer ideas about how to go about writing memos and add two writers' strategies that can make writing them easier. Then I present ways to use memos to raise focused codes to conceptual categories.

Memo-writing is the pivotal intermediate step between data collection and writing drafts of papers. When you write memos, you stop and analyze your ideas about the codes in any—and every—way that occurs to you during the moment (see also Glaser, 1998). Memo-writing constitutes a crucial method in grounded theory because it prompts you to analyze your data and codes early in the research process. Writing successive memos throughout the research process keeps you involved in the analysis and helps you to increase the level of abstraction of your ideas. Certain codes stand out and take form as theoretical categories as you write successive memos.

Memos catch your thoughts, capture the comparisons and connections you make, and crystallize questions and directions for you to pursue. Through conversing with yourself while memo-writing, new ideas and insights arise during the act of writing. Putting things down on paper makes the work concrete and manageable—and exciting. Once you have written a memo, you can use it now or store it for later retrieval. In short, memo-writing provides a space to become actively engaged in your materials, to develop your ideas, and to fine-tune your subsequent data-gathering.

Through writing memos, you construct analytic notes to explicate and fill out categories. Start by developing your focused codes. Memos give you a space and place for making comparisons between data and data, data and codes, codes of data and other codes, codes and category, and category and concept

> Memo-writing is the pivotal intermediate step between data collection and writing drafts of papers. …
> Memo-writing constitutes a crucial method in grounded theory because it prompts you to analyze your data and codes early in the research process.

and for articulating conjectures about these comparisons. Use memos to help you think about the data and to discover your ideas about them.

The quick memo below explores relationships between suffering and moral status. From time to time, I had pondered Erving Goffman's (1963) powerful analysis of stigma. His concept has inundated social scientific and nursing literatures on chronic illness and disability. My research participants talked about situations in which they felt stigmatized but somehow the concept of stigma did not quite represent all that I saw and heard. The pain and sorrow on their faces and in their voices cast deep shadows on their tales. Few people mentioned the term 'suffering' in reference to themselves; but their stories were replete with it. Nor did participants use the term 'moral status,' although it made sense of their experience.

My earlier interviews contained codes such as 'being stigmatized,' 'loss of self,' 'losing credibility,' 'feeling devalued', although I did not anchor them in an analysis of injustice, legitimacy, and suffering. That came later when certain incidents spoke to these concerns directly. I had discerned relationships between stigma, loss of self, and suffering much earlier (Charmaz, 1983) and realized that much suffering derived from how other people treated those with chronic illnesses but I focused on loss of self rather than developing an explicit analysis of suffering. Nor did I engage ideas about moral status, although a later perusal of the data revealed numerous indications of it. Having a reservoir of earlier transcribed interviews and tapes helped enormously. Had I not had them, I would have missed liminal cues and nuanced statements. By treating 'suffering as a moral status' as a category, I raised a code to a conceptual level to treat analytically. I treat it as distinctive and constituted by properties that I discern in the data and synthesize by scrutinizing and compiling initial codes. Thus, I constructed this category, and developed an abstract analysis of it that stays close to my data.

BOX 4.1   EXAMPLE OF A MEMO – SUFFERING

<u>**Suffering as a Moral Status**</u>
Suffering is a profoundly <u>moral status</u> as well as a physical experience. Stories of suffering reflect and redefine that moral status.

With suffering come **moral rights** and **entitlements** as well as **moral definitions— when suffering is deemed legitimate**. Thus, the person can make certain moral claims **and** have certain moral judgments conferred upon him or her.

> Deserving
> Dependent
> In need

Suffering can bring a person an elevated moral status. Here, suffering takes on a sacred status. This is a person who has been in sacred places, who has seen, known what ordinary people have not. Their stories are greeted with awe and wonder. The self also has elevated status. This person is special; the compelling story casts an aura of compelling qualities on the story-teller.

(Continued)

(Continued)

Ex. Bessie and her daughter. Bessie sat bent over in her wheelchair at the kitchen table and tells me of her rapid descent into life-threatening illness. When she began her tale of her risky surgery, her middle-aged daughter, Thelma, who had been tidying kitchen counters in the adjoining room, stops and joins us. Bessie tells of her near-death experience when her heart stopped. Thelma listened with rapt attention and awe. Though she had heard the tale many times before, it transformed the moment anew. Bessie told of being in the long dark tunnel, then seeing a beautiful bright light. Bessie believed that the light emanated from the face of God. As Thelma heard her mother's tale again, she gazed upon her with reverence. Afterwards, Thelma emphasized how this event had lifted Bessie's spirits and improved her attitude toward her illness.

Suffering also may present opportunities to play out the myth of the hero who emerges victorious against all odds. Thus again, suffering elevates status and sets the person apart when viewed as a hero who has emerged from battle. This person has defied death and, perhaps, doctors through resolving to act despite taking risks. Heroic status often follows facing illness and death earlier than one's peers. Such stories then become tales that entice and proclaim. They entice an audience and they proclaim a changed identity. Both person and circumstance are transformed through the heroic struggle.

Although suffering may first confer an elevated moral status, views change. The moral claims from suffering typically narrow in scope and in power. The circles of significance shrink. Stories of self within these moral claims may entrance and entertain for a while, but grow thin over time—unless someone has considerable influence or power. The circles narrow to most significant others.

The moral claims of suffering may only supercede those of the healthy and whole in crisis and its immediate aftermath. Otherwise, the person is less. WORTH LESS. Two words—now separate may change as illness and aging take their toll. They may end up as 'worthless.'

The moral status of suffering brings standards of decorum and dignity. One has to live up to these standards or suffer the consequences. However, the standards are usually taken-for-granted and relative to group and prior experience. Invoking the standards of one group can alienate another.

Christine went from silence to outburst. Silence doesn't work in some contexts; it's the only strategy in others. An outburst does attract attention, but can alienate.

The ill person may also take for granted standards that are or are not shared. One's moral status may emerge in private with spouse, parent, or adult child. It may occur in public as degradation. A groundskeeper had worked as part of a mainte-nance team for years with the same men. They had shared an esprit de corps. But now his work-mates refused to help him on the very tasks that they had always been defined as two- or three-men jobs. A professor in an understaffed department suffered a rapid decline that resulted in his colleagues taking over his classes. Though they said they did so willingly, he sensed how burdened they were and felt that he had let them down. Meanwhile his colleagues banged at the Dean's door, saying 'How can we get him out of here?'

Christine makes moral claims, not only befitting those of suffering, but of PERSONHOOD. She is a person who has a right to be heard, a right to just and fair treatment in both the medical arena and the workplace. (memo 1–04–98)

The memo in Box 4.1 outlines ideas and initiates discussion between them. I tried to jot down quickly everything that came to mind about the category, codes, and data. Ideas for the category came to me when I was coding data while traversing the continent by plane, so I stopped to write them. As I was scribbling, the links between suffering and moral status became clearer. I said to myself, Of course, this is what I've been trying to grapple with; why didn't I think of it sooner? I jotted down the short memo and typed it when I returned home. I copied my earlier capital letters and spacing and used boldface in lieu of my yellow felt-tip marker. (I use visual strategies to emphasize ideas from the start.) That way I gave myself some prompts and flagged leads to pursue. A few additions clarified points.

In the memo, I first established 'suffering as a moral status' as a category I aimed to analyze. I claimed that we need to think beyond physical pain and agony and look into moral life and moral worth. Hence, I formed a working definition of suffering as making a person's moral status problematic. Research participants dwelled on moral tales of loss and its stigmatizing consequences. The tone and body language of their telling expressed suffering and meaning, sometimes more than their words. Still, participants' tales also contained tacit claims for moral rights and legitimate moral status.

Which codes did the category 'suffering as a moral status' subsume? How did these codes fit together under the category? I saw that the category subsumed a number of initial codes that implied devaluation and the participant's response to experiences in which they felt demeaned, disbelieved, or discriminated against. I began to connect conceptions of rights, claims, and injustice with both suffering and moral status. Writing the memo helped me to clarify how moral status changes in suffering. It prompted me to look further at the conditions under which moral status rises as well as those when it plummets. I began to lay out a moral hierarchy of suffering and to ferret out how implicit rules affect someone's status in this moral hierarchy. The memo encouraged me to go back and forth between data and my emerging analysis and to relate it to other categories.

The memo contains ideas and several stories but its purpose needed fleshing out. I had been comparing situations between various research participants for some years. Recall Christine Danforth's story in Chapter 3. The line-by-line coding in Box 3.2 (p. 52) generated several potential categories, 'suffering as a moral status,' 'making a moral claim,' and 'having a devalued moral status' (Charmaz, 1999, 2001). Over the years, Christine had told stark stories of her struggles to remain independent, to manage her illness, and to have a place in the world. Several major incidents inflamed Christine's sense of moral outrage about her treatment and ignited growing concern about her moral rights. These incidents not only aroused her sense of injustice but also undermined her sense of self.

I used the memo to begin defining relationships between suffering and moral status. Hence, I first claim an expanded definition of suffering that includes social responses and I assert the relationship of this definition to self. Many people I talked with realized that other people–including professionals and family members–denied or doubted the presence and/or extent of their symptoms. These participants told stories of their attempts to be treated as persons with legitimate concerns. As you could see in Bonnie Presley's story of delaying disclosure in Chapter 3, whether and when someone discloses illness affects how other people view and treat them. Suffering can take a further twist. Receiving second-hand news can hurt loved ones and cause them to suffer. Thus, legitimacy, disclosure, fairness, and suffering become intertwined.

To which kind of theoretical analysis does the category of 'suffering as a moral status' belong? What types of conceptual connections does the memo suggest? It certainly speaks to structure, process, and experience. The notion of status assumes structure. In this case it assumes a hierarchical stratifying of social value. Structure remains implicit in the memo but I assert its presence—and its implications. Note how holding high moral status compares with low. I point out the tenuousness of high moral status and imply how it deteriorates. This process holds profound implications for self and identity. It stirs people's emotions, affects their identities, redefines their situations, and changes relationships. The category integrates disparate, as well as similar experiences, implies temporal ordering and turning points, fosters certain behavior, fits into and emerges under certain conditions, and has consequences.

The memo hints at how sensitizing concepts, long left silent, may murmur during coding and analysis. Faint echoes of Talcott Parsons (1953), Erving Goffman (1959, 1961, 1963, 1967) and Emile Durkheim (1893/1964, 1912/1965, 1925/1961), who inspired Goffman, reverberate through the memo. Parsons's conception of the sick role lingers in the background but affects the moral position from which moral expectations and edicts flow. No doubt Goffman's treatment of moral life and moral meanings throughout his opus informed and furthered my connections between moral hierarchies, moral status within them, and suffering. I had not reviewed either theorist in anticipation of writing the memo, nor thought about them when doing it. We can, however, discern how the memo complements several of their ideas. Both Goffman and Durkheim wrestle with moral rules, moral rights, and moral responsibilities. Goffman dealt extensively with how people presented themselves to others, managed impressions that others might have, and played roles during interactions. For Goffman, situations have their own moral rules and people aim to establish themselves as moral beings within them. Durkheim's analysis of the moral force of rules and of meanings of the sacred and profane illuminates the hidden strength of social bonds and shared values.

With a few additions, this memo served as the analytic core of a keynote address that would be published after the conference. Several months elapsed before I could return to the material and revise the address. Like many writers, I had misjudged the completeness of the category. Its sketchiness struck me. It needed filling out. I clarified the category a little for the article and later returned to the field to gain more ideas. Note that the published version below smoothes and tightens the memo but employs most of my original language. Because I chose this memo for a spoken address, I wanted the audience to hear the links between my ideas and the stories that gave rise to them. I also wanted them to envision the suffering that follows loss of moral status. By the time I presented the material five weeks after drafting the memo, I had articulated an explicit moral hierarchy. The chart depicts this moral hierarchy as a structure and shows movement down it. As moral status plummets, worthlessness enshrouds many people with debilitating chronic illnesses.

BOX 4.2   THE PUBLISHED VERSION OF THE MEMO ON SUFFERING

Suffering as a Moral Status

Hierarchy of Moral Status

Suffering is a profoundly *moral status* as well as a physical experience. A moral status confers relative human worth and, thus, measures deserved value or devaluation. Stories of suffering reflect, redefine, or resist such moral status. The stories form moral parables of right and wrong, of moral virtue and moral flaw, of reason and rationalization. Kleinman, Brodwin, Good, and Good (1991) argue that the current collective and professional language describing suffering takes a rationalized, routinized form rather than expressing moral and religious meaning. Granted, moral meanings of suffering may neither be directly evident nor expressed; however, they still shape thought and action.

With suffering come moral rights and entitlements as well as moral definitions—if suffering is deemed legitimate. Thus, a sick person can make certain moral claims *and* have certain moral judgments conferred upon him or her such as:

- deserving
- dependent
- in need

Suffering can award an individual an elevated, even sacred, moral status. This is someone who has been in sacred places, who has seen and known what ordinary mortals have not. His or her stories are greeted with awe and wonder. The self also has elevated status. This person is special; the compelling story casts an aura of compelling qualities on the storyteller.

Bessie Harris's experience transformed her moral status and her view of her suffering. Earlier she had plummeted into total disability from emphysema and heart disease. When I visited Bessie, I found her bent over in her electric wheelchair at the kitchen table. She proceeded to tell me of her rapid descent into life-threatening illness. As she began her tale of her risky surgery, her middle-aged daughter, Thelma, who had been tidying kitchen counters in the adjoining room, stopped and joined us. Bessie told of her near-death experience when her heart stopped. Thelma listened with rapt attention and awe. Though she had heard the tale many times before, it transformed the moment anew. Bessie told of being in the long dark tunnel, then seeing a beautiful bright light. Bessie believed that the light emanated from the face of God. As Thelma heard her mother's tale again, she gazed on her with reverence. Afterwards, Thelma declared that this experience had lifted Bessie's spirits and improved her attitude toward her illness.

Suffering also may present opportunities to play out the myth of the hero who emerges victorious against all odds. Thus, again, suffering elevates status and sets the person apart when viewed as a hero who has emerged from battle. This person has defied death and, perhaps, doctors through resolving to act despite taking risks. Heroic status often follows facing illness and death earlier than one's peers. Such stories then become tales that attract an audience and proclaim a changed identity. A heroic struggle transforms both the person and his or her situation.

(Continued)

(Continued)

A 50-year-old woman had a difficult surgical procedure for a condition seldom found among her age peers. She said, 'You go into battle and you come out wounded.' Her partner marveled with admiration, 'Whew, I could *never* go through all that.'

An elevated moral status changes. Time, toil, and trouble erode high moral status. Then, moral claims from suffering narrow in scope and power. Stories of self within these moral claims may entrance and entertain for a while, but they grow thin over time—unless someone has considerable influence or power. Social circles narrow to the person's most significant others. Love, power, money, or special knowledge sustain moral status. Loss of the crucial element decreases a person's moral status.

There is an implicit hierarchy of moral status in suffering (see Figure 1).

HIGH MORAL STATUS–VALIDATED MORAL CLAIMS

MEDICAL EMERGENCY
INVOLUNTARY ONSET
BLAMELESSNESS FOR CONDITION

SUSTAINED MORAL STATUS—ACCEPTED MORAL CLAIMS

CHRONIC ILLNESS
NEGOTIATED DEMANDS
PRESENT OR PAST POWER & RECIPROCITIES

DIMINISHED MORAL STATUS—QUESTIONABLE MORAL CLAIMS

PERSONAL VALUE

worth less

worth less

Worth Less

WORTHLESS

FIGURE 1   Hierarchy of Moral Status in Suffering

A crisis and its immediate aftermath allow the moral claims of suffering to supersede those of the healthy and whole. Otherwise, a person is less—worth less. WORTH LESS. Two words—first separate—can change as illness and aging take their toll. These words may join and with them, the person ends up as *worthless*.

The moral status of suffering brings standards of decorum and dignity that reflect a hierarchical position. One has to fulfill these standards or suffer the consequences. However, such standards are usually taken for granted and relative to specific groups and prior understandings. Invoking the standards of one group can alienate another. Christine Danforth went from silence to outburst. Silence does not work in some contexts; it is the only strategy in others. An outburst does demand attention, but it can alienate.

(Continued)

(Continued)

An ill person may also take for granted standards that are or are not shared. One's moral status may emerge in private with spouse, parent, or adult child. It may occur in public settings or at work. A person may gradually feel subtle devaluation or experience obvious degradation. A groundskeeper had worked as part of a maintenance team for years with the same men. They had shared an esprit de corps. But now his work-mates refused to help him on the very tasks that everyone agreed were two- or three-man jobs. A professor in an understaffed department suffered a rapid decline that resulted in his colleagues taking over his classes. Though they said they did so willingly, he sensed how burdened they were and felt that he had let them down. Meanwhile his colleagues banged at the Dean's door, saying 'How can we get him out of here?' Moral claims of suffering seldom long preserve a person's public status.

Moral claims and moral status become contested. Almost every aspect of Christine Danforth's life is problematic—living arrangements, family, medical care, income level, work relations. After being on a disability leave, she went back to work. She said,

And so I went back to work on March first, even though I wasn't supposed to. And then when I got there, they had a long meeting and they said I could no longer rest during the day. The only time I rested was at lunchtime, which was my time; we were closed. And she said, my supervisor, said I couldn't do that anymore, and I said, 'It's my time, you can't tell me, I can't lay down.' And they said, 'Well, you're not laying down on the couch that's in there, it bothers the rest of the staff.' So I went around and I talked to the rest of the staff, and they all said, 'No, we didn't say that; it was never brought up.' So I went back and I said, 'You know, I just was talking to the rest of the staff, and it seems that nobody has a problem with it but you,' and I said, 'You aren't even here at lunchtime.' And they still put it down that I couldn't do that any longer. And then a couple of months later one of the other staff started laying down at lunchtime, and I said, you know, 'This isn't fair, she doesn't even have a disability and she's laying down,' so I just started doing it.

Christine made moral claims, not only befitting those of suffering, but of *personhood*. She claimed a right to be heard, a right to just and fair treatment in both the medical arena and the workplace.

The paradox? Christine worked at a non-profit agency that provided advocacy services for people with disabilities. (Charmaz, 1999: 367–370)

The life of an initial memo can outlast its publication. Further analysis and development of the ideas can generate additional works. One memo can spark numerous ideas and serve varied purposes. The journal articles in which memos appear can presage books. Since publication of the address, I have refined some of my ideas about suffering to reflect how definitions of difference in my data accelerated individuals' descent down the hierarchy. As I compared incidents in my data, I learned more about how class and age differences played out in interaction and appeared in the hierarchy (see Charmaz, 2005).

Methods of Memo-writing

Methods for producing memos rely on making them spontaneous, not mechanical. Before learning about grounded theory, you may have thought of memos as formal business communications that state policies, procedures, and proposals in official, frequently opaque, bureaucratic terms. In contrast, grounded theorists write memos to serve analytic purposes, as you can see in the example above. We write our memos in informal, unofficial language for personal use. I wrote the memo above to catch my fleeting ideas about the code and to probe data, not to share with you.

The methods of memo-writing are few; do what works for you. Memos may be free and flowing; they may be short and stilted—especially as you enter new analytical terrain. What's important is to get things down on paper and stored in your computer files. Keep writing memos however you write and in whatever way advances your thinking.[1]

BOX 4.3   HOW TO WRITE MEMOS

Prerequisite: Study your emerging data!

Identify what you're talking about–title your memo as *specifically* as possible. You may sense that the words you choose do not quite capture the meaning. Flag them. Think about them. Refine them later. *Write now!*

Early Memos
Record what you see happening in the data. Use early memos to explore and fill out your qualitative codes. Use them to direct and focus further data collection. Some basic questions may help:

- *What is going on in the field setting or within the interview accounts?* Can you turn it into a pithy category? Examples: 'avoiding disclosure,' 'living one day at a time,' 'surrendering to illness'
- What are people doing?
- What is the person saying?
- What do research participants' actions and statements take for granted?
- How do structure and context serve to support, maintain, impede or change their actions and statements?
- What connections can you make? Which ones do you need to check?

A grounded theory study allows you to look for processes. The following questions help to maintain a focus on process:

(Continued)

(Continued)

- What process is at issue here?
- Under which conditions does this process develop?
- How do(es) the research participant(s) think, feel, and act while involved in this process?
- When, why, and how does the process change?
- What are the consequences of the process?

Structure memos to chart observed and predicted relationships in your data and between your emerging categories.

Advanced Memos

- Trace and categorize data subsumed by your topic
- Describe how your category emerges and changes
- Identify the beliefs and assumptions that support it
- Tell what the topic looks and feels like from various vantage points
- Place it within an argument
- Make comparisons:

  o Compare different people (such as their beliefs, situations, actions, accounts, or experiences)
  o Compare data from the same individuals with themselves at different points in time
  o Compare categories in the data with other categories—example: How does '"accepting" illness' compare with 'reconciling oneself to illness?' Which categories should become major sections? Which should be relegated minor status?
  o Compare subcategories with general categories for fit—example: Where does '"accepting" Illness' go? At what point does it become an issue? Where does it fit into the course of illness?
  o Compare sub-categories within a general category—example: What is the difference between an 'identifying moment' and a 'Significant event?'
  o Compare concepts or conceptual categories—example: Demonstrate the differences between the 'self in the past' and the 'self in the present,' compare experiencing 'intrusive illness' with 'immersion in Illness'
  o Compare the entire analysis with existing literature or the ruling ideas in a field
  o Refine the consequences of your analysis

Adapted from Kathy Charmaz (1995). 'Grounded Theory,' pp. 27–49 in Jonathan A. Smith, Rom Harré, & Luk Van Langenhove (eds), *Rethinking Methods in Psychology*. London: Sage

Memo-writing forces you to stop other activities; engage a category, let your mind rove freely in, around, under, and from the category; and write whatever comes to you. That's why memo-writing forms a space and place for exploration and discovery. You take the time to discover your ideas about what you have seen, heard, sensed, and coded.

Memo-writing forms the next logical step after you define categories; however, write memos from the beginning of your research. Memos spur you to develop your ideas in narrative form and fullness early in the analytic process. Your memos will help you clarify and direct your subsequent coding. Writing memos prompts you to elaborate processes, assumptions, and actions covered by your codes or categories. They encourage you to take your emergent categories apart and break them into their components. Memos also help you to identify which codes to treat as analytic categories, if you have not already defined them. (Then you can further develop these categories through more memo-writing.)

No single mechanical procedure defines a useful memo. Do what is possible with the material you have. Memos vary, but you may do any of the following in a memo:

- Define each code or category by its analytic properties
- Spell out and detail processes subsumed by the codes or categories
- Make comparisons between data and data, data and codes, codes and codes, codes and categories, categories and categories
- Bring raw data into the memo
- Provide sufficient empirical evidence to support your definitions of the category and analytic claims about it
- Offer conjectures to check in the field setting(s)
- Identify gaps in the analysis
- Interrogate a code or category by asking questions of it.

Grounded theorists look for patterns, even when focusing on a single case (see Strauss & Glaser, 1970). Because we stress identifying patterns, grounded theorists typically invoke respondents' stories to illustrate points–rather than provide complete portrayals of their lives or even a full narrative of an experience.[2] When you bring raw data right into your memo, you preserve telling evidence for your analytic ideas from the start. Providing ample verbatim material 'grounds' your abstract analysis and lays a foundation for making claims about it. Including verbatim material from different sources permits you to make precise comparisons right in the memo. These comparisons enable you to define patterns in the empirical world. Thus, memo-writing moves your work beyond individual cases.

> Forming the definition from your codes and data forces you to pierce the surface … Your definition of the category starts by explicating its properties or characteristics.

Begin your memo by titling it. That's easy because your codes give you titles to analyze; hence, you already have direction and focus. Define the category you intend to treat. Note how I tried to define why and how suffering is a moral status. Take your definition as far as you can. Forming the definition from your codes and data forces you to pierce the surface. Although you may establish a preliminary, working definition to get a handle on the phenomena, grappling with your material moves the definition beyond description into analysis. Thus, your definition of the category starts by explicating its properties or characteristics.

Next, think about where both the category and the data it subsumes lead you. Follow these leads, whatever they might be. I look for the underlying and—usually—unstated assumptions embedded in the category. In addition, I try to show how and when the category develops and changes and why and for whom it has relevance in the field setting. I found that people frequently referred to living one day at a time when they suffered a medical crisis or faced continued uncertainty. Subsequently, I began to ask questions about what living one day at a time was like for them. I began to define the category and its characteristics from their responses and from published autobiographical accounts. The term 'living one day at a time' condenses a series of implicit meanings and assumptions. It becomes a strategy for handling unruly feelings, for exerting some control over a now uncontrollable life, for facing uncertainty, and for handling a conceivably foreshortened future.

Memo-writing encourages you to dig into implicit, unstated, and condensed meanings. Look for codes that subsume condensed meanings. These codes give you analytic mileage and carry conceptual weight. See how I tried to get at these meanings in the section of a longer memo shown in Box 4.4.

BOX 4.4   EXAMPLE OF MEMO-WRITING

Living One Day at a Time

Living one day at a time means dealing with illness on a day-to-day basis, holding future plans and even ordinary activities, in abeyance while the person and, often, others deal with illness. When living one day at a time, the person feels that his or her future remains unsettled, that he or she cannot foresee the future or if there will be a future. Living one day at a time allows the person to focus on illness, treatment and regimen without becoming entirely immobilized by fear or future implications. By concentrating on the present, the person can avoid or minimize thinking about death and the possibility of dying.

Relation to Time Perspective
The felt need to live one day at a time often drastically alters a person's time perspective. Living one day at a time pulls the person into the present and pushes back past futures (the futures the person projected before illness or before this round of illness) so that they recede without mourning [their loss]. These past futures can slip away, perhaps almost unnoticed. [I then go and compare three respondents' situations, statements, and time perspectives.]

Begin writing memos as soon as you have some ideas and categories to pursue. If at a loss about what to write, elaborate on your most frequent codes. Keep collecting data, keep coding, and keep refining your ideas through writing more and further developed memos. Some researchers who use grounded theory methods discover a few interesting findings early in their data collection and then truncate their research. Their work

> Memo-writing frees you to explore your ideas about your categories. Treat memos as partial, preliminary, and provisional. They are imminently correctable. Just note where you are on firm ground and where you are making conjectures. Then go back to the field to check your conjectures.

lacks the 'intimate familiarity' with the setting or experience that Lofland and Lofland (1995) avow meets the standards for good qualitative research. Barney G. Glaser (2001) rightly applauds Martin Jankowski's (1991) concept of 'defiant individualism' among gang members, because Jankowski has compared hundreds of incidents.[3] Cover your topic in depth by exploring sufficient cases and by elaborating your categories fully.

Memo-writing frees you to explore your ideas about your categories. Treat memos as partial, preliminary, and provisional. They are imminently correctable. Just note where you stand on firm ground and where you make conjectures. Then go back to the field and check your conjectures.

Memos can remain private and unshared. At this point, just get your ideas down as quickly and clearly as you can. Do not worry about verb tense, overuse of prepositional phrases, or lengthy sentences at this point. You write memos to render the data, not to communicate to an audience. Use memo-writing to discover and explore ideas. You can revise the memo later.

Writing memos quickly without editing them fosters developing and preserving your natural voice. Then your memo reads as though written by a living, thinking, feeling human being rather than a pedantic social scientist. You can write memos at different levels of abstraction—from the concrete to the highly theoretical. Some of your memos will find their way directly into your first draft of your analysis. Set aside others with a different focus and develop them later.

Much of your memo-writing will be concerned with making comparisons, in keeping with Glaser and Strauss's constant comparative methods. In your successive memos, you can compare incidents indicated by each category, integrate categories by comparing them and delineating their relationships, delimit the scope and range of the emerging theory by comparing categories with concepts and write the theory, which you may compare with other theories in the same area of study. Hence, you may begin by elaborating the codes in which you compared one respondent's beliefs, stance, and actions with another respondent's, or one experience with another. If you have longitudinal data, you can compare a participant's response, experience, or situation at one point in time with that at another time. Then as you become more analytic and have some tentative analytic categories, compare new data with them. This step will help you delimit your categories and to define their properties.

As you develop categories, write further memos to detail comparisons between them. These memos help you to tease out distinctions that sharpen your treatment of the material. Such memos also aid you to weigh and locate your categories in relation to each other. Through memo-writing, you distinguish between major and minor categories and delineate how they are related. Thus, you begin to frame them into a theoretical statement. You direct the shape and form of your emergent analysis through your memos.

At each more analytic and abstract level of memo-writing, bring your data right into your analysis. Show how you build your analysis on your data in each memo. Bringing your data into successive levels of memo-writing ultimately saves time; you do not have to dig through stacks of material to illustrate your points. In the section of a memo provided above, note that I first defined the category, 'living one day at a time,' and outlined its main properties. Then I developed aspects of living one day at a time such as its relationship to time perspective, which I show in the excerpt, and to managing emotions. The memo also covered *how* people lived one day at a time, the problems it posed as well as those it solved, and the consequences of doing so.

Memo-writing helps you to:[4]

- Stop and think about your data
- Treat qualitative codes as categories to analyze
- Develop your writer's voice and writing rhythm. (Let your memos read like letters to a close friend; no need for stodgy academic prose)
- Spark ideas to check out in the field setting
- Avoid forcing your data into extant concepts and theories
- Develop fresh ideas, create new concepts, and find novel relationships
- Demonstrate connections between categories (e.g. empirical events and social structures, larger groups and the individual, espoused beliefs and actions)
- Discover gaps in your data collection
- Link data-gathering with data analysis and report-writing
- Build whole sections of papers and chapters
- Keep involved in research and writing
- Increase your confidence and competence.

Adopting Writers' Strategies: Prewriting Exercises

Delving into memo-writing can be liberating. Memo-writing can release you from the strictures of academic writing, the constraints of traditional research procedures, and the controls of teachers and supervisors. But does it? Not always. Some problems arise from within the researcher, others from without. Some researchers find that the freedom of memo-writing poses a disquieting leap of faith and practice. Memo-writing requires us to *tolerate ambiguity*. Researchers who write from an outline with a predictable beginning, middle, and end may move right into reporting and miss the discovery, exploratory phase of writing. Memo-writing exemplifies this discovery phase. Subsequently, these researchers cannot write until they have the whole picture in mind. They wait—and wait. Other people view writing as tedious drudgery. They dawdle and dread it.[5]

If either dawdling or dreading sounds like you, try building prewriting exercises into your analytic practices to help you learn to tolerate ambiguity—and to enjoy writing. Prewriting exercises consist of strategies that writers use; they are not part of the methods associated with grounded theory. These exercises can, however, help you delve into writing your grounded theory memos. You may use them as unrelated warm-up exercises or as tools to help you begin memo-writing.

Teachers and research supervisors often treat grounded theory memos as interim, but sharable reports, rather than as private analytic explorations. Thus, another scenario can stifle your efforts to write memos: that is, being evaluated on their quality. How can you write spontaneous memos subject to scrutiny when their purpose is for personal analytic building blocks? Likely, your memos lose spontaneity and their creative edge. When a watchful eye stares—or glares—over your shoulder, it may take you forever to draft a memo.

From their perspectives, teachers and research supervisors have good reasons for evaluating your memos. Many students can handle a large, unwieldy project when their teachers have divided it into steps. This pedagogical strategy fits traditional quantitative research design and much of qualitative research, but not memo-writing.

The problem now extends to the professional realm. Increasingly, research teams on large funded projects choose grounded theory methods. Collaborative research projects depend on sharing tasks and ideas. Principal investigators expect team members to prove their merit. What better way to see how team members demonstrate merit than through their memos? How can team members collaborate if they do not share their emerging analyses? Yet this kind of situation poses other pressing questions for you. How can you avoid being stifled, complete tasks on time, and preserve your analytic autonomy?

Again, consider starting with prewriting exercises. They can get you started and make memo-writing easier. You can revise your memos later for clarity and organization. For the past decade, I have introduced two prewriting exercises, *clustering* and *freewriting*, in grounded theory workshops.[6] Both blocked and fluent workshop participants have found them useful ways to get started and to rethink ideas and their organization. Peter Elbow's (1981) guidelines for freewriting resemble aspects of memo-writing but do not limit you to the data. Both clustering and freewriting are non-linear and thus liberate you from linear logic and organization.

Clustering

Clustering is a shorthand prewriting technique for getting started. As Rico (1983) explains, clustering gives you a non-linear, visual, and flexible technique to understand and organize your material. Adopt this technique to produce a tentative and alterable chart or map of your work. Like freewriting, a major objective of clustering is to liberate your creativity. You write your central idea, category, or process; then circle it and draw spokes from it to smaller circles to show its defining properties, and their relationships and relative significance.

Because it offers a diagram of relationships, clustering shares some similarities with conceptual or situational mapping in grounded theory (see Clarke,

2003, 2005; Soulliere, Britt & Maines, 2003). The configurations of clusters provide an image of how your topic fits together and relates to other phenomena. Clustering is active, quick, and changeable. You can remain uncommitted to a cluster. Try several different clusters to see how the pieces of your puzzle fit together in a variety of ways. This form of prewriting gives you a fast self-correcting way to work with ideas. Clustering makes writing less onerous for those who dread it and speeds up the process for those who enjoy it. Novices find that clustering expedites laying out the form and content of their memos.

Through clustering you gain control because you create an image of the piece before delving into writing about it. Putting together a sensible cluster can give a novice confidence to start elaborating the various sections of it. Clustering can give you a preliminary sketch of the memo you need to write. Later, you can use clustering to work out how sections of your paper fit together.

You can use clustering for all kinds of writing tasks at varied levels of analytic work. The general approach to clustering includes the directions below. You might follow a few of these directions when you first explore your codes.

- Start with the main topic or idea at the center
- Work quickly
- Move out from the nucleus into smaller subclusters
- Keep all related material in the same subcluster
- Make the connections clear between each idea, code, and/or category
- Keep branching out until you have exhausted your knowledge
- Try several different clusters on the same topic
- Use clustering to play with your material.

A nucleus word, such as a code, forms the most basic cluster. Try to construct the cluster and see where it takes you. Clustering around processes moves you further into studying actions rather than only structures. Try to draw connections between parts of your emerging pattern. When you finish, you have a plan for proceeding. Whether or not you follow your plan, you have created a way of moving in and through the material. For practice, try clustering topics unrelated to your research or writing. Explore your thoughts about an event, a film, or a book.

Treat clustering as inconsequential to lessen the seriousness of writing. If it helps you play with your material, so much the better. Writers use clustering to combat writing blocks. Clustering can get you started and keep you moving. The spontaneity and imagery in clustering can foster developing feeling, imagery, and rhythm when you begin to write.

Clustering can enable you to define essentials. It allows for chaos and prompts you to create paths through it. You gain a way of sifting and sorting your material while you create a pattern about, around, and through your category(ies). Clustering lets you make what lurks in the background jump into the foreground. Use clustering to make things explicit and order your topic. A cluster provides a direct visual, as contrasted with a solely mental, image. Hence, you can assess relative importance of the points within your cluster and relationships between them.

Clustering techniques are fast, fluid, fruitful—and fun. If they help you, adopt them. I have adapted these techniques to use with grounded theory methods. You may wish to start clustering with one code and then move on to clustering relationships between codes and then codes and categories. In any case, try the general approach to clustering as outlined above or my adaptation below. After working on a cluster for eight to ten minutes, you will sense how to begin writing about the category. Then you can begin writing a focused freewrite, or a memo.

The following are *guidelines for clustering*, and Figure 4.1 offers an example.

- Draw a circle around a main code large enough to include what it indicates
- Make the circled code the center of *this* cluster
- Divide the inside of the circle to show the defining properties of the code
- Draw spokes from your code to any codes it subsumes to signify relationships
- Use configurations of clusters to construct an image of how your main codes fit together and relate to other categories
- Make the size of your circled codes reflect their relative empirical strength
- Indicate the relative strength of the relationships between codes by the width of your lines
- Allow your clusters to be non-linear
- Work quickly and keep involved in the process
- Take a cluster as far as you can
- Treat clustering as flexible, mutable, and open-ended
- Keep clustering. Try several on the same codes. Compare them.

Freewriting

Freewriting means putting pen to paper or fingers to keyboard and writing for eight minutes to begin, longer with practice. Freewriting encourages you to: 1) compose fresh material and 2) unlearn past immobilizing habits, and 3) write in a natural voice. Freewriting liberates your thoughts and feelings. It provides an effective warm-up exercise and produces results, a freewrite. A quick ten-minute freewrite may save you hours of staring at a blank screen.

Writing teachers often urge students to use freewriting for free association— write whatever comes to consciousness. This type of freewriting opens our minds and releases our imaginations. Such freewriting can increase our receptivity to the world and our ease in writing. It releases immobilizing constraints that others place on you and you may have internalized. Regular sessions of this freewriting can help your writing flow and heighten your awareness of feeling and imagery.

How do you do freewrites? Try following these guidelines:

- Get your ideas down on paper as quickly and fully as you can
- Write to and for yourself
- Permit yourself to write freely and badly
- Don't attend to grammar, organization, logic, evidence, and audience
- Write as though you are talking.

Be receptive when freewriting. Accept anything that comes to mind. Keep writing—putting one thing down on paper leads to another. Let the process

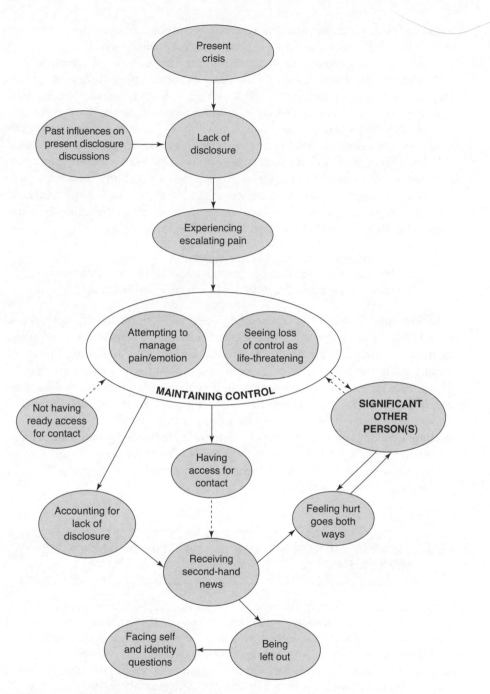

FIGURE 4.1 'Example of Clustering'

emerge. Follow those glimpses of ideas and bursts of inchoate thoughts—right now. You can assess them later. Just concentrate on what you learn or sense now.

Correct grammar doesn't matter. Neither does perfect spelling, logical organization, and clear arguments. What does matter is that you become accustomed to getting your ideas on paper, however they emerge. A freewrite is for your eyes only like a secret journal you create and share with yourself.

Once you are comfortable with freewriting, try a focused freewrite that addresses your data and categories. To help you remain open, follow the guidelines above. Doing focused freewrites can keep you from becoming immobilized and may serve as a direct precursor to memo-writing. Study these freewrites because they may contain seeds of a great memo. By adding a step or two to the writing process, you may soon be writing fluent memos for your research project.

Work in whatever way suits your style—with pad and pencil or your computer. I started to do a focused freewrite for a review essay with my (trained) voice-activated program. What medium could be faster or more spontaneous? Having a constant stream of recording errors distracted me more than the speed of talking helped. The following errors were among them:

> 'well-intentioned methods' for 'qualitative methods'
> 'the death of the analysis' for 'the depth of the analysis'
> 'the fragment-this tradition' for 'the pragmatist tradition'

In Box 4.5, 'Example of a Focused Freewrite,' I took the clustering that I made from Bonnie Presley's interview excerpt and wrote about it for about 12 minutes. Note that I brought other data right into the freewrite; the act of writing about the codes sparked comparisons with other research participants. This focused freewrite is considerably more coherent than my freewrites often are, in part because I completed the clustering first and in part because I find writing from data easier than other forms of writing. The clustering helped me to draw relationships between several intriguing codes and Bonnie's situation. Clustering is particularly helpful to those of us who gravitate to images. Many writers freewrite first or use both techniques. Experiment with freewriting and clustering and see what works for you.

BOX 4.5   EXAMPLE OF A FOCUSED FREEWRITE ON CODES FROM BONNIE PRESLEY'S INTERVIEW (EXCERPT)

The crisis sets off the chain of events and dilemmas about disclosure. Yet the past history of relationships and issues around disclosure echo in the current crisis. Lack of disclosure may be an explicit choice or a consequence of other actions or inactions. Various participants will make assumptions about the person's lack of disclosure, how long it prevailed and what it 'really' meant. In Bonnie's case, her lack of disclosure coincided with escalating pain and her increased efforts to manage, to cope, to control what was happening. If so, then disclosing implied risks of losing control if all the past conflict, disappointments, and lack of emotional support arise again. In other situations such as Bob's, disclosing meant possibly reinvoking all the past issues about obtaining help and his embarrassment—and mortification for asking for it. Such issues in disclosure raise all kinds of sticky intimacy issues and

(Continued)

(Continued)

relationship obligations anew. Bob defines not asking for help unless absolutely necessary as his relationship obligation; Bonnie sees avoiding emotional upheavals with her daughter as hers.

In some sense then, Bob only has partial and tentative access for help and partial access for contact. It is not a given. Bonnie has access for contact although she has to be proactive to realize it. Amy comes by or calls sporadically; she is not a regular part of Bonnie's day, as Linda has become. This incident with Bonnie shows how feeling hurt goes two ways. Misunderstandings build on each other.

From the family or friend's view, receiving second-hand news informs one of his or her place and significance. Being left out stings. It elicits unwelcome images of self and the relationship. It may reaffirm family hierarchies and past family feuds as in Ann's case. Identity questions emerge.

Using Memos to Raise Focused Codes to Conceptual Categories

Writing memos on your codes from the start helps to clarify what is happening in the field. In grounded theory, memo-writing relies on treating some codes as conceptual categories to analyze. Glaser and Strauss (1967: 37) define a category as a 'conceptual element in a theory.' Yet what stands as a category? But what does that mean? No need to worry; you already have your focused codes, as I note above.

Through engaging in focused coding, you begin to sketch the content and form of your budding analysis. Attempting to treat focused codes as categories prompts you to develop and scrutinize them. Then you can evaluate these tentative categories and decide whether they are categories. If you accept these codes as categories, clarify what they consist of and specify the relationships between them.

First, assess which codes best represent what you see happening in your data. In a memo, raise them to conceptual categories for your developing analytic framework—give them conceptual definition and analytical treatment in narrative form in your memo. Thus, you go beyond using a code as a descriptive tool to view and synthesize data.

What do categories do? Categories explicate ideas, events, or processes in your data—and do so in telling words. A category may subsume common themes and patterns in several codes. For example, my category of 'keeping illness contained' included 'packaging illness,' that is, treating it 'as if it is controlled, delimited, and confined to specific realms, such as private life,' and 'passing,' which means, 'concealing illness, maintaining a conventional self-presentation, and performing like unimpaired peers' (Charmaz, 1991a: 66–68).

Again, make your categories as conceptual as possible—with abstract power, general reach, analytic direction, and precise wording. Simultaneously, remain consistent with your data. By having made your focused codes active, incisive (to reflect what people are doing or what is happening), and brief, you have the material to treat them as potential categories. During coding you asked what category does this piece of data indicate? Now ask: what category does this code indicate? A little time and distance from collecting data and initial coding may help you to move another conceptual step. Processes gain visibility when you keep codes active. Succinct, focused codes lead to sharp, clear categories. That way, you can establish criteria for your categories to make further comparisons.

Grounded theorists look for substantive processes that they develop from their codes. 'Keeping illness contained,' 'packaging illness,' and 'living one day at a time' above are three such processes. As grounded theorists create conceptual handles to explain what is happening in the setting, they may move toward defining generic processes (Prus, 1987). A generic process cuts across different empirical settings and problems; it can be applied to varied substantive areas. Two codes in Chapter 3, 'avoiding disclosure' and 'assessing potential losses and risks of disclosing,' reflect fundamental, generic processes of personal information control. Although these processes describe choices people with illness make in disclosing information, people with other problems may treat information control similarly. For sociologists, generic processes are basic to social life; for psychologists, generic processes are fundamental for psychological existence; for anthropologists, these processes support local cultures. Because they are fundamental, generic processes can apply in varied professions and fields. A grounded theorist can elaborate and refine the generic process by gathering more data from diverse arenas where this process is evident. For example, personal information control and choices in disclosing are often problematic for homosexuals, sexual abuse survivors, drug-users, recovering alcoholics, and ex-convicts as well as for people with chronic conditions. Concentrate on analyzing a generic process that you define in your codes; then you can raise relevant codes to theoretical categories that lead to explanations of the process and predictions concerning these categories.[7] As you raise a code to a category, you begin to write narrative statements in memos that:

- Define the category
- Explicate the properties of the category
- Specify the conditions under which the category arises, is maintained, and changes
- Describe its consequences
- Show how this category relates to other categories.

Categories may consist of *in vivo* codes that you take directly from your respondents' discourse or they may represent your theoretical or substantive definition of what is happening in the data. Recall that my terms 'good days and bad days' and 'living one day at a time' came directly from my respondents' voices. In contrast, my categories 'recapturing the past' and 'time in immersion and immersion in time' reflect theoretical definitions of actions and events. Further, categories such as 'pulling in,' 'facing dependency,' and 'making trade-offs' address my respondents' substantive realities of grappling with a serious illness. I created these codes and used them as categories but they reflect my research participants' concerns and actions. Novice researchers may find that they rely most on *in vivo* and substantive codes. What often results is a grounded description more than a theory. Nonetheless, studying how these codes fit together in categories can help you treat them more theoretically.

By writing memos on your focused codes, you build and clarify your category by examining all the data it covers and by identifying variations within it and between other categories. You also become aware of gaps in your analysis. For example, I developed my category 'existing from day to day' when I realized that my category 'living one day at a time' did not cover impoverished people's level of desperation. In short, I had data about a daily struggle to survive that the first category, 'living one day at a time,' did not subsume. Box 4.6 provides the first paragraph of the finished narrative:

BOX 4.6   EXAMPLE OF A MEMO PROMPTED BY STUDYING AN EARLIER MEMO—THE CATEGORY OF 'EXISTING FROM DAY TO DAY'

Existing from day to day occurs when a person plummets into continued crises that rip life apart. It reflects a loss of control of health and the wherewithal to keep life together.

Existing from day to day means constant struggle for daily survival. Poverty and lack of support contribute to and complicate that struggle. Hence, poor and isolated people usually plummet further and faster than affluent individuals with concerned families. Loss of control extends to being unable to obtain necessities—food, shelter, heat, medical care.

The struggle to exist keeps people in the present, especially if they have continued problems in getting the basic necessities that middle-class adults take for granted. Yet other problems can assume much greater significance for these people than their illness—a violent husband, a runaway child, an alcoholic spouse, the overdue rent.

Living one day at a time differs from existing from day to day. Living one day at a time provides a strategy for controlling emotions, managing life, dimming the future, and getting through a troublesome period. It involves managing stress, illness, or regimen, and dealing with these things each day to control them as best as one can. It means concentrating on the here and now and relinquishing other goals, pursuits, and obligations. (Charmaz, 1991a: 185)

Note the comparisons between the two categories above. To generate categories through focused coding, you need to compare data, incidents, contexts, and categories. Try making such comparisons as suggested in the section on 'Writing Advanced Memos' in Box 4.3–How To Write Memos.

Some examples might help. Carolyn Wiener (2000) compares how professional providers, health care managers, and industry regulators define quality care and accountability for it. I compare individuals' depictions of events and their responses to them at different times (an advantage of comparing material from sequential interviews is that you can compile respondents' stories about their recent events rather than ones reconstructed from long-past incidents). In addition to comparing events and incidents, I also compared how people experience different phases of their illnesses.

As I compared different people's experiences, I realized that some people's situations forced them into the present. I then looked at how my rendering of living one day at a time did not apply to them. I reviewed earlier interviews and began to seek published accounts of illness narratives that might clarify the comparison. As is evident in the distinctions between these two categories above, focused coding prompts you to begin to see the relationships and patterns between categories.

Concluding Thoughts

Your memos will form the core of your grounded theory. Following up on ideas and questions that came up while you wrote them will push your work forward. Now you can set aside those memos that you deem to be finished and work on those that still raise nagging questions. Memos provide a record of your research and of your analytic progress. Do keep file copies of each one so that you have the chronological set and can retrieve an earlier idea that you had discarded. You can revisit, review, and revise your memos with a critical eye as you proceed. Like me, you may find that a little time and distance allows gaps and holes in your memos to appear. On returning to them you may identify your next step in an instant and, moreover, take your ideas to a more abstract analytic level.

Perhaps more often than solving our analytic problems, studying our memos—particularly early memos—points to gaps we need to fill. Our ideas are tentative and the memos reveal that we need to do more work to strengthen our categories. When we realize that our categories are weak or incomplete, we can seek more data, but how do we do that? Which data should we seek? How will this new material solve our analytic problems? The next chapter will show you how grounded theorists grapple with these problems and often solve them. Plan to return to the empirical world. In the meantime, keep writing memos.

NOTES

1 For memos that make quick preliminary comments and converse with a co-author, see Anselm Strauss's (1987: 111–112) memo.

2 In this sense, grounded theorists include fewer field anecdotes and less description than other qualitative approaches. We often fragment actions, events, and participants' stories in service to our developing analyses. Glaser (1998) lauds such fragmentation as necessary to move the theory forward. Narrative analysts, phenomenologists, and some postmodernists object to fracturing participants' stories into fragments because they believe the story needs to be preserved (although often in condensed form) in its wholeness and that the form the story takes as well as the content, provide significant insight into its meaning.

3 Glaser (2001) clarifies his stance on comparing incident to incident in this volume but argues that small sample size does not mean limited incidents because people can talk at

length and be re-interviewed. Whether and how well his logic works in actual practice is an empirical question. Telling incidents become evident during data-gathering and analysis and may not affect all participants, thereby limiting the source of comparisons. Many, if not most, grounded theory studies rely on one-shot interviews (see also, Creswell, 1998). Thus, researchers may not discover participants' other incidents that might offer sources of comparison. A researcher also loses the chance to ask more questions about the incident of original interest. Grounded theory studies with small samples seldom match the insight of detailed case studies such as Edward J. Speedling's (1982) study of eight men and their families during and after the men's hospitalizations for heart attacks. Speedling was a participant observer at the hospital for several months before choosing men for his study. After selecting the men, he visited and interviewed them and their families multiple times from their arrival in intensive care through their convalescence and reconstruction of life at home.

4 Adapted from Kathy Charmaz (1999) Stories of suffering: subjects' stories and research narratives. *Qualitative Health Research* 9: 362–382.

5 Don't castigate yourself. Some good writers procrastinate, then inch along, word by word. You may be absorbing the material at a preconscious level and need that time to have your ideas come together. Just try to flow with the process, recognize your patterns, and, if need be, build in some steps and strategies that help you move forward.

6 Those of us who have taught courses on writing routinely include these techniques. For more ideas and excellent advice, see Eide (1995) and Flowers (1993).

7 Dey (1999) is correct in arguing that categorization in grounded theory is more complex and problematic than its originators suggest. I agree with Dey that categorization involves inferences as well as classification.

5 Theoretical Sampling, Saturation, and Sorting

Turns and twists in your research journey leave you with questions about directions to take, how quickly to proceed, and what you will have when you arrive. Theoretical sampling prompts you to retrace your steps or take a new path when you have some tentative categories and emerging, but incomplete ideas. By going back into the empirical world and collecting more data about the properties of your category, you can saturate its properties with data and write more memos, making them more analytic as you proceed. Afterwards, you are ready to sort and integrate memos on your theoretical categories. You may find it helpful to chart the course with diagrams and maps that explain what you have and where you are going.

Suppose that you have arrived at some preliminary—and perhaps tentative—categories. While making earlier comparisons between data, you selected some focused codes and wrote memos on them. Now several categories look like promising abstract tools for rendering your data analytically. Yet one quick reading of these memos tells you: These categories are intriguing but thin. You have not yet defined your categories and their properties clearly. Too much still remains assumed, unknown, or questionable. Instead you want robust categories that stand on firm, not shaky grounds. What do you do? How can grounded theory strategies advance your analytic thinking at this stage of the research?

> Theoretical sampling means seeking pertinent data to *develop* your emerging *theory*. The main purpose of theoretical sampling is to elaborate and refine the categories constituting your theory. You conduct theoretical sampling by sampling to develop the properties of your category(ies) until no new properties emerge.

The answer is to gather more data that focus on the *category* and its properties. This strategy is *theoretical sampling*, which means seeking and collecting pertinent data to elaborate and refine categories in your emerging theory.

You conduct theoretical sampling by sampling to develop the properties of your category(ies) until no new properties emerge. Thus, you *saturate* your categories with data and subsequently *sort* and/or diagram them to integrate your emerging theory.[1] Conducting theoretical sampling can keep you from becoming stuck in unfocused analyses. Glaser and Strauss (1967; Glaser, 1978, 1998, 2001; Strauss, 1987) created the strategies of theoretical sampling, saturation, and sorting. Despite Glaser's continued efforts to explicate what theoretical sampling and saturation entail and Strauss and Corbin's (1990, 1998) explanations, researchers commonly misunderstand how grounded theorists use these strategies.

This chapter consists of guidelines for conducting theoretical sampling, saturating your categories and sorting them into an integrated theoretical statement. I draw upon an interview with Jane Hood[2] and her book *Becoming a Two-Job Family* (1983), as well as on other published materials to illustrate theoretical sampling. Hood is one of the very few authors whose grounded theory analysis and methodological decisions are both explicit. Because qualitative researchers routinely adopt the term 'saturation,' I qualify its meaning in grounded theory, show how it differs from standard understandings and suggest where some grounded theorists themselves have taken it amiss. The chapter ends with ideas about how to do theoretical sorting.

In the interview excerpt below, Jane Hood recounts how she used grounded theory strategies in her study. In her book, she specifies that these were not dual-career families. Rather they were working and lower-middle-class parents both of whom had full-time jobs or were one-career-one-job families. The thrust of Hood's research shifted as she studied her initial data. Originally, she had planned to study married women's self-concepts and friendship networks when they returned to work after having children. Early in Hood's fieldwork, however, she discovered an intriguing family issue: how couples negotiated childcare and housework when women returned to the workforce. As a result, she shifted her data collection to address this issue. Hood's data include 1) material from a small pilot study, 2) in-depth first interviews of 16 wives, 3) in-depth second interviews of these wives, 4) interviews with their husbands, 5) a follow-up questionnaire six years later, 6) telephone interviews she conducted six to seven years after the second round of interviews, and 7) fieldnotes about each interview and its setting, phone call, and informal meeting.

When I talked with her, Hood described how she adopted grounded theory strategies from the beginning of her research:

> It looks like I have something going on here [in her data]. Let's say, in my case it was with women who were working because they really wanted to. Women who were working because they wanted to weren't getting much help from their husbands with housework in my two-job family study. I began to wonder whether women who were working because they *had* to and whose income was really valued by their husbands might get more help but the way I had done my [initial] sampling I had asked for volunteers to be interviewed about the experience of going back to work after having been home full-time. So the volunteers tended to be people who wanted to tell me how wonderful it was to work. I wasn't getting people who were going to work more reluctantly because they had to. But since I was really interested in how women who returned to work kind of bargained with their spouses about getting help with childcare and housework, it was critical that I look at people with a little more bargaining power, who went to work

because their husbands really *needed* them to work. So then I went out and *looked* for those women and lo and behold it made a big difference.

I did have already one or two women in my original collection of seven or eight interviews who were working because they had to and that gave me a clue that that was an important distinction. Then I *expanded* on that category and that was theoretical sampling. Because I had a category of women who went back to work because they wanted to—for self-fulfillment— and another category who went back to work because their family really needed the money.

[The categories] came out of analyzing the data ... I would ask them, 'Why did you go back to work?' Some of the women would say 'Well I went back to work because I was bored at home,' 'I went back to work because I was getting eczema and I went to the doctor and the doctor told me that I had to get out of the house,' or 'I went back to work because I really needed more than just staying at home'... —for self-fulfillment reasons.

I coded reasons for going back to work. I was also coding the kind of help they were getting from their husbands and the kinds of things their husbands were saying about their income. When they went back to work because they wanted to, their husbands were more likely to be saying, 'Well we don't really need you to work. If you can't handle the housework, then you can just quit,' etc. They didn't have much bargaining power because their husbands weren't recognizing their income as necessary. They had gone back to work for self-fulfillment.

Then I realized that when husbands would say—because I would ask husbands, 'What would happen if she quit?' and they would say 'Well, I'd have to take a second job' or 'I don't know *what* we'd do if she quit.' In those cases, husbands *couldn't* say, 'Well, you know, she just can quit whenever she wants.'

'Quit whenever she wants' became a really important analytical code as far as reasons for going back to work: self-fulfillment vs. economic necessity— a few people did both. But what was really important is that the husband recognized and was willing to say that they couldn't easily get along without her income. And that they would have to make major changes—maybe sell their house, cut back on lots of things or—major changes in their lifestyle would be required if the wife quit work. If she could quit whenever she wanted, if that's what the husband basically said, then they described her income as 'icing on the cake.' That was another category that developed from the work. It's funny how many guys referred to it that way, 'icing on the cake.' 'It's a little extra.' When they thought of it that way, they didn't see her as a coprovider—that was part of the definition of a secondary provider, they described her income as 'icing on the cake' ... Even when a woman's salary was paying the whole mortgage payment, this guy said, well he was really putting the bread on the table; he wouldn't recognize her as a coprovider. She made the same amount of income as many women who were recognized as making a necessary contribution. He wouldn't let go of the provider role.

This is what's different [about grounded theory], I suppose, when we're developing these categories and developing an analysis as we go along, we are really looking at the data as we code and developing a grounded concept. We call them categories but it's really grounded in the data.

Hood's coding and sampling methods shaped her substantive study from its beginnings.[3] Because she had initially expected to study changes in women's self-concepts and friendship networks, she only interviewed wives during her first round of interviews. Yet her early analysis revealed that she needed to interview husbands as well as focus more on women who had financial pressures to return to work. Her *in vivo* codes such as 'quit whenever she wants' and 'icing on the cake' provide vivid indicators of certain husbands' stances toward having their wives' work. Such codes also gave Hood strong clues about how these husbands' views played out in interaction.

Note how Hood traced the conditions under which women gained bargaining power. Through following what she defined in her data, she linked bargaining power to marital roles. In Hood's book, role analysis in marriage emerges as a dominant theme. Her work fits into the family of theoretical codes on roles and extends knowledge of how couples enact roles. Granted, other researchers might construct the study differently, according to what they saw in the data. Another researcher, for example, might also identify the bargaining issues but pursue a different line of analysis with them, such as the partners' emotions about bargaining. Still another researcher might interview lesbian or gay couples who take neither the concept of gender nor conventional gender roles for granted. Rich data can spark multiple directions of inquiry.

Hood built on her interest in marital roles and developed a theoretical framework and proposed testable hypotheses that locate bargaining power within the context of the marriage. She showed how these wives' bargaining power varied in relation to each spouse's commitment to and investment in the marital relationship, work and family priorities, the extent of the wife's role overload, and the couple's style of resolving conflicts. Hood's work reveals how a researcher acts on her theoretical and substantive interests and engages her data as she constructs a grounded theory through making comparisons at each analytic level. Consider several of Hood's concluding remarks in her book:

> None of the couples in this book decided to become coproviders in order to adopt a more equal division of labour. Instead they became two-job couples either because the wife needed to get out of the house or the family needed money, or both. In the process of becoming a two-job family, some couples also developed a more equal balance of power in their marriages and a more equal division of labour in the household. This move towards equality was, however, an unforeseen and unintended consequence of becoming coproviders.
>
> ... Couples who purposefully decide to share roles are like couples who began to share roles 'without really thinking about it' in at least one important respect, however. Most find that the new common ground created by role sharing and the increased communication necessary to maintain role-sharing relationships brings them closer together. (1983: 197–198)

Theoretical Sampling

Distinguishing Theoretical Sampling from Other Types of Sampling

To understand and to use theoretical sampling, we must relinquish our preconceptions about what sampling means. Sampling to develop a researcher's emerging theoretical categories distinguishes theoretical sampling from other forms of sampling. Sometimes qualitative researchers claim to use theoretical sampling but do not follow the logic of grounded theory. They mistake theoretical sampling for the following types of sampling:

- Sampling to address initial research questions
- Sampling to reflect population distributions
- Sampling to find negative cases
- Sampling until no new data emerge.

These sampling strategies mistake theoretical sampling for conventional qualitative research approaches. Of course anyone who writes a research proposal seeks data to address his or her research questions—but this sampling is of an initial type. Initial sampling provides a point of departure, not of theoretical elaboration and refinement. We cannot assume to know our categories in advance, much less have them contained in our beginning research questions. Grounded theory logic presupposes that we will construct categories through the comparative methods of analyzing data.

Remember that criteria for initial sampling differ from those you invoke while theoretical sampling. Initial sampling in grounded theory is where you start whereas theoretical sampling directs you where to go. For initial sampling, you establish sampling criteria for people, cases, situations, and/or settings before you enter the field. You need to find relevant materials for your study whether that leads you to sampling people, settings, or larger structures such as government agencies or organizations.

> Initial sampling in grounded theory is where you start, whereas theoretical sampling directs you where to go.

If, for example, you plan to study customer service relationships, gaining access to observe actual encounters is a prerequisite. What you will see and hear depends, of course, on your position in the organization and how you negotiate it. You will have access to some things but not others.[4] If you obtain permission to interview customer service agents but not to observe them, then your study shifts in another direction.

Seemingly straightforward topics may soon become complex. If you wish to explore drinking among people with disabilities, then you must start with at least a provisional definition stating what the term 'disability' will cover. Then you need to find out what drinking—and disability—mean to your participants and find out if you need to talk with their families or friends. You must decide whether you will include people with disabilities who view themselves as recovering alcoholics. Topics that prompt you to contact certain people but not others already circumscribe what you address. You should explicate and, not least among your tasks, examine your own preconceptions about drinking.

Theoretical sampling also follows a different logic than sampling techniques for traditional quantitative research design. The purpose of theoretical sampling is to obtain data to help you explicate your categories. When your categories are full, they reflect qualities of your respondents' experiences and provide a useful analytic handle for understanding them. In short, theoretical sampling pertains only to conceptual and theoretical development; it is *not* about representing a population or increasing the statistical generalizability of your results. Many quantitative studies require random samples of people whose characteristics are representative of the population under study. Whereas quantitative researchers want to use their data to make statistical inferences about their target populations, grounded theorists aim to fit their emerging theories with their data. Quantitative researchers test preconceived hypotheses; grounded theorists sometimes offer the grist for emergent hypotheses that other researchers might pursue.

Colleagues and teachers who invoke the logic of quantitative research often mistakenly advise qualitative researchers to make their samples represent distributions of larger populations. The error of this advice lies in assuming that qualitative research aims for generalizability. Although this strategy may be useful for initial sampling, it does not fit the logic of grounded theory and can result in the researcher collecting unnecessary and conceptually thin data.[5] During our talk, Jane Hood commented on understanding theoretical sampling:

> Very few people do [understand it]. I really think it's a craft ... You need somebody to give you feed-back as you're trying to learn how to do this because there is a subtle difference between theoretical sampling and other kinds of purposeful sampling. Theoretical sampling is purposeful sampling but it's purposeful sampling according to categories that one develops from one's analysis and these categories are not based upon quotas; they're based on theoretical concerns. And—the authors of textbooks don't get it. The authors of textbooks typically say [something like], 'Oh, you don't have enough women; go get more.' No, that's not theoretical sampling. That's basically quota sampling or sampling on demographic characteristics. There's nothing wrong with starting out that way *but* that's your first step. Theoretical sampling really makes grounded theory special and is the major strength of grounded theory *because* theoretical sampling allows you to tighten what I call the corkscrew or the hermeneutic spiral so that you end up with a theory that perfectly matches your data. Because you choose the next people to talk to or the next cases to find based upon the [theoretical] analysis and you don't waste your time with all sorts of things that have nothing to do with your developing theory.[6]

As Hood states, many researchers sample different settings or individuals to reflect empirical distributions or situations but they are not conducting theoretical sampling. For example, a specialist in organizations may plan to sample different businesses with both strict and loose systems of authority. This plan may produce interesting contrasts in data but it does not constitute theoretical sampling. Again, until researchers construct conceptual categories from the data and sample to develop these categories, they are not conducting theoretical sampling.

The search for negative cases raises more ambiguous questions. Whether or not sampling negative cases complements or contradicts grounded theory depends on the situation. Qualitative researchers often use negative cases to find new variables or to provide alternative explanations from their developing theory. The logic of negative cases assumes asking whether the data include individuals, situations, or themes that do not fit your analysis. Virginia Olesen asks a further question: Did you try to find those cases? (Personal communication, June 5, 2005).

The source of the negative cases and how the researcher uses these cases shapes their relative fit with grounded theory. Did these cases arise in the data or did the researcher *import* them into the research process as though they furthered theoretical sampling? If the researcher does not define negative cases in the comparative analysis of his or her data, a search for them may result in importing them. If negative cases emerge in the data, however, these cases may indicate the need to refine one's emerging theory. Examining negative cases comes close to the emphasis on variation in a category or process and analytic density in grounded theory (Strauss & Corbin, 1990). Becker (1998) points out that some researchers consider hypothetical negative cases or draw on fiction for possibilities. To the extent that such practices cause the researcher to stray from their studied empirical world, they remain inconsistent with the grounded theory emphasis on building one's analysis from it.[7]

Perhaps the most common error occurs when researchers confuse theoretical sampling with gathering data until they find the same patterns reoccurring. This strategy differs from theoretical sampling because these researchers have not aimed their data-gathering toward explicit development of *theoretical* categories derived from analyses of their studied worlds. Instead, the patterns describe empirical *themes* in their studied worlds.

Some forms of sampling come much closer to theoretical sampling than others. Pertti Alasuutari's (1996) sampling strategies share similarities with theoretical sampling. He notes that his strategic selection of case study examples resembled theoretical sampling; however, his objective differed. Alasuutari's ethnographic study of a local Finnish tavern focused on the lives of regular male patrons who were heavy drinkers. Through his studies of alcohol use (1992, 1995), he aimed to gain a 'unified picture of different cultural logics within which the same historical structural conditions are viewed in people's lived experience,' not to develop a general theory (1996, p. 376). Nevertheless, his focus on cultural logics led to a sophisticated cultural theory of alcoholism (1992). When discussing the research process involved in this project, Alasuutari states:

> In ethnographic research the testing of hypotheses may have to do with more than just the kinds of thing you're making observations about or the kinds of subjects that you raise with the informants. On the basis of your results you may decide to move on and collect a new data set, as I did in the AA group project. When I learned that A-Guilds in Finland had their own journal, it seemed a good idea to go through all its back volumes to determine whether the 'treatment philosophy' I had discovered in Tampere was a local or a more national phenomenon. (1995: 172)

The Logic of Theoretical Sampling
Theoretical sampling involves starting with data, constructing tentative ideas about the data, and then examining these ideas through further empirical inquiry.

Consider how Hood (1983) kept moving back and forth between data collection and data analysis throughout her research. Codes became categories. Early categories were suggestive but not yet definitive. Further data collection strengthened them but Hood then saw new gaps in her nascent analysis. She returned to the field and asked further questions—and kept writing and analyzing.

Memo-writing leads directly to *theoretical sampling*. Theoretical sampling is strategic, specific, and systematic. Because you intend to use it to elaborate and refine your theoretical categories, conducting theoretical sampling depends on having already identified a category(ies). This pivotal grounded theory strategy helps you to delineate and develop the properties of your category and its range of variation.

Writing memos has already enabled you to flag incomplete categories and gaps in your analysis. Engaging in theoretical sampling prompts you to *predict* where and how you can find needed data to fill gaps and to saturate categories. Like Hood's hunches, your predictions arise from your immediate analytic work. They are not off-hand conjectures. Rather, they emerge from your grounded comparative analysis of earlier data. Follow hunches about where to find data that will illuminate these categories and then go *collect* these data. Next, code them and compare your codes with each other, earlier codes, and your emerging categories. Write increasingly more abstract and conceptual memos as you proceed to record your new comparisons—and all those flashes of insight you have while filling out your categories. Theoretical sampling ensures that you construct full and robust categories and leads you to clarify relationships between categories.

Theoretical sampling not only helps you fill out the properties of your major categories, you can learn more about how a basic process develops and changes. When you engage in theoretical sampling, you seek statements, events, or cases that will illuminate your categories. Like Hood, you may add new participants or observe in new settings. Quite possibly, you may ask earlier participants further questions or inquire about experiences that you had not covered before.

How does theoretical sampling benefit your analysis from the start? From early in the research process, you check emerging questions as you compare data with data. Note how Hood's comparisons between data led her to make conjectures about her categories that she subsequently checked out through further data collection. Her story about how she used theoretical sampling reveals how she formed analytic questions and used deductive logic. For example, Hood predicted that married women's bargaining power increased with their husbands' awareness and open acknowledgment of the wives' vital financial contribution to the household. Then Hood checked her hunches and found them confirmed in subsequent data collection. In this sense, theoretical sampling entails both of what we commonly refer to as inductive and deductive reasoning.

The particular form of reasoning invoked in grounded theory makes it an abductive method, because grounded theory includes *reasoning* about experience for making theoretical conjectures and then checking them through further experience.[8] Abductive reasoning about the data starts with the data and subsequently moves toward hypothesis formation (Deely, 1990; Fann, 1970; Rosenthal, 2004). In brief, abductive inference entails considering all possible

theoretical explanations for the data, forming
hypotheses for each possible explanation, checking them empirically by examining data, and pursuing the most plausible
explanation.

> In brief, abductive inference
> entails considering all possible
> theoretical explanations for the
> data, forming hypotheses for
> each possible explanation,
> checking them empirically by
> examining data, and pursuing
> the most plausible explanation.

At this point, researchers take their ideas
emanating from experience, form a follow-up
hypothesis, and then move back to check
this hypothesis in experience (Peirce, 1958).
Thus after you examine cases, you make a logical inference that offers a theoretical interpretation of the relationships between these cases, and then you
return to the field to check and evaluate your inference. These processes are
central to theoretical sampling and are apparent in Hood's reflections during the
interview about how she did theoretical sampling.

> You ... go back and forth between data collection and analysis and as your
> theory develops through the constant comparative method, you know with
> each step which data you need to collect in order to refine your theory. So
> in a way I see grounded theory as a combination of inductive and, to some
> extent, deductive work. You're inductively developing theory and then
> you're at least trying out your hunches here continuously ... We can call it
> an abductive method. ... I wouldn't say we are exactly testing theory,
> depending what you mean by testing, but we are testing our hunches.

As Hood's remarks imply, conducting theoretical sampling advances your
analysis. Simultaneously it keeps you from getting stuck in either unfocused
data collection or foiled analyses. Use theoretical sampling to keep you moving
toward such emergent objectives such as:

- To delineate the properties of a category
- To check hunches about categories
- To saturate the properties of a category
- To distinguish between categories
- To clarify relationships between emerging categories
- To identify variation in a process.

Theoretical sampling is *emergent*. It follows constructing tentative categories.
You cannot know which ideas you will need to sample before you begin analysis. The specific reason why you conduct theoretical sampling depends on the
analytic problems you are grappling with and what ideas, gaps, ambiguities,
and questions subsequently arise.[9]

Identifying problems and seeking solutions for them takes a certain amount
of candor and distance. Are your categories analytically thin? Insufficiently
supported? Are your ideas about the relationships between categories hazy?
Are they indistinct but perhaps suggestive? Good researchers learn to recognize
such analytic problems—and work to resolve them. Theoretical sampling
in grounded theory provides a valuable tool for developing your analysis and

correcting trouble spots. Grappling with analytic problems is part of the research process. Feeling confused and uncertain–but learning to tolerate the ambiguity–shows your growth as a researcher. Researchers who treat the analytic process as transparent often have superficial analyses.

Conducting theoretical sampling encourages you to follow up on analytic leads. As a result, you improve your study through:

- Specifying the relevant properties of your categories
- Increasing the precision of your categories
- Providing the substance to move your material from description to analysis
- Making your analysis more abstract and generalizable
- Grounding your conjectures in data
- Explicating the analytic links between or among categories
- Increasing the parsimony of your theoretical statements.

Theoretical sampling gives you the data to delineate the properties of a category. When I was trying to sort through how people experienced a serious chronic illness, their accounts abounded with tales of uneven days, troublesome symptoms, and lost time. When comparing these accounts, I devised the category, 'experiencing intrusive illness.'[10] Certainly the category itself is mundane and specific to illness as stated, but what does it include? How might I conceptualize it? For what types of experiences beyond illness might experiencing unwanted intrusions have relevance?

After gathering more data through theoretical sampling, I defined the category of intrusive illness by its analytic properties as demanding continued attention, allotted time, and forced accommodation. Note how these properties fit the following account:

> There's a lot of things I can't do. ... When I go to night school ... I have to go straight home to lay down before I do, or I can't go, where years ago I wouldn't have had to do that.
> And I have really had problems with lights. I can't be in a room that has fluorescent lighting without wearing special glasses. So if I go to class at night, I have to sit there with sunglasses on. Then that makes me even more tired. It makes my eyes swell shut ... And I've also missed three classes and before I've never missed class. (Charmaz, 1991a: 43)

As I examined many cases and incidents, I aimed to make the properties of the category of intrusive illness reflect the actions people took toward their illness and reveal meanings they attributed to it. In their view, the intrusiveness of their illness imposed special demands on them if they were to maintain some semblance of their earlier lives. The properties of this category seem straightforward although they provide grist for making abstract statements about time and self. When conducting theoretical sampling about experiencing an intrusive illness, I gathered more data on how people defined their uneven days, what allotting time to illness-related tasks to get through the day meant to them, when they felt forced to accommodate to illness, which accommodations they made, and how they saw themselves. For example, one woman wanted to minimize her co-workers' knowledge of her condition. She felt forced to complete her work assignments early in the day before fatigue overtook her and tried to camouflage her symptoms in the afternoon. As her problems with getting through the workday increased, she realized that she could no longer hope to hold on until retirement eight years hence. When asking about such accommodations, few questions elicited many stories. Moreover, I witnessed events that illuminated how intrusive illness affected my research participants and was able to piece their implicit views and actions together as I developed the analysis.

Note that theoretical sampling gives you the material to compare theoretical category with category. Think about whether you have lumped properties under one category that might call for constructing separate, distinctive categories. Experiencing intrusive illness differs from the other two ways of experiencing illness, as an interruption or immersion in it. By defining each category by its properties, I raise the analytic level of the category and sharpen the definitions of each.

Delineating links between views and actions is one way of sharpening your ideas. Subsequently, an analysis of mundane experiences in a field setting became more analytic, abstract and potentially generalizable. Theoretical sampling gives your work analytic depth and precision. As you engage in theoretical sampling, your work gains clarity and generality that transcends the immediate topic. By focusing on your *theoretical categories* rather than on a single empirical topic, theoretical sampling leads you to sample across substantive areas. Thus, engaging in theoretical sampling can encourage you to raise your theory to a formal, more abstract level that cuts across different substantive areas.

If we moved the analysis of having an intrusive experience across substantive fields, where would we take it? Certainly some types of caregiving demand continued attention, allotted time and forced accommodation—and may be unwelcome, similar to having a serious illness. A few weeks ago, a caregiver whose father was dying of cancer read portions of my book. She commented on how my analysis of time applied to her caregiving experience as well as to her father's situation. People who find themselves mired in unexpected, unpleasant legal or bureaucratic battles might offer insights on how an intrusive experience encroaches on their lives. Experiencing identity theft or obtaining special services at school for a child with learning disabilities are two examples. In each situation, we could explore how properties of experiencing an unwanted and persistent situation shape qualities of time—and subsequent selves and situations. We might compare what began as an unwelcome, sometimes shocking disruption with situations that began as inconvenient and became intrusive. We could look at how and when the intrusive experience takes over people's lives. Depending on how encompassing it is, life changes may occur that have consequences for these individuals' development of self. Had I taken my analysis of self and time beyond the experience of illness, I could have constructed a formal theory of them.

Anchoring your categories in a solid substantive base first gives you leads about where and how to proceed in other areas. Jane Hood's book provides a substantive grounded theory of marital bargaining about family work.[11] Through her analysis, she builds a foundation from which further research across fields could generate a formal theory of both silent and strategic bargaining. She might establish, for example, a theoretical continuum between gradual accommodation and explicit negotiations. In any case, she has the initial material to seek new individuals and groups involved in bargaining. Then she could check how participants' relative equal or unequal power and different stakes in the outcome of bargaining affect how it proceeds and what happens as a result of it.

Using Theoretical Sampling

You can use theoretical sampling in both early and later stages of your research—*if* you have categories to direct your sampling. Use theoretical sampling as a strategy to narrow your focus on emerging categories and as a technique to develop and refine them. Begin theoretical sampling when you have some preliminary categories to develop. Theoretical sampling helps you to check, qualify, and elaborate the boundaries of your categories and to specify the relations among categories. Initially, theoretical sampling helps you to fill out the properties of a category so that you can create an analytic definition and explication of it. Later, theoretical sampling may help you demonstrate links among categories.

Some attempts to conduct theoretical sampling may not be particularly theoretical. In this case, researchers pursue an interesting finding but they may not theorize its significance. They fail to push the boundaries of a substantive finding and answer the 'So what?' question. Of what larger, more abstract theoretical category or problem is this finding a part? Theoretical sampling means more than following up on intriguing earlier codes, which good researchers routinely do. Conduct theoretical sampling after you have already defined and tentatively conceptualized relevant ideas that indicate areas to probe with more data. Otherwise, early theoretical sampling may result in one or more of the common grounded theory pitfalls:

- Premature closure of analytic categories
- Trite or redundant categories
- Over-reliance on overt statements for elaborating and checking categories
- Unfocused or unspecified categories.

Textbook authors often treat theoretical sampling as a procedure that researchers conduct through interviews. Theoretical sampling is less of an explicit procedure than a *strategy* that you invoke and fit to your specific study. Methods for conducting theoretical sampling vary accordingly. Theoretical sampling can entail studying documents, conducting observations, or participating in new social worlds as well as interviewing or reinterviewing with a focus on your theoretical categories.

What you look for through theoretical sampling and *how* you conduct it depends on your purposes in doing it. Consistent with the logic of grounded

theory, theoretical sampling is emergent.
Your developing ideas shape what you do,
areas you tap and questions you pose
while theoretical sampling.

> *What* you look for through
> theoretical sampling and *how*
> you conduct it depends on your
> purposes in doing it. Consistent
> with the logic of grounded
> theory, theoretical sampling is
> emergent. Your developing
> ideas shape what you do and
> the questions you pose while
> theoretical sampling.

When I was trying to figure out how
people with chronic illnesses defined the
passage of time, I went back to several participants whom I had interviewed before to
ask them more focused questions about
how they perceived times of earlier crisis
and when time seemed to slow, quicken,
drift, or drag. Because such topics resonated with their experiences, they
responded to esoteric questions and offered numerous insights about meanings of
temporal duration. For example, when I studied their stories, I realized that chronically ill adults implicitly located their self-concepts in the past, present, or future.[12]
These timeframes reflected the form and content of self and mirrored hopes and
dreams for self as well as beliefs and understandings about self. Hence, I made 'the
self in time' a major category. Thereafter, I asked more people how they saw themselves in relation to the past, present, or future. An elderly working-class woman
said without hesitation:

> I see myself in the future now. If you'd asked where I saw myself eight
> months ago, I would have said, 'the past.' I was so angry then because I
> had been so active. And to go downhill as fast as I did—I felt life had been
> awfully cruel to me. Now I see myself in the future because there's some-
> thing the Lord wants me to do. Here I sit all crumpled in this chair not
> being able to do anything for myself and still there's a purpose for me to
> be here. [*Laughs.*] I wonder what it could be. (Charmaz, 1991a: 256)

Through theoretical sampling you can elaborate the meaning of your categories, discover variation within them, and define *gaps among categories*. By gaps
between categories, I mean that your current categories do not account for the
full range of relevant experience. Theoretical sampling relies on comparative
methods for discovering these gaps and finding ways to fill them. These methods
are particularly helpful when you attempt to analyze liminal experience and tacit
views. For example, as I talked with people about their experiences of illness and
time and wrote memos about the properties of locating one's self in time, I realized that meanings of the past differed (Charmaz, 1991a). For some people, the
past was a tangled web in which they felt ensnared. They sought to explain and
account for past events that had brought them to the present. Other people
located themselves in a familiar past because the present seem so alien and inexplicable. Still others located themselves in a reconstructed past that shone bright
with happiness, fullness, and vibrancy when juxtaposed against a lived present
with which they did not identify. As I analyzed differences in how people located
themselves in the past, my subcategories depicting their pasts, 'the past as a tangled web,' 'the familiar past and the inexplicable present,' and 'the reconstructed
past,' refined the larger category of the self in the past and showed how living in
the past varied.

Discovering Variation

Variation within a process usually becomes apparent while you are conducting theoretical sampling. For example, when living with physical impairment, people show considerable variation in how they act and feel about it. They may ignore impairment, minimize it, struggle against it, reconcile themselves to it, embrace it, or adapt to it.[13] Not only may these ways of living with impairment differ among people, but also they may differ over time with the same individual. I wanted to see what changes occurred over time, so I talked with a subset of my interview participants for a number of years. Being selective about which data you seek and where you seek them aids you to see variation in the studied process. You focus on certain actions, experiences, events, or issues, *not on individuals per se*, to understand how, when, and why your theoretical categories vary. However, you will likely gain more knowledge about those experiences, events, or issues that you seek to treat theoretically through observing or talking with certain individuals. For example, one of my main categories was 'immersion in illness' (Charmaz, 1991a). Major properties of immersion include recasting life around illness, slipping into illness routines, pulling into one's inner circle, facing dependency, and experiencing an altered (slowed) time perspective. Activities of all sorts took longer but not everyone's time perspective changed, despite being immersed in illness.

How could I account for this phenomenon? What supported maintaining the time perspective of a former workaday world? By going back through my data, I gained some leads. Then I talked with more people about specific experiences and events that influenced their time perspective. Theoretical sampling helped me to refine the analysis and make it more complex. I then added a category 'variations in immersion' to highlight and account for different experiences of immersion in illness.

My earlier interviews contained hints that immersion in illness varied and affected experiencing time but the significance of this variation only occurred to me after I developed the larger category of immersion in illness. I had begun to see variations in what being immersed in illness was like when I compared telling events and specific experiences of people with different illnesses, with different life situations, and different ages. Subsequently, theoretical sampling helped me to define more specific forms of variation. For example, I sampled to learn how illness and time differed for people who spent months in darkened rooms and how both varied when people anticipated later improvement or defined their situations as facing continued uncertainty. Demarcations of time stretched when people had few activities, little companionship, and minimal responsibilities. Making comparisons explicit through successive memos enabled me to draw connections that I did not initially discern. The memo became a short section of a chapter that begins as follows and then goes on to detail each remaining point:

Variations in Immersion

A lengthy immersion in illness shapes daily life and affects how one experiences time. Conversely, ways of experiencing time dialectically affect the qualities of immersion in illness. The picture above of immersion and time has sharp outlines. What sources of variation soften or alter the picture of immersion and time? The picture may vary according to the person's 1) type of illness, 2) kind of medication, 3) earlier time perspective, 4) life situation, and 5) goals.

The type of illness shapes the experience and way of relating to time. Clearly trying to manage diabetes necessitates gaining a heightened awareness of timing the daily routines. But the effects of the illness may remain much more subtle. People with Sjögren's syndrome, for example, may have periods of confusion when they feel wholly out of synchrony with the world around them. For them, things happen too quickly, precisely when their bodies and minds function too slowly. Subsequently, they may retreat into routines to protect themselves. Lupus patients usually must retreat because they cannot tolerate the sun. Sara Shaw covered her windows with black blankets when she was extremely ill. Thus, her sense of chronological time became further distorted as day and night merged together into an endless flow of illness. (Charmaz, 1991a: 93)

Theoretical sampling focuses further data collection to refine key categories in your research. You can then define these categories quite explicitly and identify their properties and parameters. Your subsequent memo-writing becomes more precise, analytic, and incisive. Theoretical sampling keeps you moving between targeted data collection and analytic memo-writing. You follow leads, check out hunches, and refine your ideas in successive memos. Because theoretical sampling forces you to check your ideas against direct empirical realities, you have solid materials and sound ideas with which to work. You gain confidence in your perceptions of your data and in your theorizing about them.

The logic of theoretical sampling implies a quick, focused method of gathering pinpointed data. Some grounded theorists present it as an unproblematic step in refining theory. Yet conducting theoretical sampling entails more than technical and analytic procedures. It brings you back into empirical worlds with all their ambiguities and tensions.

Empirical worlds have their own rules and traditions. Theoretical sampling may not fit them. Textbook explanations of theoretical sampling seldom take into account interactional reciprocities and situational demands. These technical explanations ignore relationships and reciprocities in the field and all the actual work it takes to gain ready access to information. You may not be able to dash in, grab the needed data, and dart back to your desk. The lines between involvement and distance in field research often blur and may require continual renegotiation. Remember that human beings are unlikely to relish being treated as objects from which you extract data. Reciprocities are important, and listening and being there are among them. Some researchers may command access on the basis of their authority and the prestige of their projects. Many other researchers cannot. Instead we gain access through the trust that emerges through establishing on-going relationships and reciprocities. Ignoring such reciprocities not only weakens your chances of obtaining telling data but, moreover, dehumanizes your research participants—and yourself.

The logistics of legitimacy, formal access, and entry also pose problems. During a recent presentation on grounded theory, one researcher asked me, 'How do you do theoretical sampling when you have to have approval of IRBs (institutional review boards)?"[14] An excellent question. Depending on the situation of your participants and your situation, conducting theoretical sampling may require further clearance with institutional committees. Biomedical models of experimentation may well guide these committees. Through their decisions, they attempt to enact principles of doing no harm to research subjects, anticipating potential harm, and articulating strategies for minimizing and handling whatever harm arises. Funded research proposals receive careful scrutiny before their principal investigators can gather any data. Most researchers and students who pursue unfunded research also must receive approval from institutional committees before proceeding with their studies. How can they reconcile the emergent process of doing grounded theory with institutional constraints on research?[15]

Given the current practices of institutional review committees, many qualitative researchers try to anticipate all possible contingencies and account for them in their research proposals. Taken literally, theoretical sampling poses obstacles because you cannot anticipate what your core categories will be beforehand. You can, however, create a rationale to justify using theoretical sampling later without explaining the logic of theoretical sampling or specifying core categories in advance. Just seek approval for a possible second and perhaps third set of interviews and observations from the start. It helps to include participant observation at interview and field sites as part of your methodological approach. Multiple interviews and observations give you access. A discourse of clarification and confirmation should then suffice to gain approval of your proposal. By delineating key grounded theory steps, you show how you plan to increase the conceptual precision of your emerging ideas and to focus your data-gathering to achieve this precision as you proceed. Thus, your later observations, interviews, cases, or other data are pinpointed to address conceptual issues. In short, building plans to return to the field settings and key 'informants' into your original proposal gives you some leeway to gather further data to develop properties of categories. Similarly, when you design an interview study, plans to conduct follow-up interviews on the major ideas will allow for theoretical sampling.

Adopting the language of member-checking in your research proposal may also help, as a large literature on member-checking has made it an accepted– and sometimes expected–practice. Although member-checking generally refers to taking ideas back to research participants for their confirmation, you can use return visits to gather material to elaborate your categories. Cheryl Albas and Dan Albas[16] devised a clever method of checking and refining their categories late in their research. They explain their major categories to certain participants they have studied and then inquire whether and to what extent these categories fit each participant's experience. Albas and Albas observe the participant's expressions given in the conversation and those unwittingly given off. When a participant offers bland agreement with their analysis, Albas and Albas conclude that their categories have not penetrated the core of the participant's experience. Subsequently, Albas and Albas engage the participant in a discussion to generate new properties of a category or a range of categories. They report that they have gained some of their best data from this technique.

Alasuutari (1992, 1996) invokes a similar strategy but turns it inside out. Instead of aiming to discover what he might have overlooked or under-analyzed, as

Albas and Albas did, he confronts his research participants with their tacit actions. Thus, Alasuutari aims for what *they* have overlooked or understated. He speaks from the standpoint of the researcher when he points out that informants typically provide meaningful but partial interpretations. The researcher must dig deeper to develop a more complete explanation. Alasuutari's strategies for constructing this explanation resemble theoretical sampling. See how he brought his observations back to his informants:

> In one particular conversation I raised the issue of why members were always so eager to compete for the title of heaviest drinker and at the same time to belittle the drinking of other members:
>
> PA: Somehow I feel there's this feeling in this group that there's someone here who hasn't drunk as much as the others or who's been down and out for a shorter while than others, that you tend to belittle that person's drinking, that, you know that's nothing really, I drank a lot more than he did.
> A: Where've you heard that?
> PA: I have you know.
> B: I see.
> PA: Even during these sessions right here.
> C: It's always better the sooner you have the sense to go and get help isn't it.
> A: That's right.
> C: The longer you drink the more stupid you are, there's no doubt about that.
> PA: But do you brag about being more stupid?
> C: You tend to color things a bit, like I've been drinking longer than you have. You've only been drinking for a year but I've been there two years. So the one who's been drinking a year realizes that this is the point where I need to go and get help for myself. I'm so stupid that I didn't have the sense to come and get help, I had to carry on. So this is how I describe the situation so that there you are, I'm a bit better, *I know these things*, a bit better.
>
> When I raised this question, the members of the group first wanted to deny my interpretation, even though I had clear examples of these sorts of situations in my field notes. When at long last it is admitted that the phenomenon really exists, member C (in the italicized section of his speech) renders further support to my interpretation that the emphasis on the seriousness of one's earlier alcohol problems is associated with the respect that members show for practical experience. (1995: 170–171)

In this instance, Alasuutari offered his interpretation and pushed for a dialogue about it.[7] He gained confirmation of his view then pushed further later in the same conversation. In my view, Alasuutari's effectiveness relied on dual sources: strong bonds with group members and solid data from which to speak. Strong bonds build trust and foster open conversations with research participants about areas ordinarily left unspoken. Solid data ground the questions–*despite their provocative nature*. What might be a preconceived leading question by an unskilled observer can become an incisive strategy by a practiced ethnographer. Interestingly, Alasuutari did not take the men's support for his interpretation at face value. Rather he took it a few analytic steps further. He located his confirmed interpretation in the context of the group culture and concluded that it also reflected the group members' contradictory relationships with staff and lack of trust in professionals.

Saturating Theoretical Categories

When do you stop gathering data? What criteria do you use? The standard short grounded theory answer to the criteria question dictates: stop when your categories are 'saturated.' The longer answer is that categories are 'saturated' when gathering fresh data no longer sparks new theoretical insights, nor reveals new properties of your core theoretical categories.

> Categories are 'saturated' when gathering fresh data no longer sparks new theoretical insights, nor reveals new properties of these core theoretical categories.

As implied above, grounded theory saturation is not the same as witnessing repetition of the same events or stories, although many qualitative researchers confuse saturation with repetition of described events, actions, and/or statements. The common use of the term saturation refers to nothing new happening. 'I kept finding the same patterns.'

In contrast, Glaser (2001) takes a more sophisticated view of saturation than implied by common research parlance.

> Saturation is not seeing the same pattern over and over again. It is the conceptualization of comparisons of these incidents which yield different properties of the pattern, until no new properties of the pattern emerge. This yields the conceptual density that when integrated into hypotheses make up the body of the generated grounded theory with theoretical completeness. (p. 191)

Glaser's perspective on saturation forms the foundation for treating theoretical concepts in grounded theory. When you treat categories theoretically, you raise them to an abstract and general level while preserving their specific connections to the data from which you constructed these categories. When assessing whether you have saturated your categories, consider asking such questions as the following:

- Which comparisons do you make between data within and between categories?
- What sense do you make of these comparisons?
- Where do they lead you?
- How do your comparisons illuminate your theoretical categories?

- In what other directions, if any, do they take you?
- What new conceptual relationships, if any, might you see?

Grounded theory logic invokes saturation as the criterion to apply to your categories. As such, some grounded theorists (Glaser, 1992, 1998, 2001; Stern, 2001) argue that you keep sampling until your categories are saturated and that this logic supercedes sample size–which may be very small.

Other considerations may supercede sample size. Think about how your claims of saturation affect the credibility of your study. A small study with modest claims might allow proclaiming saturation early. Researchers who make hefty claims should be circumspect about the thoroughness of their data and the rigor of their analyses. A study of 25 interviews may suffice for certain small projects but invites skepticism when the author's claims are about, say, human nature or contradict established research.

Theoretical saturation is what grounded theorists aim for–or should aim for, according to the canons. Yet grounded theorists often invoke the term, 'saturation' uncritically. Disagreements arise about the meaning of saturation. As Janice Morse (1995) observes, researchers often proclaim saturation rather than prove that they have achieved it. Thus, like other qualitative approaches, the grounded theory approach shares the hazard of assuming that categories are saturated when they may not be.

The kinds of initial research questions and the analytic level of the subsequent categories matter. Mundane research questions may rapidly produce saturated but common or trivial categories. For example, a researcher who asks whether obese women experience stigma may find that all of her interviews indicate that they do and claim that her category of 'experiencing stigma' is saturated without beginning to analyze what stigma means and how it is enacted. Uncritical or limited analytic treatment may also result in early saturation of categories. Novel questions may demand more complex categories and more sustained inquiry.

Dey (1999) challenges the notion of saturation on two counts: the meaning of saturation and its consequences. First, he points out that grounded theorists produce categories through partial–not exhaustive–coding. Dey views the term 'saturation' as 'another unfortunate metaphor' (p. 257) because of its imprecise usage. For him, the term saturation is incongruent with a procedure that 'stops short of coding all of the data' (p. 257) and relies on the researcher's *conjecture* that the properties of the category are saturated. In short, you cannot produce evidence to support this conjecture without doing the work. Rather than establishing categories saturated by data, Dey contends that we have categories *suggested* by data. Instead of claims of achieving saturation, Dey's preferred term, '*theoretical sufficiency*' (p. 257), better fits how researchers conduct grounded theory.

Second, Dey implies that following grounded theory methods may lead to unanticipated consequences for saturating categories. He wonders if saturation of categories itself is an artifact of how grounded theorists focus and manage data collection. Such concerns spark further questions. Are our claims to having saturated categories legitimate? If so, when? Is the method a teleological closed system? When researchers treat grounded theory guidelines like recipes, they do foreclose possibilities for innovation without having explored their data. Strauss and Corbin's (1990, 1998) axial coding matrix may force data into preconceived frameworks, as any set of Glaser's theoretical codes may also. Adopting and applying these frameworks takes the focusing inherent in grounded theory and renders it directive and prescriptive. Subsequently, researchers undermine the value and legitimacy of their analyses.

By extension, Dey's argument complements my concerns about foreclosing analytic possibilities and about constructing superficial analyses. My solution? Be open to what is happening in the field and be willing to grapple with it. When you get stuck, go back and recode earlier data and see if you define new leads. Use grounded theory guidelines to give *you* a handle on the material, not a machine that does the work for you.

Theoretical Sorting, Diagramming, and Integrating

Sorting, diagramming, and integrating your memos are inter-related processes. Your sorting may integrate the analysis and a diagram may simultaneously sort and integrate it. The visual image of a diagram may suggest the content and direction of the analysis as well as its form. All qualitative researchers use such methodological strategies as sorting, diagramming, and integrating their materials; however, grounded theorists use these strategies in service of the *theoretical* development of their analysis. I treat sorting, diagramming, and integrating separately below for clarity although they are intertwined in grounded theory practice.

Theoretical Sorting

Analytic memos provide the substance for creating first drafts of papers or chapters. Writing memos during each analytic phase prompts you to make the analysis progressively stronger, clearer, and more theoretical. You already have developed categories in your written memos and have titled them in as concrete, specific, and analytic terms as possible. Now you are ready to sort them.

In grounded theory, sorting goes beyond the first step in organizing a paper, chapter, or book: sorting serves your emerging theory. It gives you a means of creating and refining theoretical links. Through sorting, you work on the theoretical integration of your categories. Thus, sorting prompts you to compare categories at an abstract level.

> Grounded theory sorting gives you a logic for organizing your analysis and a way of creating and refining theoretical links that prompts you to make comparisons between categories.

Think of the logic of your emerging theory. It became apparent in my research on the experience of chronic illness that certain events reverberated in people's consciousness long after their occurrence and became turning points. I called them 'significant events' and treated them as a major category because they shaped meanings of time and self. My treatment[18] of the category reads:

Significant Events as Turning Points

Relived moments. Retold stories ... recurring feelings. Significant events echo in memory. Whether validating or wholly disrupting, a significant event reveals images of present or possible self and evokes feelings. Thus, these events mark time and become turning points.

A significant event stands out in memory because it has boundaries, intensity, and emotional force. Furthermore, a significant event captures, demarks, and intensifies feelings. Frequently, those feelings are unhappy ones such as bewilderment, humiliation, shame, betrayal, or loss. The event flames and frames these feelings. The emotional reverberations of a single event echo through the present and future and therefore, however subtly, shade thoughts and feelings about self and alter meanings of time (cf. Denzin, 1984).

Significant events transcend the actors within them and the stage on which they occur. These events are emergent realities, events *sui generis*; they cannot be reduced to component parts (Durkheim, 1951). Thus, a significant event reflects more than a relationship or another's actions. When, where, and how the event occurs, and who participates in it, contribute to the force of the event and affect subsequent interpretations of it. Sorting what the event means and the 'correct' feelings to hold about it shapes self-images and self-worth.

A significant event freezes and enlarges a moment in time. Because of inherent or potential meanings of self within the event, people grant obdurate qualities to it. They reify it. To them, the event supercedes past meanings and foretells future selves. (Charmaz, 1991a: 210)

In the narrative above, I spelled out the properties of the category. Then I addressed two processes subsumed by it: finding positive events and reliving negative events. When research participants defined specific positive or negative events as turning points that held meaning for self, I treated them as significant events. Next I considered how a person's present emotions were tied to a past self. In this case, sorting proceeded from a straightforward logic but became more complex as I brought the analysis from past to present with memos about subcategories of 'experiencing present emotions and a past self' and 'transcending past emotions.'

Researchers construct how they sort and compile memos. The closer your sorting reflects your depiction of the flow of empirical experience, the smoother it will seem to you and likely to your readers. When you have a logic that makes sense, sorting and integrating memos falls into place. When you include several processes or pursue multiple categories, how to sort and integrate your memos may not always be so clear-cut. Try several different sortings and think through how each portrays your analysis. When you are working out the implications of each way of sorting, it may help to diagram them.

Sorting, comparing, and integrating memos seem like simple steps. Each memo on a category may become a section or subsection of the draft. If so, integrating memos may merely reproduce the theoretical logic of the analysis, or stages of a process. However, sorting, comparing, and integrating memos may be more complicated. Take a memo from your pile and compare it with another, then another (see also Glaser, 1998). How do the memos compare? Does your comparison spark new ideas? If so write another memo. Do you discern new relationships between memos? What leads do you gain by sorting the memos? If it helps, take your related memos and form quick clusters with them. How do they fit together? What makes most sense? Some sets of memos fit together so well that the answers seem obvious. But for many analyses, you must create the order and make the connections for your readers. The first draft of your paper represents how you sort, compare, and integrate a set of memos into some kind of coherent order.

How does one go about sorting, comparing, and integrating memos?

- Sort memos by the title of each category
- Compare categories
- Use your categories–carefully
- Consider how their order reflects the studied experience
- Now think how their order fits the logic of the categories
- Create the best possible balance between the studied experience, your categories, and your theoretical statements about them.

Some practical advice may help. Sort your memos by hand in an area where you can see and shuffle them. Turn the computer off for now. A large table works well; the floor can too if you have no cats or children to disrupt your sorted designs. I once plastered my dining room walls with cards containing the titles of my memos. Be willing to experiment with different arrangements of your memos. Treat these arrangements as tentative and play with them. Lay out your memos in several different ways. Draw a few diagrams to connect them. When you create a sorting that looks promising, jot it down and diagram it.

Continue to compare categories while you sort memos. Sorting fosters your efforts to refine comparisons between categories. As a result of sorting, you can see relationships between your categories more clearly. For example, sorting memos about time and self, clarified a major shift in how people with serious chronic illnesses viewed themselves. I saw how easily they went from trying to live in the present to situating their selves in the past as the present became more problematic. Relationships between categories form an outline of what you cover and *how* you cover it. They give your future readers important information. And studying and sorting these categories helps you learn when and where you go astray.

Diagramming

Diagrams can offer concrete images of our ideas. The advantage of diagrams is that they provide a visual representation of categories and their relationships. Many grounded theorists, particularly those influenced by Clarke (2003, 2005), Strauss (1987) and Strauss and Corbin (1998), treat creating visual images of their emerging theories as an intrinsic part of grounded theory methods. They use various types of diagrams–including maps, charts, and figures–to tease out relationships while constructing their analyses and to demonstrate these relationships in their completed works.

Diagrams can enable you to see the relative power, scope, and direction of the categories in your analysis as well as the connections among them. You may find that diagrams can serve useful and diverse purposes at all stages of analysis. You might revise an early quick clustering about a category into a more exacting form as a diagram illustrating the properties of a category. You might develop a conceptual map that locates your concepts and directs movement between them.

Maps show positions and processes (Clarke, 2003, 2005). Conceptual maps can plot the relative strength or weakness of relationships. Adele Clarke (2003, 2005) uses maps to create sophisticated situational analyses that offer a fresh alternative to the earlier grounded theory emphasis on basic social processes. She argues that we already know much about our research sites and problems before officially collecting data and that maps are one way to make fruitful use of this knowledge.

Through mapping situations, social worlds and their arenas, and positions in discourses, Clarke intends to develop grounded theory methods in ways that preserve empirical realities and complexities without resorting to reductionist analyses or wholly relying on the basic social process model that Glaser (1978) long argued was essential to grounded theory. Consider Clarke's techniques (see Figures 5.1 and 5.2) for sorting conventional grounded theory memos in addition to explicating the social arenas and social worlds' levels of analysis for which she devised them.

Clarke's situational maps take Glaser's (1998) dictum 'All is data' seriously because she builds structural properties right into her maps and positions them in social worlds and arenas. The structural elements that shape and condition the situation being studied can be plotted on the map. Her strategy allows us to move from micro to organizational levels of analysis and to render invisible structural relationships and processes visible. Similarly, this approach fosters making relationships and processes between different social worlds and arenas visible that ordinarily might be hidden from view. The situational analysis that follows provides provisional, flexible, interpretive theorizing about the construction of the studied social worlds.

Strauss and Corbin (1990, 1998) introduce the conditional/consequential matrix as a way of providing a visual representation of the observed transactions in the empirical world and their interactions and inter-relationships. In particular, they offer this matrix as an analytic device for thinking about macro and micro relationships that might shape the situations the researcher studies. They provide a depiction of the conditional/consequential matrix as concentric but connected circles that place the individual at the core in their 1998 edition (as contrasted with placing action at the core in the 1990 edition). The concentric circles represent increasingly larger social units.

A major purpose of the conditional/consequential matrix is to help researchers to think beyond micro social structures and immediate interactions to larger social conditions and consequences. Strauss and Corbin propose that the conditional/consequential matrix can aid researchers in making theoretical sampling decisions as well as in locating the contexts in which the conditions occur and the paths between them. They present this matrix as offering a means for developing theory that advances the researcher's work beyond describing phenomena. The conditional/consequential matrix is a technique to *apply*; therefore, it may force

FIGURE 5.1 Abstract Situational Map, Messy Working Version

Source: Clarke, 2003: 564. © 2003 by the Society for the Study of Symbolic Interaction. Used with permission.

moving your data and analysis in a pre-established direction. If, however, your emerging analysis indicates that mapping conditions, contexts, and consequences in this way fits your data, you might wish to use this matrix.

Integrating Memos

How do you integrate the memos? Ordering for process is one obvious solution to integrate the piece. If you build your paper on a major category, then you must decide how the memos about it best fit together. Processural analyses have a

HUMAN ELEMENTS/ACTORS	NON HUMAN ELEMENTS
e.g., individuals	e.g., technologies
collective actors	material infrastructure
specific organizations	specialized knowledges
	material 'things'
POLITICAL/ECONOMIC ASPECTS	SOCIO-CULTURAL ASPECTS
e.g., the state	e.g., mass media
particular industry/ies	religion
local/regional/global orders	ethnicity
political parties	race
TEMPORAL DIMENSIONS	SPATIAL DIMENSIONS
e.g., historic aspects	e.g., geography
seasonal aspects	
crisis aspects	
DISCURSIVE CONSTRUCTION(S)	DISCURSIVE CONSTRUCTION
OF NON HUMAN ACTANTS	OF HUMAN ACTORS
As found in the situation	As found in the situation
MAJOR ISSUES/DEBATES	MORE SYMBOLIC
[USUALLY CONTESTED]	DIMENSIONS
As found in the situation, and	e.g., aesthetic elements
see positional map	affective/sentimental elements
	moral/ethical elements
OTHER KINDS OF ELEMENTS	DISCOURSES
As found in the situation	e.g., normative expectations of actors, actants, and/or other particular elements; popular cultural discourses; situation-specific discourses

FIGURE 5.2   Abstract Situational Map, Ordered Working Version

Source: Clarke, 2003: 564. © 2003 by the Society for the Study of Symbolic Interaction. Used with permission.

built-in logical order, but analytic categories may have a subtle one that will make sense to your readers. For example, in my analysis of disclosure, it made sense to talk first about avoiding disclosure of illness followed by assessing the risks and then disclosing illness. Taking this example into another realm, avoiding and risking disclosures—personal, professional, and organizational disclosures—occur in work settings of all kinds. A corporate manager who knows that downsizing lies on the horizon may first avoid disclosure, and then risk it with trusted staff, and later make strategic general announcements. In this case, disclosure dilemmas relate to the type and extent of public release of information or potential discoveries of hidden information, and other conditions that affect disclosure.

Much of the grounded theory literature emphasizes writing about a single category. You may, however, need to juggle several categories. If so, then your sorting attends to how these categories fit—or do not fit—together. The subsequent integration may reflect what you found in the empirical world. The integration makes relationships intelligible. Early grounded theory studies stressed causal relationships but now many scholars aim for interpretive understandings. Such understandings remain contingent on contextual conditions.

Through sorting and integrating memos, you may explicate implicit theoretical codes which you may have adopted without realizing it. In addition, these strategies may force you to think through theoretical links among categories that may have been left implicit. Diagramming sharpens the relationships among your theoretical categories. All three strategies can spark ideas for constructing your written report and shaping the introduction and writing the theoretical framework.

Concluding Thoughts

Like coding and memo-writing, theoretical sampling occupies a crucial place in grounded theory. It articulates a practice that the best qualitative researchers may follow but may not define. The movement back and forth between category and data in theoretical sampling fosters raising the conceptual level of your categories and extending their reach. As you develop your categories, you can see which ones to treat as major concepts in your analysis.

By engaging in theoretical sampling, saturation, and sorting, you create robust categories and penetrating analyses. Capturing what you have gained in successively more abstract memos gives you the grist for the first draft of your finished piece. Sorting and diagramming gives you its initial analytic frame. Now you are ready to write the first draft of your report but first you may wish to think a bit more about theorizing in grounded theory.

NQTES

1 Strauss (see Strauss, 1987; Strauss & Corbin, 1990, 1998) emphasized diagramming as a way of laying out conceptual relationships. Since then, this approach is most developed in Adele Clarke's (2003, 2005) works. As a graduate student, I wrote a paper, 'Conceptual Mapping' (1969), that addressed ways to integrate theoretical analyses by showing relationships between concepts and by offering a visual representation of their relative significance.

2 Interview with Jane Hood, November 12, 2004.

3 Hood's use of theoretical sampling built directly on grounded theory guidelines; however, her coding strategies diverged. She began coding with open-ended codes and quickly went to a formal procedure with code sheets to sort and organize the material into more general categories (see 1983: 200–202). Hood stated that she might have done something different had she had access to something like The Ethnograph, a computer-assisted program. She said that she used the code sheet approach as a way of 'interviewing' her data and holding herself accountable for patterns in the data as well as to check properties of categories. Although the code sheets may look like survey coding, she said that she was not using survey coding because the point was not to count but to establish category boundaries. Social scientists frequently draw on several methodological approaches simultaneously, depending on the research problem and/or the researcher's proclivities. Some nurse researchers disdain such methodological ecumenicalism as method slurring (see Baker, Wuest, & Stern, 1992).

4 Should customer service representatives define your presence as a management plant, they will likely conceal their concerns and perhaps their usual practices. Moreover, they may see you and your research as an extension of organizational forms of domination consistent with Dorothy E. Smith's (1999) warnings about researchers reproducing domination that participants already experience in the setting. If they see you as an ally, then you may gain a different picture, and gain still another view on the scene if you talk with customers about their experiences.

5 Doctoral students might negotiate with their advisors by building several stages of data collection into their research proposals. That way, they could begin by taking population distributions into account but plan to follow the leads in their emerging analyses thereafter.

6 Jane Hood edited this passage for clarity.

7 Fiction can provide great data for all kinds of projects when researchers treat them as texts to analyze, rather than as substitute realities. For example, we could look at how authors represent women and men, collective values, or individual quests during specific time periods. Hypothetical negative cases are trickier. The extent of researchers' knowledge about their studied worlds and how they use these cases matters here. Superficial knowledge and scant further inquiry can derail a grounded theory analysis. Researchers who rely on hypothetical negative cases risk slipping into armchair theorizing.

8 Charles Sanders Peirce (1878 [1958]) developed abductive reasoning. It underlies the pragmatist tradition of problem-solving and supports the notion that the borders between scientific discovery and justification are indistinct. Strauss was heavily influenced by Peirce and John Dewey as well as George Herbert Mead. The creative, cognitive dimensions of abductive reasoning in grounded theory may be most emphasized by Strauss and his followers.

9 As I pointed out in earlier chapters, you can revisit and recode earlier data from the vantage point of a new idea, which expedites theoretical sampling of your new category.

10 I chose to make experiencing illness the focus of the book because it would speak to broader audiences than a book on time. This focus did, however, allow developing the analyses of time and self.

11 For a study in which married women in middle-class dual-earner families took the lead in time negotiations and indirectly maintained control over family tasks, see Kerry Daly (2002). The couples worked in managerial or professional positions for fifty hours a week or more. Daly found that by controlling the family schedule, these women obtained their husbands' participation in childcare and household work.

12 Gubrium (1993) has observed that nursing home residents similarly locate themselves in time. While some saw their lives as in the past, others were rooted in their nursing home experience, and still others looked over their current situations to the future.

13 I developed these subcategories from depictions of my participants' statements and actions. Hence they import fewer implied judgments than the psychological concepts of acceptance and denial that pervade professionals' discourse about illness and impairment.

14 Her question arose during a presentation titled, 'Constructing Qualitative Research through Grounded Theory,' at the Center for AIDS Prevention Studies (CAPS), University of California, San Francisco, September 7, 2004.

15 Qualitative researchers in a number of disciplines and professions are challenging narrow institutional directives that hinder their research. They are engaged in educating colleagues who adhere to a biomedical model about its limitations for qualitative research. Changes in ethics policies and institutional reviews should result.

16 Personal communication, March 29, 2004. Albas and Albas found that they obtained some of their most compelling data with this method and, simultaneously, they expedited and strengthened their analyses. See also, D. Albas & C. Albas (1988, 1993) and C. Albas & D. Albas (1988).

17 Alasuutari's strategy is reminiscent of advice that Anselm Strauss once gave me about not taking textbook prescriptions of conducting neutral interviews too seriously. He found that sometimes provocative questions worked and field researchers could ask them, as long as they did not get kicked out of the setting.

18 The copy editor changed my final wording about relived moments and recurring feelings without consulting me. My original rendering is included here.

6 Reconstructing Theory in Grounded Theory Studies

Grounded theorists talk much about theory and about constructing theory, but what do they mean? In this chapter, we stop for a sojourn to contemplate what theory means and how grounded theorists engage in theorizing as a *practice*. I begin with an excerpt of theorizing in grounded theory research and then step back and ask: What is theory? By viewing general definitions of theory as two distinct traditions, we clarify how the antecedents of constructivist and objectivist grounded theory reflect these traditions. Reconsidering critiques of grounded theory helps to refresh our thinking and reaffirm our theoretical tasks. To encourage your development of theoretical sensitivity, I suggest ways you might plumb the depth of your ideas while expanding the reach of your theory. We close by inspecting how three different grounded theories demonstrate theorizing in practice and end by reflecting on how grounded theorists are part of their theorizing.

What stands as *theory* in grounded theory? How do researchers make their grounded theory analyses theoretical; that is, how do they move from the process of analysis to production of a grounded theory? Which directions do grounded theories typically take? To assess if, how, why, and when grounded theory studies offer 'bona fide' theories, requires taking a step back and asking: What is theory? The term theory remains slippery in grounded theory discourse. Many grounded theorists talk about theory but few define it. A number of grounded theorists claim they construct theory, but do they? A closer look may help. By taking several grounded theories apart, I will reconstruct their logic with you.

To begin thinking about reconstructing theory in grounded theory research, consider the excerpt below from my study of the experience of chronic illness. It is part of a paper that contains an explicit theoretical logic. In the analysis, I focused on how people with serious chronic illnesses struggled to have a valued self.[1] They struggled with both how they defined themselves and how other people identified them. I realized that people who suffered physical losses developed identity goals for their future, particularly when their losses occurred during a short period of time. I grappled with these sometimes overt, but often covert, meanings and implications of identity goals to develop a theoretical rendering. A number of people planned to struggle against illness and to compete in conventional worlds. They espoused these goals when illness and disability were new. As time elapsed, they usually scaled down their identity goals. The short excerpt below captures the logic of my substantive theory of relationships between identity goals and the emerging identity hierarchy.

> An identity hierarchy becomes visible as ill people, over time, choose different types of preferred identities, reflecting relative difficulty in achieving specific aspirations and objectives. The types of preferred identities constitute particular identity levels in the identity hierarchy. These identity levels include: (1) the supernormal social identity, an identity demanding extraordinary achievement in conventional worlds; (2) the restored self, a reconstruction of previous identities before illness; (3) contingent personal identity, a hypothetically possible, though uncertain, identity because of further illness; and (4) the salvaged self, retaining a past identity based on a valued activity or attribute while becoming physically dependent. Experiencing progressive illness often means reducing identity goals and aiming for a lower level in the identity hierarchy. In short, reducing identity goals means aiming for a less preferred identity. (Charmaz, 1987: 285)

In the narrative, I point out that my research participants struggled for a valued self because they did not want to be invalids. For them, being an invalid meant being an invalid person. This assumption informed the identity goals they made and the actions they took. An important property of the identity hierarchy concerns movement in it. People do not always plummet down the identity hierarchy; some climb up identity levels. I observed a few people with serious illnesses without much hope, move from being immersed in illness to realizing extraordinary accomplishments. They may start from different points, depending on how they define their situations, and they may move up and down the identity hierarchy through the course of their illness.

Part of my task involved accounting for these chronically ill people's identity goals and the actions they took, if any, to realize them. Hence, I aimed to fulfill the following objectives: 1) to develop the properties of each category in the identity hierarchy and demonstrate how they fit together; 2) to specify conditions under which my research participants selected a preferred identity; 3) to take into account the resources they could pull together to realize their identity goals; 4) to define when they moved up or down the identity hierarchy; 5) to delineate social contexts in which they attempted to negotiate and establish their preferred and potential identities; and 6) to suggest how different identity levels presuppose different selves. These analytic objectives contributed to the theoretical level and density of the analysis. See how I began to weave them into the paper:

> The person's *expectations of and for self* are significant sources of his or her definitions of preferred identities for the future. People maintain self consistency and continuity through their expectations as well as their actions. Age alone affects such expectations. Younger adults confront all the usual identity issues of their age cohorts clustering around career,

intimacy, and lifestyle. These young adults typically made valiant efforts to realize their preferred identities. Profoundly disturbed by the threat of a life of invalidism, they also thought it unsuitable for persons their age. Many others echo this woman's remark: 'I expected to have a chronic illness which interfered with my life at seventy-five, but at twenty-nine? Who would have guessed it?' (p. 292)

My analysis of movement up and down the identity hierarchy takes a neutral, objective tone in presenting the ideas and their relationships. These excerpts obscure the constructivism in my analysis, which since then has become more visible in my work. My neutral writing style above separates my ideas about the identity hierarchy from their analytic construction but links them as theoretical conceptions. The neutral tones of analytic discourse in much qualitative research erase the interpretive acts that produced them and, moreover, eradicate ambiguities in both the studied scenes and their analytic treatment (Charmaz & Mitchell, 1996).

Now we need to interrogate the excerpts above and ask what makes the line of analysis in them theory—or theoretical. What kind of presuppositions about theory does this type of analysis assume? How can we reconcile the creative process of developing grounded theories with their objectivist presentations in theoretical reports? How might we take grounded theory in a constructionist direction? To make theorizing transparent, we need to see how grounded theorists construct their theories.

What Is Theory?

What does 'theory' mean in social scientific thinking? What should stand as a bona fide theory exemplifying a grounded theory? Disagreements about how to do grounded theory and what a completed theory should look like often arise from unsettled notions about what theory means. These disagreements resonate with grumblings—and ideological clashes—throughout the social sciences that grounded theorists echo without necessarily realizing their epistemological underpinnings. Such disagreements may be played out and intensified in discussions and directions about how to construct grounded theory. When we look beneath the surface, we can discern different meanings of theory among grounded theorists. Some of these definitions of theory remain firm, some are elastic.

When thinking about concepts of theory in grounded theory, it helps to look at broader definitions of theory in the social sciences. I touch upon theoretical perspectives in classical sociological theory and cultural studies to exemplify these broader definitions and to identify major themes in them.

Positivist Definitions of Theory

Perhaps the most prevalent definitions of theory derive from positivism. Positivist definitions of theory treat it as a statement of relationships between abstract concepts that cover a wide range of empirical observations. Positivists view their theoretical concepts as variables and construct operational definitions of their concepts for hypothesis testing through accurate, replicable empirical measurement. These definitions exert considerable influence for two reasons: 1) they reach across fields and 2) authors of research textbooks widely adopt and promulgate them.

In this view, the objectives of theory are *explanation* and *prediction.* Positivist theory aims for parsimony, generality, and universality and simultaneously reduces empirical objects and events to that which can be subsumed by the concepts. Positivist theory seeks causes, favors deterministic explanations, and emphasizes generality and universality. In short, positivist theories consist of a set of inter-related propositions aimed to:

> Positivist theory seeks causes, favors deterministic explanations, and emphasizes generality and universality.

- Treat concepts as variables
- Specify relationships between concepts
- Explain and predict these relationships
- Systematize knowledge
- Verify theoretical relationships through hypothesis-testing
- Generate hypotheses for research.

With their emphasis on parsimony, these theories are elegant in form and direct in their statements; however, these theories can result in narrow, reductionist explanations with simplistic models of action.

Interpretive Definitions of Theory

An alternative definition of theory emphasizes *understanding* rather than explanation. Proponents of this definition view theoretical understanding as abstract and interpretive; the very understanding gained from the theory rests on the theorist's interpretation of the studied phenomenon. Interpretive theories allow for indeterminacy rather than seek causality and give priority to showing patterns and connections rather than to linear reasoning. George Ritzer and Douglas J. Goodman's (2004) discussion of criteria for classical sociological theory (which assumes abstract, general concepts) illustrates this view. For Ritzer and Goodman, theory has a far-ranging scope, offers wide applications, and deals with fundamental issues in social life. Given their focus on classical theory, it has also withstood the test of time. They declare that their definition contrasts with theories that aim for explanation and prediction. Ritzer and Goodman's definition of theory has strong interpretive elements in its emphasis on understanding and scope.

Interpretive theory calls for the imaginative understanding of the studied phenomenon. This type of theory assumes emergent, multiple realities; indeterminacy; facts and values as

> Interpretive theory calls for the imaginative understanding of the studied phenomenon. This type of theory assumes emergent, multiple realities; indeterminacy; facts and values as linked; truth as provisional; and social life as processual.

inextricably linked; truth as provisional; and social life as processual. Thus interpretive theory is fully compatible with George Herbert Mead's symbolic interactionism, which shares these assumptions. Mead takes a sophisticated view of action as the starting place for analysis that includes the person's imagined understanding of the other person's role and response during interaction.

We interpret our participants' meanings and actions and they interpret ours. The interpretive turn in theory has gained attention as social constructionist principles gained advocates among diverse scholars, particularly since the 1960s. This theoretical approach emphasizes practices and actions. Rather than explaining reality, social constructionists see multiple realities and therefore ask: *What* do people assume is real? *How* do they construct and act on their view of reality? Thus knowledge–and theories–are situated and located in particular positions, perspectives, and experiences. In brief, interpretive theory aims to:

- Conceptualize the studied phenomenon to understand it in abstract terms
- Articulate theoretical claims pertaining to scope, depth, power, and relevance
- Acknowledge subjectivity in theorizing and hence the role of negotiation, dialogue, understanding
- Offer an imaginative interpretation.

Interpretive theories are often juxtaposed against positivist theories, which I do below in my discussion of constructivist and objectivist grounded theory. For now, consider that grounded theory as *theory* contains both positivist and inter-pretivist inclinations. Glaser's (1978, 1992, 1998, 2003) treatment of theory contains strong positivist leanings. He emphasizes the development of theoretical categories that serve as variables, assumes an indicator-concept approach, seeks context-free but modifiable theoretical statements, and aims for 'the achievement of parsimony and scope in explanatory power' (1992: 116). Glaser stresses the work of using comparative methods and attributes the analytic development of theory to emergence from this comparative work; however, he treats emergent categories almost as its automatic result. The place of interpretive understanding remains less clear in his position than the positivist elements.

Strauss and Corbin's (1998) view of theory has some positivist leanings but emphasizes relationships among concepts. For them, theory means 'a set of well-developed concepts related through statements of relationship, which together constitute an integrated framework that can be used to explain or predict phenomena' (p. 15). Their stance toward constructing theories, however, also acknowledges interpretivist views. Corbin (1998) recognizes that analysis means that researchers interpret data but implies that such interpretation is an unavoidable limitation. She writes, 'How can one remove who and what one is from the comparative process? An analyst can only compare based on how s/he reads the data. One would hope that by 'sticking to the data' the analyst is left out of the interpretive process, but this is highly unlikely' (p. 123). Strauss and Corbin draw clear distinctions between theory and description, which they see as a person's use of words to invoke mental images of objects, events, and experiences. For them, theory is much more abstract and explanatory.

If we turn to cultural theory, Alasuutari (1996) further distinguishes between how lay people ordinarily make sense of their worlds and what the concept of theory means. By adopting a sophisticated view of theory consistent with Schutz (1967), Alasuutari argues that theoreticians examine lay persons' rules of interpretation and therefore move beyond lay persons' conceptions.

> One takes a one-step distance from the members' perspective, not by arguing that it is narrower or incorrect, but by studying how it works in con-stituting social realities. Theories are thus deconstructions of the way in which we construct realities and social conditions and ourselves as sub-jects in those realities. They cannot compete with lay thinking, because their very objective is to make sense of it in its various forms and in dif-ferent instances. (1996: 382)

Alasuutari explicitly departs from definitions of theory as generalized state-ments about universals from which researchers deduce hypotheses to explain local, specific phenomena. Instead, to him theories provide interpretive *frames* from which to view realities. Although Alasuutari's comment recognizes that lay persons and researchers hold different interpretive frames, we might note that both make sense of lay persons' ideas and actions.

Alasuutari's careful explication of the local scenes and specific incidents com-bined with his theorizing of them gives his work theoretical reach and depth. His work combines the sensibilities of a skilled ethnographer with the kind of theoretical sensitivity possessed by the best grounded theorists.

The Rhetoric, Reach, and Practice of Theorizing

Whether positivist or interpretive, theories are rhetorical—although interpretive theorists more likely acknowledge this point than their positivist counterparts. A theorist attempts to convince readers that certain conclusions flow from a set of premises (Markovsky, 2004). Thus, theories present arguments about the world and relationships within it, despite sometimes being cleansed of con-text and reduced to seemingly neutral statements. For those who espouse posi-tivist notions of objectivity, such cleansing and neutrality only adds to their persuasiveness.

When we consider either positivist or interpretive theory, we need to think of its theoretical reach and power within, beyond, and between disciplines. Randall Collins says, 'Theory is what you remember' (2004a; see also Davis, 1971). Theories flash illuminating insights and make sense of murky musings and knotty problems. The ideas fit. Phenomena and relationships between them you only sensed beforehand become visible. Still, theories can do more. A the-ory can alter your viewpoint and change your consciousness. Through it, you can see the world from a different vantage point and create new meanings of it. Theories have an internal logic and more or less coalesce into coherent forms.

My preference for theorizing—and it is for theorizing, not theory—is unabashedly interpretive. Theorizing is a *practice*. It entails the practical activity of engaging the world and of constructing abstract understandings about and within it. The fundamental contribution of grounded theory methods resides in offering a guide to interpretive theoretical practice not in providing a blueprint for theoretical products.

Interpretive theorizing arises from social constructionist assumptions that inform symbolic interaction, ethnomethodology, cultural studies and phenomenological discourse, and narrative analysis. Such theorizing is not limited to individual actors or micro situations. Nor should it be. Rather, interpretive theorizing can move beyond individual situations and immediate interactions. Maines (2001) makes this argument about symbolic interactionism and Alasuutari's (1995, 1996, 2004) vantage point in cultural studies points a way. Speaking from the theorists' camp, Collins (2004b) argues for situations rather than individuals as starting points for theorizing continuities between classical nineteenth-century theory and contemporary theoretical questions. He views the social in the individual and explores how the varied intensity of rituals shape forms of social participation and ideas at local levels that collectively involve larger social structures. Strauss's analyses of negotiated orders (1978; Strauss, Schatzman, Bucher, Ehrlich, & Sabshin, 1963) and social worlds (1978a) initiate interpretive inquiry at organizational and collective levels. Rather than studying the structure of the hospital as static, Strauss and his colleagues (1963) revealed its dynamic, processual nature by analyzing negotiations within and between people and departments at varied organizational levels in the hospital. Their interpretation of the hospital as a negotiated order and analysis of this order assumed considerable significance because Strauss et al. showed how researchers could study the construction of individual and collective action and the intersections between them.

Interpretive theorizing can infuse network analysis with the tools to bring meanings into view. Both Collins (2004b) and Clarke (2003, 2005) suggest methodological strategies for studying meso and macro levels of analysis. Collins endorses using network analysis to study situations, although grounded theorists would find that Clarke's methods give them more access to specific contexts and types of interactions. When researchers use both methods, they may find that Clarke's situational analysis and positional mapping can broaden network analysis and make it more interpretive.

Constructivist and Objectivist Grounded Theory

Throughout this book, I have treated using grounded theory methods and theorizing as *social actions* that researchers construct in concert with others in particular places and times. In addition to our research participants, colleagues, teachers, students, institutional committees and untold others may live in our minds and influence how we conduct our studies long after our immediate contact with them. We interact with data and create theories about it. But we do not exist in a social vacuum.

How might our conceptions of theory and research influence what we do and the allegiances we hold? As I have implied, a number of the disputes among grounded theorists and critiques by other colleagues result from where various authors stand between interpretive and positivist traditions.

I have explicated those differences by arguing that grounded theory has taken somewhat different forms since its creation: constructivist and objectivist grounded theory (Charmaz, 2000, 2001). Constructivist grounded theory is part of the interpretive tradition and objectivist grounded theory derives from positivism. I juxtapose these forms here for clarity; however, whether you judge a specific study to be constructivist or objectivist depends on the *extent* to which its key characteristics conform to one tradition or the other.

> I juxtapose constructivist and objectivist forms of grounded theory here for clarity; however, whether you judge a specific study to be constructivist or objectivist depends on the *extent* to which its key characteristics conform to one tradition or the other.

Constructivist Grounded Theory

As consistent with my stance in earlier chapters, a constructivist approach places priority on the phenomena of study and sees both data and analysis as created from shared experiences and relationships with participants and other sources of data (see Charmaz, 1990, 1995b, 2000, 2001; Charmaz & Mitchell, 1996). Constructivist grounded theory lies squarely in the interpretive tradition.

> A constructivist approach places priority on the phenomena of study and sees both data and analysis as created from shared experiences and relationships with participants (see Charmaz, 1990, 1995b, 2000, 2001; Charmaz & Mitchell, 1996).

Constructivists study *how*–and sometimes *why*–participants construct meanings and actions in specific situations. As I explained in Chapter 2, we do so from as close to the inside of the experience as we can get but realize that we cannot replicate the experiences of our research participants. A constructivist approach means more than looking at how individuals view their situations. It not only theorizes the interpretive work that research participants do, but also acknowledges that the resulting theory is an interpretation (Bryant, 2002; Charmaz, 2000, 2002a). The theory *depends* on the researcher's view; it does not and cannot stand outside of it. Granted, different researchers may come up with similar ideas, although how they render them theoretically may differ.

Grounded theorists may borrow an insight from Silverman's (2004) observation of conversational analysis. He contends that only after establishing how people construct meanings and actions can the analyst pursue why they act as they do. Certainly a fine-grained analysis of how people construct actions and meanings can lead a grounded theorist to establishing some reasons for it, although occasionally the why may emerge with the how.

The logical extension of the constructivist approach means learning how, when, and to what extent the studied experience is embedded in larger and, often, hidden positions, networks, situations, and relationships. Subsequently, differences and distinctions between people become visible as well as the hierarchies of power, communication, and opportunity that maintain and perpetuate such differences and distinctions. A constructivist approach means being alert to conditions under which such differences and distinctions arise and are maintained. Having the material to anchor the experience takes rich data and entails having sufficient knowledge so one can see differences and distinctions. When grounded theory studies are extremely small, they risk being disconnected from their social contexts and situations. Thus, researchers can diminish the potential power of their analyses by treating experience as separate, fragmented, and atomistic.

Constructivist grounded theorists take a reflexive stance toward the research process and products and consider *how* their theories evolve, which involves reflecting on my earlier point that both researchers and research participants interpret meanings and actions. Constructivist grounded theorists assume that both data and analyses are social constructions that reflect what their production entailed (see also Bryant, 2002, 2003; Charmaz, 2000; Hall & Callery, 2001; Thorne, Jensen, Kearney, Noblit & Sandelowski, 2004). In this view, any analysis is contextually situated in time, place, culture, and situation. Because constructivists see facts and values as linked, they acknowledge that what they see—and don't see—rests on values. Thus, constructivists attempt to become aware of their presuppositions and to grapple with how they affect the research. They realize that grounded theorists can ironically import preconceived ideas into their work when they remain unaware of their starting assumptions. Thus, constructivism fosters researchers' reflexivity about their *own* interpretations as well as those of their research participants.

Objectivist Grounded Theory

An objectivist approach to grounded theory contrasts with the constructivist approach. Objectivist grounded theory resides in the positivist tradition and thus attends to data as real in and of themselves and does not attend to the processes of their production.

> Objectivist grounded theory resides in the positivist tradition and thus attends to data as real in and of themselves and does not attend to the processes of their production.

This stance erases the social context from which data emerge, the influence of the researcher, and often the interactions between grounded theorists and their research participants. Note that most interview excerpts in published reports, including mine, do not give you a sense of how interviewers and their research participants produced the data. An objectivist grounded theorist assumes that data represent objective facts about a knowable world. The data already exist in the world; the researcher finds them and 'discovers' theory from them.

In this approach, the conceptual sense the grounded theorist makes of data derives from them; meaning inheres in the data and the grounded theorist discovers it (see, for example Corbin & Strauss, 1990; Glaser, 1978; Glaser & Strauss, 1967). This view assumes an external reality awaiting discovery and an unbiased observer who records facts about it. Objectivist grounded theorists believe that careful application of their methods produces theoretical understanding. Hence their role becomes more of a conduit for the research process rather than a creator of it. Given these assumptions, objectivist proponents would argue for a stricter adherence to grounded theory steps than would constructivists.[2]

Objectivist grounded theorists remain separate and distant from research participants and their realities, although they may adopt observational methods. Claims of value-free neutrality assume, paradoxically, a value position. Consistent with their assumption of neutrality, these grounded theorists treat how they portray research participants in their written reports as unproblematic. They assume the role of authoritative experts who bring an objective view to the research.

Glaser (see, for example, 1978, 1992, 1998, 2001, 2003) articulates crucial aspects of an objectivist position, despite his disdain of quests for accurate data and insistence that grounded theory is not a verification method.[3] I agree with Glaser on the issue of verification. Checking hunches and confirming emergent ideas, in my view, does not equal verification, particularly if one defines verification as entailing systematic quantitative procedures that presuppose establishing firm definitions of the phenomena before studying them. Rather than contributing verified knowledge, I see grounded theorists as offering plausible accounts.

Glaser (2002) treats data as something separate from the researcher and implies that data are untouched by the competent researcher's interpretations. If, perchance, researchers somehow interpret their data, Glaser argues that then these data are 'rendered objective' by looking at many cases. This point contradicts Glaser's vigorous defence of small samples in discussion of saturation. Granted, the number of 'cases' may not always equal sample size but in many grounded theory studies they come close and are minuscule.

Studying many cases is crucial, in part because researchers may become aware of their preconceptions about their topics. Yet such study may not challenge their fundamental assumptions about the world, ways of knowing it, or actions in it. Here, researchers' entrenched assumptions grind the lens for viewing the world and filter their resulting images of it. *What* we define as data and *how* we look at them matters because these acts shape what we *can* see and learn. Without engaging in reflexivity, researchers may elevate their own tacit assumptions and interpretations to 'objective' status. Our assumptions, interactions—and interpretations—affect the social processes constituting *each* stage of inquiry.

Glaser is correct about the value of looking at many cases. Many theorists, including those whose unexamined assumptions predetermine what they see, benefit from looking at many cases because they can strengthen their grasp of their empirical worlds and discern variation in their categories. Surely we learn as we proceed, particularly when we strive to find out what our research participants say and do and what their worlds are like.

A constructivist approach does not adhere to positivist notions of variable analysis or of finding a single basic process or core category in the studied phenomenon. The constructivist view assumes an obdurate, yet ever-changing world but recognizes diverse local worlds and multiple realities, and addresses how people's actions affect their local and larger worlds. Thus, those who take a constructivist approach aim to show the complexities of particular worlds, views, and actions.

Theorizing in Grounded Theory

Critique and Renewal

Where's the theory in grounded theory? Although more researchers claim to have used grounded theory methods than profess to have constructed substantive or formal theories, most hold some sort of conception of theory. If you peruse articles whose authors claim allegiance to grounded theory to see how they construe a finished grounded theory, you might find such varied views as: 1) an empirical generalization, 2) a category, 3) a predisposition, 4) an explication of a process, 5) a relationship between variables, 6) an explanation, 7) an abstract understanding, and 8) a description. Recently, Glaser (2001) described grounded theory as a 'theory of resolving a main concern' that can be theoretically coded in many ways.[4] Assertions abound about what stands as theory in grounded theory, and that, of course, complicates assessing the extent to which grounded theorists have produced theories. Some observers look at what researchers have done in the name of grounded theory (see, for example, Becker, 1998; Charmaz, 1995b; Silverman, 2001) and note that most studies are descriptive rather than theoretical. Granted, description entails conceptualization but theoretical treatment is also analytic and abstract.

Other observers address the logic of grounded theory. Certainly numerous critics (see, for example, Atkinson, Coffey, & Delamont, 2003; Bulmer, 1979; Dey, 1999, 2004; Emerson, 1983, 2004; Layder, 1998) have challenged presuppositions and prescriptions that they find in grounded theory concerning preconception, pure induction, and procedures. Of course, grounded theorists from different variants have critiqued each other's approaches, as is evident throughout this book (see, for example, Bryant, 2002, 2003; Charmaz, 2000, 2001c, 2005; Clarke, 2005; Corbin, 1998; Glaser, 1992, 2002, 2003; Melia, 1996; Robrecht, 1995; Stern, 1994a; Wilson & Hutchinson, 1996).

Several more criticisms merit discussion. Burawoy (1991) says that grounded theory produces empirical generalizations that lead to generic explanations abstracted from time and place.[5] Three points are relevant here. First, in contrast to Burawoy, a major strength of grounded theory resides in its applicability across substantive areas. Still, we should reconsider *how* and *when* we move our analysis and ask whether we have gained intimate familiarity with the phenomenon before transporting an analysis.[6] Second, Burawoy argues that unlike grounded theory, his extended case method (1991) uncovers the particulars of situations, explains how macro foundations shape them, and grounds the reproduction and maintenance of globalization (Burawoy, 2000). He sees grounded theory as leading to astructural analyses and implies that inductive methods and decontextualized generalizations contribute to that result.

What Burawoy suggests that grounded theory cannot do, I argue, is exactly what grounded theory gives us the methods to do (Charmaz, 2005). A contextualized grounded theory can start with sensitizing concepts that address such concepts as power, global reach, and difference and end with inductive analyses that theorize connections between local worlds and larger social structures.

The issue of decontextualized analyses raises further concerns that Burawoy does not mention. Grounded theorists may produce decontextualized analyses when they disattend to context or are unaware of or unclear about it. Such analyses mask the significance of constructivist elements in grounded theory. Objectivist grounded theorists strive to attain generality and decontextualization typically results. While constructing decontextualized analyses by moving across fields, these grounded theorists may ironically force their data into their earlier generalizations because they lack sufficient contexts with which to ground their new data. Similarly, seeking decontextualized generalities also can reduce opportunities to create theoretical complexity because decontextualizing fosters (over)simplification. Third, Burawoy is right that some empirical generalizations from specific studies do become taken as *generic* statements about larger realities. We might consider at what point these generalizations are granted theoretical status. Who grants them theoretical status—or doesn't? For what purposes? The stress on theorizing leads to consideration of who does the theorizing and with what sort of claims of authority or of conferred authorization.

Burawoy asserts that grounded theory does not consider power in micro contexts and that 'it represses the broader macro forces that both limit change and create domination in the micro sphere' (1991: 282). Burawoy is correct that the originators of grounded theory did not address power. Yet it is quite another issue to attribute the lack of attention to power as a weakness residing within the method itself. The *method*? The method does not preclude attending to power. Layder (1998: 10) raises a similar questionable criticism when he states that grounded theory 'is committed epistemologically (the validity of knowledge) and ontologically (its view of social reality) to denying the existence of phenomena that are not only or simply behavioural (like markets, bureaucracies, and forms of domination).' Not necessarily. Merely because earlier authors did not address power or macro forces does not mean that grounded theory methods cannot. It might mean pursuing mixed methods forms of data collection that include use of documents. Chang's (2000) study of the social transformation of class in China offers valuable clues as to how grounded theorists might study power and macro processes. Adopting grounded theory methods in these areas could wring a new twist to old theoretical clothes.

Burawoy's focus on the objectivist elements in grounded theory leaves out its constructivist potentials. In contrast to Burawoy and Layder's claims, I contend that we should use grounded theory methods in precisely these areas to gain fresh insights in social justice inquiry (Charmaz, 2005b). Clarke's (2005) extensions of grounded theory also encourage pursuing such directions.

Critics from within grounded theory debate what should stand as grounded theory and which directions it should take. Critics from without sometimes reify statements in the early works and turn them into static pronouncements, rather than treating them as starting points or as now historical statements of an evolving method. Most critics have not engaged the full range of sources about grounded theory and a few read no further or deeper than the rhetoric they find in the *Discovery* book (Glaser & Strauss, 1967). Others interpret the method narrowly. These critics commonly miss four crucial points: 1) theorizing is an activity; 2) grounded theory methods provide constructive ways to proceed with this activity; 3) the research problem and the researcher's unfolding interests can shape the *content* of this activity, not the method; and 4) the products of theorizing reflect how researchers acted on these points.

Critics' reifications about the nature of grounded theory spawn further reifications about its presumed limits. Critics often reify early grounded theory statements. Subsequently, *their* pronouncements are sometimes reified as inherent truths about what grounded theory is and what we can do with it. These reifications influence other interpreters, practitioners, and students of the method. Untested notions about what grounded theory can address spawn reifications about boundaries circumscribing the content of grounded theory studies, such as the belief that grounded theorists cannot use their methods to theorize power. Limited ideas about the form of inquiry grounded theory takes also produce other kinds of reifications. Treating grounded theory as only a variable analysis, for example, can lead to reductionist frames and encourage favoring those 'variables' within ready grasp. Hence, a superficial study can result that may skirt the border of a category without explicating it.

Theory generation continues to be the unfilled promise and potential of grounded theory. As Dan E. Miller (2000: 400) states, 'Although grounded theory (Glaser & Strauss, 1967) is often invoked as a methodological strategy, ironically too little grounded theory is actually done.'

Developing Theoretical Sensitivity through Theorizing

Like other recent texts (see Glaser, 1998; Goulding, 2002; Locke, 2001; Strauss & Corbin, 1998), this volume clarifies the logic and sequence of grounded theory methods. Early grounded theorists predicated constructing theory on developing 'theoretical sensitivity' (Glaser, 1978), but how might grounded theorists acquire it? Which clues can we discover through studying grounded theorists' actions? What do acts of theorizing entail?

Theorizing means stopping, pondering, and rethinking anew. We stop the flow of studied experience and take it apart. To gain theoretical sensitivity, we look at studied life from multiple vantage points, make comparisons, follow leads, and build on ideas. Because you chart your direction through acts of theorizing, you may not be able to foresee endpoints or stops along the way.

The acts involved in theorizing foster *seeing* possibilities, *establishing* connections, and *asking* questions. Grounded theory methods give you theoretical openings that avoid importing and imposing packaged images and automatic answers. How you practice theorizing and how you construct the content of theorizing vary depending on what you find in the field. When you theorize, you reach down to fundamentals, up to abstractions, and probe into experience. The content of theorizing cuts to the core of studied life and poses new questions about it.

> When you theorize, you reach down to fundamentals, up to abstractions, and probe into experience. The content of theorizing cuts to the core of studied life and poses new questions about it.

Although tools may help, constructing theory is not a mechanical process. Theoretical playfulness enters in. Whimsy and wonder can lead you to see the novel in the mundane. Openness to the unexpected expands your view of studied life and subsequently of theoretical possibilities. Your hard work reins in those ideas that best fit the data and brings them to fruition.

Consistent with Glaser's (1978) guidelines, I have stressed using gerunds in coding and memo-writing. Adopting gerunds fosters theoretical sensitivity because these words nudge us out of static topics and into enacted processes.[7] Gerunds prompt thinking about actions—large and small. If you can focus your coding on *actions*, you have ready grist for seeing sequences and making connections. If your gerunds quickly give way to coding for topics, you may synthesize and summarize data but the connections between them will remain more implicit. Thus, I suggest renewed emphasis on actions and processes, not on individuals, as a strategy in constructing theory and moving beyond categorizing types of individuals.[8] In my analysis of identity levels in an identity hierarchy, the categories result from people's objectives and actions rather than being pinned to certain individuals. Individuals can and do move up and down the hierarchy and certain social conditions foster such movement while other conditions hinder it.

Taking a closer look at processual analyses may aid your efforts to construct theory.[9] Studying a process fosters your efforts to construct theory because you define and conceptualize relationships between experiences and events. Then you can define the major phases and concentrate on the relationships between them. Major events and often the pacing may be clear when you study an identifiable process, such as becoming a member of a profession.[10] Graduate degree programs in social work, for example, have definite beginnings and endings and you can discern the pacing and sequencing that lie between. From early on, you know the path and can watch for markers and transitions in the passage. Other processes, such as being selected for lay-off from work or dying of cancer may not be so clear—at least to those who experience these processes and researchers who study them. If so, you may have to do considerable observational and analytic work to define phases that make empirical and theoretical sense.

In their substantive grounded theory of bereavement, Hogan, Morse, and Tasón (1996) outline processes of surviving a death of a close family member. They present their theory as somewhat sequential major processes that may overlap or reemerge:

1. Getting the news
2. Finding out
3. Facing realities
4. Becoming engulfed with suffering
5. Emerging from the suffering
6. Getting on with life
7. Experiencing personal growth

These authors qualify the process according to whether the deceased person had experienced an illness or sudden death. Survivors of a person who suffered a sudden death entered bereavement at the second major phase, finding out, while those whose loved one died of an illness experienced the shock of the terminal diagnosis and a caregiving process. Hogan et al. connect descriptions of grief to specific phases in the process, and to sub-processes that constitute a particular phase. Thus they treat 'enduring hopelessness,' 'existing in the present,' and 'reliving the past' as part of the 'missing, longing, and yearning' that characterizes how bereaved people experience being engulfed in suffering. Note the strong parallels between these processes and my 1991 analysis of experiencing a serious chronic illness. Both studies tap fundamental phases in suffering and properties of meanings of loss.

If grounded theorists have the methods to construct theory, why do many studies remain descriptive? Coding for themes rather than actions contributes to remaining at a descriptive level. In contrast, grounded theorists have the tools for explicating actions that constitute a process, as Clarke demonstrates in *Disciplining Reproduction* (1998). She persists in analyzing these actions in her treatment of each phase of the two-edged process of scientists establishing their field as a legitimate discipline and exerting controls over women's bodies. Such works keep the *analytic momentum*, and thus extend their theoretical reach further than those that identify a process, outline its phases, and then describe them. One hazard of grounded theory approaches is constructing a list of connected but under-analyzed processes.

Star (1989) keeps the analytic momentum in her analysis of establishing scientific certainty among early brain researchers who believed that mental functions were localized to specific areas of the brain. In her discussion of their tactics for dismissing opponents who argued mental functions were diffuse, she simultaneously shows us localizationists' strategies and theorizes how their actions establish scientific dominance. See how Star maintains her analytic momentum as she discusses the following process:

Manipulating Hierarchies of Credibility

A hierarchy of credibility refers to the differential weight given to the word of people or organizations with different status. That is, a person or institution at the top of a hierarchy is intrinsically more 'believable' than someone at the bottom (Becker, 1967). All else being equal, the word of a Nobel Prize winner is likely to be taken as more plausible than that of a vagrant, even if the content of the statements is the same.

Scientific arguments that manipulate hierarchies of credibility are not sanctioned by scientific method. Yet they are common. The localization debate was not won because localizationists were more sarcastic or *ad hominem* than diffusionists. Instead, localizationalists could more effectively manipulate hierarchies of credibility as they gained professional power in medicine and physiology.

'More Scientific than Thou'

Among the types of claims that manipulate hierarchies of credibility are claims on the part of one side or another to [greater] scientificity. These are claims that one procedure or approach is more scientifically viable, or technically astute, than another. Such claims are often opposed to designations like 'metaphysical,' 'poetic,' 'impressionistic,' or 'soft science ...' (1989: 140)

Star starts with a clear definition of her category of 'manipulating hierarchies of credibility,' and then builds its structure by showing how localizationists built the architecture of their argument. Hence, she reaches down into the data and shows how localizationists established that they were 'more scientific than thou,' as one tactic supporting the more general category of 'manipulating hierarchies of credibility.' Subsequently, she fits together being more scientific than thou with other tactics that support and specify the larger category, including 'arguments from authority' and 'ignoring, censorship, and sarcasm.' In each case, she shows how localizationists used these tactics and gave reasons why they invoked them. Because Star gives her categories and subcategories imagery and substance, she constructs a dense theoretical statement that readers remember. This excerpt shows how writing style and theoretical significance merge in the narrative. Star's engaging style persuades readers and involves them in her theoretical arguments.

To maintain analytic momentum, try to remain open to theoretical possibilities. Recall that Glaser (1978, 1998) advises you to begin the analytic process by asking, 'What is this data a study of?' (1978: 57). If we ask the question at *each* stage of the analytic process and seek the most fundamental answer that fits, we might discover that particular meanings and actions in our studied world suggest theoretical links to compelling ideas that had not occurred to us. As we pursue theoretical possibilities, we may make connections between our theoretical categories and ideas concerning the core of human experience. If so, our study may be about fundamental views and values such as those concerning human nature, selfhood, autonomy and attachment, moral life and responsibility, legitimacy and control, and certainty and truth. For example, my study of struggling for self in the identity hierarchy linked selfhood, autonomy, legitimacy, and control.

Any field contains fundamental concerns and contested ideas, whether or not they have yet been theorized. As we code data and write memos, we can think about which ones, if any, our materials suggest and how our completed theories address them. In my field of sociology, such concerns include:

Embodiment and consciousness
Individual and collective action
Cooperation and conflict
Choice and constraint
Meanings and actions
Standpoints and differences
Ritual and ceremony
Positions and networks
Power and prestige
Structure and process
Opportunities and inequalities
Rights and resources
Moral life, moral action, and moral responsibility

Discerning connections to such concerns opens possibilities for theorizing. What deflects them? Analytic starting points matter. The early grounded theory texts prescribed discovering a single basic process. If numerous 'basic' social processes occur in a setting, determining 'the' most fundamental process can be daunting, even for an objectivist grounded theorist. While I had no difficulty defining loss of self (Charmaz, 1983b) as more basic than 'managing illness' or 'disclosing illness' in my study of experiencing chronic illness, I could not define a single basic process that unified everything I was learning. For several years I wrestled with trying to identify one basic social process that captured everything I learned about experiencing illness.[11] I tried to find a more specific process than 'experiencing illness'; however, people experienced many processes ranging from learning to live with chronic illness to experiencing time in new ways to recreating or reestablishing a self they could accept.

Once the analytic work begins, all the potential problems mentioned above may arise. Thus, some grounded theories suffer from what John Lofland (1970) calls 'analytic interruptus' in qualitative research. The analytic work begins but comes to an abrupt ending. A disjuncture arises between the analytic level in these grounded theory studies and the goal of theorizing. Cathy Urquhart (2003) attributes this disjuncture in her field of information systems to subjective elements in coding. She states:

> Experience with using GTM [Grounded Theory Methods] shows that it is essentially a 'bottom up' coding method. Therefore, it is not unusual for researchers to find that GTM gives them a low level theory which they find difficult to 'scale up' appropriately.
>
> One issue then, in our use of GTM in IS [Information Systems] is to clearly identify what we are using it for: a) a coding method or b) a method of theory generation. There is ample evidence in IS literature for the first use, much less for the second. One useful side effect of using GTM in IS could be a much more detailed consideration of the role of theory – and generation of our own theories specific to IS. (2003: 47)

Urquhart's astute assessment applies to many grounded theory researchers throughout the disciplines who stop their analytic work after coding and constructing elementary categories. In contrast to Urquhart, however, I argue that the bottom-up approach gives grounded theory its strength. The subjectivity of the observer provides a *way* of viewing. Instead of arresting analysis at the coding stage, researchers can raise their main categories to concepts.

Categories are major and minor. Which categories does a researcher raise to theoretical concepts? Consistent with grounded theory logic, you raise the categories that render the data most effectively. Clarke views these categories as having 'carrying capacity' because they carry substantial analytic weight.[12] These categories contain crucial properties that make data meaningful and carry the analysis forward. We choose to raise certain categories to concepts because of their theoretical reach, incisiveness, generic power, and relation to other categories. Raising categories to concepts includes subjecting them to further analytic refinement and involves showing their relationships to other concepts. For objectivists, these concepts serve as core variables and hold explanatory and predictive power. For constructivists, theoretical concepts serve as interpretive frames and offer an abstract understanding of relationships. Theoretical concepts subsume lesser categories and by comparison hold more significance, account for more data and often are more evident. We make a series of decisions about these categories after having compared them with other categories and the data. Our actions shape the analytic process. Rather than discovering order *within* the data, we create an explication, organization, and presentation *of* the data (Charmaz, 1990).

Inspecting Grounded Theories

While keeping meanings of theory and theorizing practices in mind, we can take a fresh look at theory construction in several grounded theories I introduced earlier. Each theory bears the imprint of its author's interests and ideas and reflects its historical context as well as the historical development of ideas—and of grounded theory—in its parent discipline. Each of the theories published in the 1980s mirrors the form and style of the era. Before Clifford and Marcus's (1986) postmodern challenge in *Writing Culture*, most qualitative researchers strove to be objective and positivist. As Van Maanen (1988) suggests, Glaser and Strauss (1967) created methods that emulated the natural sciences and provided researchers with a defense against accusations of subjectivity.[13]

Jane Hood's Substantive Theory

Jane Hood's (1983) book stands out because she outlines specific theoretical conditions that explain substantive problems and processes. Compared to today, more working- and middle-class women with children married their male partners at the time Hood collected her data and fewer married women felt forced to reenter the workforce after having children. Many women—married or not—must work now and earlier cultural values have changed that both dissuaded mothers from working and fostered fathers' lack of involvement in family work.

As I pointed out in the pervious chapter, Hood found that husbands' awareness and acknowledged value of their wives' significant contributions to family finances became underlying conditions for sharing family work. Those husbands who valued their wives' financial contribution participated in housework and childcare. Those husbands who did not see their wives as coproviders did not view housework and childcare as a joint effort.

Thus the husband's definition of the situation and in particular of the wife's financial contribution became variables on which outcomes rested. Note that Hood specifies what happens when the husband acknowledges and values his wife's financial contribution *and* what happens when he does not.

Hood was influenced by Glaser and, not surprisingly, her mode of analysis reflects that influence. Like other grounded theories of the early 1980s, Hood's analysis has an objectivist cast. She seeks explanations and offers predictions. Although she engages her participants in lively discussions and raises occasional pointed questions, she offers crisp, straightforward assessments of her data from an expert's vantage point. Hood identifies variables, specifies conditions under which events and actions occur, and examines consequences. Her statements are parsimonious and integrated and she deduces testable hypotheses from them. Hood shows what people do and identifies the source of further action. She maintains analytic momentum throughout her research. As she studied her data and engaged in theoretical sampling, Hood made her theory more dense by addressing whether work-oriented spouses were more or less likely to stay together; which kinds of wives remained in the workforce, how their relative commitments to work and their wage ratios affected their bargaining power; and what categories of husbands correspondingly increased their household responsibilities. Consider this set of hypotheses that Hood deduced after she had articulated her theory:

1. Wives working for 'self' as opposed to 'family' reasons will be more likely to remain in the labor force after the need for their incomes has diminished.
2. Couples with competing goals will experience more strain than those with complementary goals.
3. Increased work commitment on the part of a wife (accompanied by a decrease in the amount of companionship she is able to offer her husband) will cause most problems in husband- and couple-centered marriages and least in child-centered marriages.
4. Wives working for self reasons married to job-oriented men are most likely to move toward recognition as coproviders (and increase their wage ratio).
5. Couples who are most ambivalent about their definition of the wife's responsibility to provide will be likely to resolve this inconsistency either by having the wife quit work or by accepting her as a coprovider.
6. Job-oriented husbands will have an easier time accepting their wives' increased work commitment than will career-oriented husbands.
7. Job-oriented husbands and families with younger children will be most likely to increase their share of household responsibility, where career-oriented husbands and fathers of older children will be less likely to.
8. Regardless of her share of the family income, a wife's bargaining power will be improved by gains in self-esteem and increased social support outside the marriage. (1983: 138)

These hypotheses follow Hood's theory of the role bargaining process based on her analysis of outcomes concerning specific research participants. If we conducted a similar study today we might cast a wider initial net to discover if, how, when, and to what extent other factors such as race or ethnic identification, religious beliefs, and geographical location might affect what happens during the bargaining process and, should patterns emerge, subsequently earn their way into the analysis. For that matter, we would want to see what contemporary couples bargain about and learn whether and to what extent they have reframed the issues since Hood's original study. A contemporary researcher likely would attend to the range of variation in the bargaining process and to situating the subsequent analysis.

A further examination of Hood's type of analysis shows its usefulness in defining *what* happened and in theorizing its implications. She reveals how implicit rules and tacit agreements about rights and obligations shape bargaining. She points out that her research participants share a tacit agreement that a wife cannot expect help with housework unless she has to work for family survival. Children, in contrast, result in joint responsibilities that spouses must cover if one partner cannot fulfill his or her tasks. Hood's couples assumed that children must receive a certain amount of parental attention and thus a spouse felt compelled to maintain that level commensurate to his or her partner's reduced involvement with the children.

Interview data may provide accounts indicating *how* couples negotiate family work from the perspectives of the men and women involved but interviews are just that—retrospective accounts subject to reconstruction in view of present exigencies and purposes. Nevertheless, Hood's multiple methods of data collection do much to counteract the limitations of interviews. Her interview accounts indicate hypothetical conditions concerning *when* negotiation is possible. We learn *why* wives may be effective or ineffective in obtaining their husbands' participation in family work. We certainly gain a sense of *whose* perspectives and prerogatives prevail first, but we don't know how strongly women whose husbands did not participate in family work felt that they should. Nor do we know how these women may have tried to impose their definitions. Interestingly, Hood did discover that men's participation in family work had the consequence of couples becoming closer. Her data may not open up the process of becoming closer but certainly points the way for further research to examine how this process may unfold.

Hood's analysis shows the social conditions at play with remarkable clarity. Not only does Hood maintain analytic momentum but also she is unwavering in her focus. Once she discovers her core variables, she proceeds to trace out their permutations and implications and integrate them in a logically precise framework. Her hypothetical statements supply tools for making predictions and for transporting the analysis to study other types of situations. For example, we could observe whether and to what extent the analysis holds for two-career couples without children.

By developing integrated conditional statements, Hood moves her analysis from empirical generalizations about a small sample to a substantive theory of an empirical problem. The conceptual level of this theory is specific and immediate. Hood shows how we can theorize concrete relationships in ways that provide a useful handle to evaluate actual situations.

Hood built early comparisons into her research that gave her the foundation to make distinctions and to pursue differences about her major concerns of role overload and marital equity. Consistent with Glaser's current emphasis on studying how people resolve a pressing problem in their lives, she stuck with analyzing if and how working women could negotiate the constant problem of family work. Take note that Hood completed her study long before Glaser's (1998) definitive statements appeared about studying how people resolve a problem.

Because of her systematic approach to data-gathering, making comparisons, and theoretical sampling, Hood could generate conditions that characterized her emerging substantive theory and contributed to its coalescence. Her theory readily permits researchers and readers alike to check empirical instances.

Hood conducted her study as an independent research project although we can easily envision transporting her approach to a large multi-method project that combines qualitative research with comprehensive national quantitative surveys. This study suggests how well certain qualitative grounded approaches could work with multi-method and multi-disciplinary research teams that address specific research problems.

Patrick Biernacki's Theory of a Basic Social Process

Patrick Biernacki's *Pathways from Heroin Addiction* (1986) offers a theoretical explication of a basic social process, as consistent with early grounded theory texts (Glaser, 1978; Glaser & Strauss, 1967). His theory accounts for the identity transformation from 'addict' to 'ex-addict' among individuals who did not seek treatment. Biernacki demonstrates the phases in the process and treats them as conceptual categories. He arrives at these categories by pulling together processes defined in his codes. I present a diagram (Figure 6.1) to show the logic of Biernacki's processual theory but only detail the last crucial phase of the process, which I discuss below.

Biernacki's theory has a strong objectivist foundation with some interpretivist elements. He traces the sequence of events and shows how sub-processes build on each other. After ex-addicts quelled their drug cravings and stayed abstinent, Biernacki argues that they underwent subtle social psychological processes involving symbolic and social reconstructions of their lives and worlds. These reconstructions required making a place in the conventional world. Such symbolic and social reconstructions usually presented addicts with harrowing problems and continued troubles—but overcoming them remained a prerequisite for completing their identity transformation. Thus, the category of 'becoming and being "ordinary"' (p. 141) became an integral concept in Biernacki's theory. He shows how his research participants experienced this phase of the transformation process. Recovering addicts had to adopt and maintain conventional lives. Yet they felt reluctant to interact with conventional people and simultaneously faced stereotyped views of addicts as untrustworthy, loathsome individuals.

To make his theory coalesce, Biernacki needed to explain the pivotal role that 'becoming and being "ordinary"' played in the recovery process to *theorize* how addicts' identity transformation became real. What happened to make this transformation possible? How did social circumstances and personal choices congeal to lead to a complete identity transformation? Biernacki's categories below refer to three different identity paths that addicts traversed to become ordinary:

- Emergent identities (pp. 144–148)
- Reverting to unspoiled identities (pp. 149–155)
- Extending identities (pp. 155–160).

Thus in the first case, recovering addicts' new identities emerged as they adopted new pursuits that absorbed their attention and spawned identity change. In the second case, constructing a former conventional identity eventually

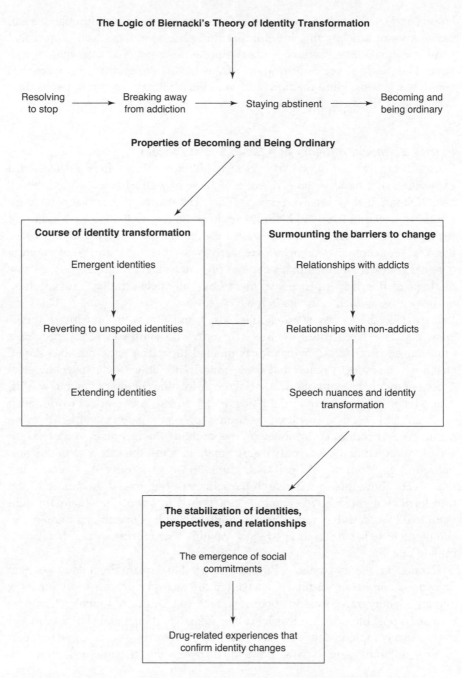

FIGURE 6.1   Patrick Biernacki's theory of identity transformation in
recovery from addiction without treatment

allowed leaving the addict identity behind, and in the third, expanding an
unspoiled identity that had remained intact during addiction created possibilities for identity change. Emergent identities developed through circumstance
and action, often without forethought. Reverting to an unspoiled identity and

extending a present one were more apt to result from conscious choices. Each category maps an identity path to becoming and being ordinary.

Biernacki's identity categories exhaust the range of empirical instances that he discovered in the field. Thus, his concept 'being and becoming "ordinary"' derives from empirical indicators and accounts for them. Biernacki had to address simultaneous processes to have his theory coalesce. While engaged in these kinds of identity-work, addicts involved themselves in 'surmounting the barriers to change,' the next major problem that Biernacki defines in their transformation. Last, ex-addicts had to stabilize their new or revised identities, perspectives, and relationships (pp. 161–180). If we take a closer look at Biernacki's category 'surmounting the barriers to change,' and examine how he treats it, we can see how he wove his data, codes, and categories into a theoretical explanation that builds directly from the data. Recovering addicts had to reject enticements offered by their addicted peers and, moreover, resist the power and pervasiveness of the drug world and its discourse. Meanwhile, addicts had to surmount the stigma of addiction in conventional worlds and prove that they had changed. Biernacki has already defined *when* surmounting these barriers becomes crucial. Next he looks at *how* ex-addicts established proof of their changed identities.

> How can this be done? Well, proof might be found in the ex-addicts' maintaining some of the involvements thought of as typical of a conventional, 'ordinary' life over an extended period of time. For example, ex-addicts are expected to be steadily employed, to maintain their own places of residence, and to keep reasonably 'normal' hours. They should also possess the material things that are common in the nonaddictive world—say, a television set and a stereo. Ex-addicts must avoid, or at least not be seen in, 'deviant' places, especially those areas known to be frequented by drug addicts. They should frequent 'normal' places—the cinema, restaurants, or sports events—and when they do, they should pay their own way.
>
> These may seem like small concerns, but they are important because they go against the stereotypic images that non-addicted people have of addicts … By the addicts' actions and even their possessions, others assess whether their claims that they are no longer using drugs and have changed their lives are true. (Biernacki, 1986: 166–167)

Biernacki provides an integrated substantive theory of identity change among addicts who do not receive treatment. His theory is sufficiently abstract to cover the range of empirical situations. Biernacki tackles the theoretical concept of identity by systematically constructing categories that synthesize and explain his research participants' accounts of their experiences. As he defined and conceptualized patterns in the data, he sought further data to specify conditions that affected the recovery. Not surprisingly, Biernacki discovered that a major factor was the extent to which a person's participation in the world of addiction excluded conventional pursuits. But Biernacki did not stop there. Rather, he also juxtaposed immersion in the drug world again against access and costs, and discovered how they varied. Biernacki found that addicts' immersion in the drug world seemed to be most complete when their drug costs were high and access was difficult. Subsequently, he began theoretical sampling among doctors and nurses. These professionals not only had low drug costs and relatively easy access but possessed valued identities with demanding involvements. By pursuing patterns in his data, Biernacki explains *why* certain addicts recover without treatment.

The theoretical reach of Biernacki's analysis extends beyond drug addiction. He addresses a generic process of identity transformation in a particular category of people that we could transport across fields to develop the concepts further. Other forms of deviant behavior, such as delinquency and prostitution, offer possibilities for advancing or modifying Biernacki's theory.

Kathy Charmaz's Constructivist Theory

The discussion below clarifies how a constructivist approach encourages you to theorize in the interpretive tradition. Interpretive theorizing may cover overt processes but also delves into implicit meanings and processes and is most evident then. To follow my reasoning, take another look at the category 'living one day at a time'. The idea of living one day at a time appeared in my data as part of the taken-for-granted discourse among chronically ill people. People stated the need to live one day at a time as an obvious fact but did not elaborate on it. A constructivist approach leads you to explore and interpret such implicit statements or actions.

Living One Day at a Time

Living one day at a time means dealing with illness—each day—but only one at a time. When people do so, they hold future plans and even ordinary pursuits in abeyance. For most people, living one day at a time tacitly acknowledges their fragility.

Living one day at a time also allows people to focus on illness, treatment, and regimen without being overcome by dashed hopes and unmet expectations. Taking this stance provides guidelines for functioning each day and confers some sense of control. By concentrating on the present, the person can avoid or minimize thinking about further disability and death.

The felt need to live one day at a time can drastically alter one's time perspective. Living one day at a time pulls the person's attention into the present and pushes once projected futures further away. Earlier visions of the future recede without disruption and slip away, perhaps almost unnoted. The present is compelling and, eventually, may seem rewarding. If so, the content of time changes; moments become longer and fuller.

Living one day at a time is a strategy for managing chronic illness and structuring time. Moreover, it also provides a way of managing self while facing uncertainty. It gives a sense of control over one's actions and, by extension, a sense of control over self and situation. Embracing this strategy also alters time perspective. ...

Living one day at a time reveals emotions embedded in the experience of illness. Many ill people, especially older people, express greater fear of dependence, debility, and abandonment than of death. Living one day at a time helps to reduce their fear that the future will be worse than the present. During a series of setbacks, Mark Reinertsen murmured, 'I try to live one day at a time because it is just less frightening.' Later he observed, 'I could just get really tied up in what might happen [death or further deterioration] since so much has happened in the last six months [multiple complications and iatrogenic diseases]. But what good does it do? I can only handle today?' (1991a, pp. 178, 180–181)

This excerpt represents an instance of constructivist analysis because it pieces together and interprets implicit meanings that constitute the category, thereby showing how a mundane statement alludes to an array of meanings and experiences. I point out actions that people take although the content of the category *relies* on how I assemble these actions and stated feelings and the interpretation I give to participants' statements and actions. When we delve into tacit meanings, not everyone we talk with is equally adept at describing them or of linking their actions to these meanings. Thus, the researcher may develop special methodological as well as analytic strategies to learn about relevant meanings and actions.

The narrative above pulls together disparate experiences in the category and elucidates the range of its tacit meanings. An interpretive analysis invites the reader's imaginative participation in related experiences through the *theoretical rendering* of the category. In this sense, the theoretical understanding of the category creates its significance; without it, research participants' unexplicated statements about living one day at a time would remain unexamined asides that happened to occur during the course of conversation. Pure description, in contrast, invites readers into scenes and invokes interest in and, often, identification with research participants' stories. The significance of the experience is often straightforward, as when Hood and Biernacki offer telling descriptions of their research. Their descriptions underscore the plausibility of their explanations.

Consistent with a constructivist approach, the view I have of the data is part of their rendering. That is also true of Hood and Biernacki's grounded theories, but it is a matter of extent. Hood and Biernacki's theories both cover definitive events with clear markers and tangible experiences. Other trained observers in their respective fields could see and chart similar processes, once they made the respective initial empirical and conceptual leaps that Hood and Biernacki made. (In Hood's case that meant ferreting out the reasons why working women received little household help from husbands and in Biernacki's case, if and how heroin addicts recover from addiction without treatment.)

My analysis above remains more intuitive and impressionistic than Hood's or Biernacki's. Whether or not its interpretive frame strengthens or weakens it redounds back to critics' allegiances to constructivist or objectivist grounded theory. Would other researchers have drawn out the relationship between past and future or treated it as a strategy to maintain emotional control? Conceivably—if they already possessed some theoretical sensitivity toward concepts of self, time, emotions, and life disruptions. If not, it's hard to say because the properties of the category remain implicit until theoretical sampling and interpretive rendering make them explicit. The further we go into implicit experience, the longer it may take to make such empirical and conceptual leaps. Might other researchers have seen different things in the experience and by extension, the category? Yes, that's possible. Perhaps the kinds of theoretical sensitivities that the researcher brings to studied life assume special significance here. The analysis results from the researcher's involvement at every point in the research process.

Part of the interpretive task is being alert to possibilities for moving the analysis beyond the definitive evidence you currently have. That's why subsequent entering or reentering the experience is crucial. Rather than viewing living one day at a time as a convenient slogan, I sampled further to find out if and how people acted on it. Observers may be able to reenter the scene; interviewers can only seek access to stories that might illuminate the category. In this case, theoretical sampling became a means of gaining access to this specific experience. By going back and exploring further questions, the fragments of experience took form.

What place do categories have in constructivist analyses? Although categories do not serve as core variables, researchers may show relationships among them. In this case, I conveyed how my category 'living one day at time' connected with three major concepts: 'Time Perspectives,' 'Time Structures,' and 'Situating the Self in Time.' Thus, living one day at a time shapes the time structure of someone's days and weeks. Taking this stance for long periods alters the person's time perspective as the past fades and the future wanes. As a result, the person locates his or her self in the present.

Like Hood and Biernacki, I specify conditions, show conceptual relationships, and forecast consequences. Rather than making explicit theoretical propositions, I weave them into the narrative. Although the theory is more diffuse than either Hood's or Biernacki's, simultaneously, it is more abstract and general. Certainly the content of inquiry influences the theoretical outcomes. The elusive nature of my dual emphases on the self and time contributes to how I developed my theoretical statements. Still, a constructivist grounded theory informed my emerging analysis and inspired making fresh theoretical connections.

Concluding Thoughts

Throughout this chapter, I drew firm lines between positivist and interpretive inquiry, constructivist and objectivist grounded theory, and the subsequent distinctions and directions they suggest. In research practice, however, the lines may not be so clear. Positivist researchers may explore elusive topics with ephemeral meanings. Constructivist grounded theorists may investigate overt processes in painstaking detail. In research practice, theorizing means being eclectic, drawing on what works, defining what fits (see also Wuest, 2000). For that matter, neither positivist nor constructivist may intend that readers view their written grounded theories as *Theory*, shrouded in all its grand mystique, or acts of theorizing. Instead they just are doing grounded theory in whatever way they understand it.

Like Star's early brain researchers, however, grounded theorists sometimes invoke a 'more theoretical than thou' form of invidious comparison. An elegant parsimonious theory may offer clear propositions but have limited scope. An imaginative diffuse theory may spark bursts of insight but offer interpretive frames with porous borders. Each presupposes different objectives and favors certain ways of knowing and types of knowledge. A theory allows us to cut through ordinary explanations and understandings and to attend to certain realities and not to others. Theories cannot be measured like bank statements although we can establish criteria for different kinds of theorizing. The balance of If–Then theoretical propositions and the number and density of abstractions depends on a grounded theorist's audience and purpose as well as on his or her theoretical proclivities. As my above discussions of theorizing in grounded theory reveal, theories serve different purposes and differ in their inclusiveness, precision, level, scope, generality, and applicability.

The subjectivity and ambiguity I portrayed in constructivist grounded theory permeates objectivist approaches as well. These approaches mask subjectivity and ambiguity through shared assumptions about the world and established formats for conducting research. In the end, inquiry takes us outward yet reflecting about it draws us inward. Subsequently, grounded theory leads us back to the world for a further look and deeper reflection—again and again. Our imaginative renderings of what we see and learn are interpretations, emanating from dialectics of thought and experience. Whether we adhere to positivist or interpretive traditions, we do not gain an autonomous theory, albeit one amenable to modification. Rather we are *part* of our constructed theory and this theory reflects the vantage points inherent in our varied experiences, whether or not we are aware of them.

NOTES

1 After completing a chapter-length analysis of this material by 1983, the published version appeared in 1987. I had laid out the central ideas in my dissertation (1973) but in the interim I had collected more data to refine the categories.

2 For a more complete statement of contrasts distinguishing constructivist and objectivist grounded theory, see Charmaz, 2000; 2006a.

3 I agree with Glaser (1992) on the issue of verification, despite its appearance in the *Discovery* (1967) book. Checking hunches and confirming ideas, in my view, does not equal verification. Rather than contributing verified knowledge, I see grounded theorists as offering plausible accounts.

4 Glaser (2001) now argues that researchers identify this main concern, which represents a significant departure from his (1992) assertion that researchers should analyze the main concern in the setting and that participants will tell them what it is.

5 Burawoy calls for 'grounded globalizations' (2000: 341) and an agenda for 'grounding globalization' later in *Global Ethnography* (2000: 337–373). Although his concepts allude to grounded theory, he does not engage or cite it.

6 My point here complements Silverman's (2004) argument cited above.

7 An emphasis on gerunds may seem like a trivial point; instead I see it as a pivotal point but one that grounded theorists do not always adopt. Perhaps the much greater emphasis on structure than process in the English language makes thinking with gerunds unfamiliar; however, researchers often find that gerunds fit much of their data in ways they had not— and could not have—fully anticipated.

8   Learning to focus on processes instead of on individuals and topics was one our first lessons in our grounded theory analysis seminars during my graduate years. We learned to go beyond static typologies labeling individuals into analyzing basic social processes to give the studied phenomenon fuller analytic treatment. Many qualitative studies at the time relied on labeling individuals, so developing explicit analyses of social processes in grounded theory marked a decided advance.

9   Numerous grounded theory studies offer insightful observations of subjective experience or organizational processes (see, for example, Hogan, Morse, & Tasón, 1996; Lempert, 1996; Melia, 1987; Thulesius, Håkansson, & Petersson, 2003; Tweed & Salter, 2000) and increasingly more grounded theory studies provide useful treatment of larger social processes (see for example Clarke, 1998; Star, 1989, 1999).

10   The level we address figures here. Although many grounded theorists study process as indicated in narratives or natural settings, to my knowledge we have not addressed interactional sequences as closely as conversational analysts (see, for example, Maynard, 2003; Silverman, 1997). Urquhart's (1998) study, which builds on system analysis, takes a step in this direction.

11   In my dissertation (1973), which addressed the same substantive area, I made 'remobilizing' the major process. Besides being an ugly word that evokes mechanistic and militaristic images, the term did not account for the range of experience. This decided limitation became increasingly apparent when I gathered additional and more complete data after the dissertation. By then, I had improved my interviewing skills and routinely tape-recorded the interviews.

12   Personal communication, February 28, 2005.

13   In the 1960s, many scholars dismissed qualitative research as impressionistic, unsystematic, and subjective.

7 Writing the Draft

A grounded theory journey extends through the process of writing, as you will see in this chapter. Writing your manuscript presents opportunities for drafting new discoveries with each revision and making your mark in your field with grace and style. I suggest ways to pull together the pieces of your manuscript, construct a compelling argument that fits your grounded theory, and scrutinize your categories again to gauge how they shape the core of the manuscript. After drafting your grounded theory, we grapple with the disputed literature review and often troublesome theoretical framework. I offer solutions to the tensions between these standard scholarly requirements and grounded theorizing that will serve your theoretical analysis and the argument you make about it. The chapter ends with writers' strategies and rhetorical devices to render your grounded theory accessible— and to make it matter.

Grounded theory writing preserves and presents the form and content of the analytic work. Rather than spotlighting actors or authors, grounded theory places ideas and analytic frameworks on center stage. In a sense, our concepts become 'actors' who create the analysis of actions in the scene. What tensions arise between constructing our grounded theory analyses and our writing tasks? How might we recapture the fullness of events through our analytic renderings? How can we merge the analytic demands of grounded theory with the standards of good writing?

As I have argued, the potential strength of grounded theory lies in its analytic power to *theorize* how meanings, actions, and social structures are constructed. Analytic memos grab readers' attention. These memos pierce our understandings and puncture our preconceptions about it. We can pull such memos together in an integrated analysis that theorizes the realm of studied action.

Grounded theories dig deep into the empirical and build analytic structures that reach up to the hypothetical. Thus, straightforward categories about ordinary experiences shine with bright meanings–through our analytic renderings. My excerpt below depicts ordinary experiences of having a chronic illness with an analytic lens that focuses and sharpens our views of these experiences. Think about the widespread incidence of common chronic illnesses. Many adults know about early symptoms, progression, current treatments, and more. If so, would they not foresee what having an illness entails? What could be more mundane than understanding what having a chronic illness means? But learning what it means is not so easy. Grounded theory research can illuminate *how* people learn the difference between having a diagnosis and an illness. By studying how people learn about chronicity, we also gain ideas about what having the illness means to them.[1]

Learning about Chronicity

Weeks and months of unrelenting symptoms teach ill people about chronicity. Further, learning about chronicity means discovering its effects on daily life. By attempting to manage their usual activities, ill people discover the meaning of their altered bodies. After his first heart attack, Harry Bauer recalled that 'when I was laying on the bed there [at the hospital], I told the doctor I was going to work. He said, "No way." He said, "When you get up from there, you'll find out how weak you are." I used to be able to pick up 100 pounds in each hand. When I got up from there, I found what he meant, I couldn't hardly hold myself up.'

The meaning of disability, dysfunction, or impairment becomes real in daily life. Until put to test in daily routines, someone cannot know what having an altered body is like. Heather Robinson did not have her first serious episode until ten months after her diagnosis but others mistook having a diagnosis with dealing with the disease. She recounted:

'People said, "You deal with this so well [immediately after diagnosis]." I just said, "I haven't really dealt with this because I haven't been ill." I mean you can't deal with something until you've experienced something, you don't have to. So as soon as I got sick with it and had to deal with it then, that I think is when I realized I had MS [multiple sclerosis] ... now I am learning where I can go and how much I can do without knocking myself out.'

The yardsticks of the past, not of an altered present and future, measure distances to walk, tasks to complete, and plans to make. Lessons about chronicity come with discoveries that those yardsticks pose arduous or impossible standards.

Frequently, ill people must abandon their hopes and their plans, and relinquish their former activities. Illness and disability force lowering expectations of self—at least for a while. Yet doing so shocks and unsettles people. In his book, psychiatrist Clay Dahlberg recounts his feelings when he learns that he can go home after having a CVA [cerebrovascular accident]: 'That was a glorious day. I started planning all the things I could do with the incredible amount of free time I was going to have. Chores I had put off, museums and galleries to visit, friends I had wanted to meet for lunch—so many joyful things. It was not until several days later that I realized that I simply couldn't do them. I didn't have the mental or physical strength and I sank into depression' (Dahlberg & Jaffe, 1977: 30).

The difference between past and present functioning contrasts sharply, for the past remains so close ... (Charmaz, 1991a: 21–22)

The example above blends analytic statements with supporting description and illustration. It thus moves back and forth between theoretical interpretation and empirical evidence. Grounded theory works can be written in a variety of ways. What steps expedite finishing the grounded theory report? How do you manage tensions between an inductive grounded theory and the deductive logic inherent in standard formats for scholarly writing? Which writing strategies enhance producing a powerful theory and vivid narrative? How can you best handle writing your report?

Regarding Writing

Making Your Mark

How do you say something original? New scholars need to make their mark on their disciplines. Senior scholars need to prove that they are still up to the mark. Old and new scholars want to show that they haven't missed the mark in their fields. Robert F. Murphy (1987: 81) proposes his 'Murphy's First Law of Academic Careers' as having two phases: 'In the first, young academics are anxious over whether they will be discovered; in the second, the established ones are worried about whether they will be found out.'

What does an 'original contribution' mean? If you offer a fresh or deeper understanding of the studied phenomena, you can make an original contribution. All too frequently researchers' assertions of an original grounded theory amount to a trite list of common-sense accounts (see also, Silverman, 2000). Of course, what stands as original depends in part on the audience. Authors invoke several strategies to claim originality. They provide 1) an analysis in a new area, 2) an original treatise in an established or fading area, and 3) an extension of current ideas.

In the past, a number of scholars made their mark by exploring significant new terrain. Like a first explorer on distant shores, they claimed the turf—and have been cited ever afterwards. The new turf may have been a field such as sociology of emotions or an intriguing topic such as the work of laboratory scientists (Clarke, 1998; Latour & Woolgar, 1979; Star, 1989). As a field develops, however, the areas narrow in which scholars can claim originality. In many disciplines, the days have long past when an author could make a breakthrough by constructing a new field.

Grounded theorists can contribute to a speciality field and simultaneously extend general theoretical interpretations that cut across fields. Theoretical ideas with grab reach further than treatment of a specific empirical problem. Patrick Biernacki's (1986) questions about accepted notions of recovery from opiate addiction not only resulted in a contribution to the study of drug abuse but also to our knowledge of identity change. Biernacki's fresh questions produced new insights in two established areas. If you can't claim new turf, you may be able to mine an overlooked area.

Some scholars develop original grounded theories in areas that have relied on other forms of study or methods of inquiry. Carolyn Wiener (2000) brought grounded theory into the field of accountability for hospital care, an area dominated by economists and quantification. Monica Casper's (1998) grounded theory ethnographic study entered the field of bioethics in which philosophers had studied hypothetical cases rather than exploring empirical circumstances.

Whether you dove into a new area or plunged into an established one, now it's time to pinpoint the original ideas in your analysis. Subsequently, use these ideas to form an argument that will speak to your intended audience.

Drafting Discoveries

The discovery process in grounded theory extends into the writing and rewriting stages. You'll gain further insights and create more ideas about your data while you're writing. You'll see clearer connections between categories and draw implications from them. Thus writing and rewriting become crucial phases of the *analytic* process. Writing demands more than mere reporting. Through writing and rewriting drafts, you can bring out implicit arguments, provide their context, make links with extant literatures, critically examine your categories, present your analysis, and provide data that support your analytic arguments. Each successive draft grows more theoretical and comprehensive.

Similar principles apply to writing your manuscript as in doing grounded theory analysis itself. Let your ideas emerge *before* you make decisions about what to do with the manuscript. Whether you intend to write a grounded theory class report or book, draft it first. Decide what to do with the manuscript and how to do it *after* you have a solid analytic draft. Take one step at a time. When reassessing your manuscript later, you may discover that it could serve a lofty goal. The grounded theory class report may make a stunning student competition submission. With revision, a thesis chapter might work as a journal submission. A dissertation could be rewritten to fit a particular series for a publishing house.

> Let your ideas emerge *before* you make decisions about what to do with the manuscript. Whether you intend to write a grounded theory class report or book, draft it first. Decide what to do with the manuscript and how to do it *after* you have a solid analytic draft.

The emergent character of grounded theory writing may conflict with class report or dissertation requirements. Residuals of positivist dominance cast shadows over how we frame our research reports–sometimes long shadows.

Required formats often presuppose a traditional logico-deductive organization. Thus, we need to rethink the format and adapt it to our needs and goals rather than pour our work

> Required formats often presuppose a traditional logico-deductive organization. Thus, we need to adapt the format rather than pour our work into standard categories. Do it in ways that work for your ideas rather than compromise your analysis.

into standard categories. Rethink and adapt a prescribed format in ways that work for your ideas rather than compromise your analysis.

Revising Early Drafts

A trade secret: writing qualitative research is an ambiguous process. Writing our analysis entails more than mere reporting. We may not realize what we've got or know where we're going. Grounded theory gives us more guidelines and, yes, grounding, than most approaches. Yet we may still feel as though we step on shaky terrain. Perhaps we wonder if our analysis has value. At this stage, learn to tolerate ambiguity but keep moving in the process. That will keep you progressing toward your goals. You'll discover rewards at the end. Learning to trust in the writing process, if not in ourselves, is like learning to trust in the grounded theory analytic process: our writing, like our analyses, is emergent. Involvement in these processes can take us where we need to go.

Similar to constructing a grounded theory analysis, writing the finished report may be filled with ambiguity and uncertainty. Finished work is replete with impression management as writers' voices exude certitude and authority (Charmaz & Mitchell, 1996). Published writers often act as if they proceeded on a single path with a clear destination from choosing their topics to writing their conclusions. More likely, the path is not single, or the destination clear. And today you can write about the bumps in the road as well.

Pulling the Pieces Together

Enthusiastic researchers might pin three lovely memos together and tack on a short introduction and conclusion. This ploy might produce a sparkling presentation but does not suffice for a completed report or published article. Carefully sorted and selected memos give you compelling content for a presentation. How you present the material matters. In an oral presentation, you impart significance through the rhythm and pacing of your speech, emotional nuances and enthusiasm, body language, and eye contact with the audience. In your written paper, the powerful ideas, subtle meanings, and graceful transitions, so apparent in your talk, all disappear. What happened? Your spoken words fade and flatten in written texts. Your analysis gave you superb material to work with—but it still needs work. What should you do?

Order your memos according to the logic of your sorting and the most telling diagram or clustering that you made. Study them. Then put your memos together in a first draft that integrates them and demonstrates the relations between them. As you work with the material, try to make the analysis more abstract. You form the core of your report with it. Take your grounded theory as far as you can before working on other sections.

Look at your theory and think about the following questions:

- Are the definitions of major categories complete?
- Have I raised major categories to concepts in my theory?
- How have I increased the scope and depth of the analysis in this draft?
- Have I established strong theoretical links between categories and between categories and their properties, in addition to the data?
- How have I increased understanding of the studied phenomenon?
- What are the implications of this analysis for moving theoretical edges? For its theoretical reach and breadth? For methods? For substantive knowledge? For actions or interventions?

- With which theoretical, substantive, or practical problems is this analysis most closely aligned? Which audiences might be most interested in it? Where shall I go with it?
- How does my theory make a fresh contribution?

Then start writing an introduction and conclusion that takes these problems into account. These sections will be rough. Just keep refining them. Your first draft of an introduction or conclusion is merely that–a draft. You can–and should–rework each section multiple times. Nothing is perfect in the early stages.[2] By reworking your draft several times, you catch vague statements and confusing sentences, and moreover craft a tight, convincing statement.

Now you can work with the whole draft. You may have generated an absorbing grounded theory analysis, but it may not contain an explicit purpose or argument. Involved researchers often assume that their purposes are obvious and their arguments, clear. They may be wrong. New authors may believe that the purpose that steered their study suffices to drive the argument and make a disciplinary contribution. That's unlikely. To make a contribution, you need to position your analysis in a specific purpose that drives your argument for *this* manuscript. We all make mistakes about the purpose and argument when immersed in our work. Just be aware that confusing an initial purpose for a contribution and assuming your argument speaks for itself, are standard pitfalls.

Constructing Arguments

Much scholarly writing consists of arguments–whether explicit or implicit. Ostensibly straightforward data analyses rely on arguments and invoke rhetorical devices to form them. We persuade readers to accept a new theory or interpretation. We convince researchers that we have solid data and sound analyses. A strong argument persuades the reader to accept the writer's viewpoint. Think about why a reader should attend to your ideas, much less accept them.

> Writers must address the 'So what?' question. A strong argument answers the 'So what?' question because you explicitly claim why your grounded theory makes a significant contribution.

You think you have an argument. The material fascinates you; therefore, you presume that anyone would want to read it. But why should your reader care? So what?

Writers must address the 'So what?' question. A strong argument answers the 'So what?' question because you explicitly claim why your grounded theory makes a significant contribution. Nonetheless, answering this question can lead to quandaries because arguments can be elusive–or stale. That means finding your argument and making it original and meaningful.

Most likely, you've buried the argument in the initial drafts. Find it. Get help in finding it. Your actual argument likely differs from what you originally set out to do. That's fine. That indicates that you've grown. An initial purpose brings you into the study but seldom suffices for an argument for a finished manuscript. New authors often mistake their initial purpose for a developed argument when they submit manuscripts for publication. You can make a more intriguing argument now, so go ahead and revise and reorganize your draft around it. Build your argument into each section, point by point, step by step. Our arguments do not stand like parked cars, waiting for us to find them. We rarely begin with an overriding argument that drives our writing. If it happens, appreciate your good fortune. If not, don't stop and wait for an argument to pop up and put the pieces of your analysis together for you.

Instead, work at it. Your argument will emerge. It develops as your thinking progresses. An argument is a product of grappling with the material. Writing short successive memos about your emerging argument can help you focus it. Some researchers benefit from talking out loud about their ideas at this point. Talking to yourself may give nebulous arguments form. Go through your manuscript and write:

- My argument here is that _____.
- My reasoning is _____.
- I support this argument by including _____.

Talking with other people is riskier than talking to yourself in writing. They may encourage you to tell what you already know or you may focus on what they wish to know, not on your remaining analytic work with the argument. My advice? If you must talk with other people, then explain the logic of your analysis to them, and bring a tape recorder. You might capture the essence of an argument and its ordering during the conversation that you had not stated or left implicit in your manuscript.

> An argument is a product of grappling with the material. You create it from points embedded in your analysis.

You create your argument from points embedded in your analysis. Outlining your paper for the main point in each paragraph can help you identify a nascent argument. Sometimes it may help to begin with a tentative initial argument. Keep refining it; see how it works. But don't commit yourself to it until you know that it accounts for your most important ideas. You may abandon the argument with which you started–that's alright. You'll gain a far more thoughtful argument than you had anticipated through wrestling with the ideas.

Questions to Help You Find Arguments:

- What sense of this process or analysis do you want your reader to make?
- Why is it significant (even practiced writers often *assume* the significance of their work rather than making it clear and explicit)?
- What did you tell your readers that you intended to do? Why did you tell them that?
- In which sentences or paragraph do your major points coalesce?

Go back and look for your argument(s)–color-code it with highlighters. Better yet, outline it. What are your sub-arguments? How closely aligned are they with your main argument? Are they integral to it? If the sub-arguments seem loosely aligned to your main argument, can you chop them out without changing it? If so, do so. Pick them up in another piece of work. If not, clarify and strengthen the connections to your main argument.

Look for the telling sentence or paragraph that makes your points coalesce. That's where you'll find your argument. Writers may not sense what is significant in their analyses. Your argument may hide where you least suspect–buried in the conclusion. You articulated your argument at the last minute. Now put it in the first moment, early in the introduction, and build it up throughout the paper.

To substantiate your argument, provide vivid description, examples, evidence that *shows* the point, rather than tells the reader what it is. Mere assertions bore readers; they do not convince them. Consider providing a balance of analytic statements anchored in concrete empirical instances. Can you see the difference between the excerpt at the beginning of this chapter ('Learning about Chronicity') and the following excerpt? Which do you find more theoretical? Which excerpt is most persuasive?

Learning What Illness Means

In order to be ill, someone has to feel sick. Merely being informed that one has a disease seldom suffices. Until a person defines changes in bodily feeling or function, he or she may postpone dealing with a diagnosis, even a serious one, and, subsequently, ignore medical advice and regimen. Illness does not seem real. Then the person may claim that the diagnosis is wrong, secondary, or inconsequential and relations with practitioners suffer accordingly.

People learn what illness is through their experience of it (Charmaz, 1991; Davis, 1963). Lessons in chronicity come in small everyday experiences such as difficulty in opening a can, bending over to pick up a newspaper, folding bedsheets, weeding the garden. Comparisons with past effortless performance can be shocking. Such jolts later become measures explicitly sought and then assessed ... (Charmaz, 1999: 282)

Granted, the two excerpts represent different genres and serve different audiences. The first is for a university press cross-over book that presents the original study. Cross-over books not only offer sound scholarship but are selected to reach general audiences as well as academic experts. The second excerpt summarizes the point for an essay in a handbook designed to serve social scientists in health and medical professionals. After writing a grounded theory, you may present your ideas in subsequent writings for different objectives, as is evident in the second piece. How you frame each rendering depends on your objective for writing it and the audience that will read it.

To keep your analysis at the forefront, write for your audience and professional standards *after* you have established your argument and garnered your evidence. Write in successive drafts. With each draft, adopt simpler, more direct words and tighter phrasing and logic. As a result, you will improve the analytic precision, clarity, and flow of the piece.

Scrutinizing Categories

Inspect your categories again to see how they shape this manuscript. Scrutinize these categories for their power, purpose, and pattern. Then you can clean them up and make them clear and crisp. Compelling categories give you a fresh handle on your material. Be judicious in your use of categories; don't abuse them or your readers. One grounded theory pitfall is overloading your work with clumsy jargon. Whittle and smooth those categories and turn the most significant ones into your concepts for *this* manuscript.

You have already treated your categories to analytic scrutiny several times. With each successive memo, your ideas grew stronger and more coherent. Thus, you already have a rhythm and flow to much of your work. Grounded theory methods prompt making connections within and between categories as an inherent part of the analytic process. Thus, your sentences already flow together to create a section.

Now examine your categories for their power, purpose, and patterns. Consider collapsing categories that lack power. Ask yourself: what purpose do they serve *here*? If you do not need them for *this* analysis, argument, or audience, drop them. In the excerpt from an early memo in Box 7.1 my categories read like a list and sound like a lecture. They do reveal, however, how I ordered and integrated the ideas in the narrative.

BOX 7.1 EXCERPT FROM AN EARLY MEMO ON DISCLOSURE

The Dilemmas of Disclosing Illness

Chronically ill people often wonder what they *should* tell and what they *need* to tell others about their illnesses. As Kathleen Lewis (1985) who has lupus erythematosus begins her book, '"How are you?" can perhaps become the most difficult question a chronically ill person needs to learn to answer (p. 3) ...'

Avoiding Disclosure

Given the potential costs, avoiding disclosure entirely can be a natural response to illness. Social circumstances as well as specific relationships may shape or intensify someone's proclivity to avoid disclosure. Perhaps the most basic reason for avoiding disclosure turns on whether someone grants illness a level of reality at all, and, if so, what kind of reality ...

Forms of Telling

Telling means to relate thoughts, actions, or feelings and to state them clearly. Here, telling often includes announcing and recounting professionals' accounts of one's illness and prognosis ...

1.   Disclosing

Disclosing represents a subjective form of telling, which brings one's experiencing, feeling self into the foreground. A disclosure reveals crucial facts and feelings about self. Private views of self and personal concerns seldom made public in middle-class American life may emerge. The very process of disclosing is risky ...

(Continued)

(Continued)

I found two types of disclosure in the data: protective disclosures and spontaneous disclosures ...

2.   Informing

When informing, in contrast, ill people assume an objective stance, almost as if their bodies and their situations remain separate from themselves ... Informing decreases emotional risks. Compared to disclosing, informing permits greater control over emotions, over others' responses, and over possible negative labels.

3.   Strategic announcing

By making strategic announcements, ill people extend their control over the information, themselves, and another's response. They *plan* what they will tell, to whom they will tell it, and when they will do it. Strategic announcing may protect self, control interaction, and preserve power ...

4.   Flaunting illness

The logical extension of making strategic announcements is flaunting illness. When flaunting illness, people extend further control over another's response and try to extract a specific response, often shock or guilt, from their audience ...

Strategies for disclosing

Ill people develop strategies for disclosing which protect others, themselves, and their relationships. They may not wish to avoid disclosing. But, they may not want to handle another's response, particularly if it taps deep feelings of anger, remorse, or fear in self. Their strategies turn on *what* they disclose and *how* they disclose it ...

1.   The content of disclosure

Softening the news teaches others a tempered view of illness. Ill people, like professionals, soften the news by stressing the positive, by glossing over any dark feelings, by claiming an active stance toward their treatment ...

2.   Structuring protective disclosures

Structuring protective disclosures includes using the following four strategies: 1) invoking the assistance of others, 2) setting the stage, 3) building progressive clues and 4) selective informing ...

The categories in Box 7.1 are straightforward and their ordering makes sense. They cover experiences that spark readers to make comparisons. Everyone has had to make problematic disclosures of some sort. Assess your readers' familiarity with analogous experiences and understanding of the categories. Then decide whether to dispense with the formal titling and treatment of each category. Box 7.2 shows how the categories collapsed in the published version.

BOX 7.2 THE PUBLISHED VERSION OF THE MEMO ON DISCLOSURE

Dilemmas of Disclosing Illness

Chronically ill people often wonder what they **should** tell and what they **need** to tell others about their illnesses ...

Avoiding Disclosure

Given the potential costs, avoiding disclosure entirely can be a natural response to illness ...

Potential Losses and Risks

In addition to the ultimate risks of losing acceptance and autonomy, ill people face immediate interactional risks: 1) being rejected and stigmatized for disclosing and for having an illness, 2) being unable to handle others' responses, and 3) losing control over their emotions ...

Forms of Telling

Telling means relating thoughts, actions, or feelings with sufficient clarity to be understandable. Telling usually includes announcing and recounting professionals' accounts of one's illness and prognosis. Because disclosing represents a subjective form of telling, the person's experiencing, feeling self is brought into the foreground. Private views of self and personal concerns seldom made public in middle-class American life may emerge ... (Charmaz, 1991a, pp. 109–119)

Use your categories as tools to build context. Make every subcategory fit under your major headings. Then think about including your subcategory titles. Carefully crafted grounded theory categories work well as signposts for student papers and professional journals. Social science and professional journal articles include multiple signposts. Essays have fewer, if any, formal breaks. A copy editor may delete all the subheadings in one quick read. As signposts disappear, the narrative style changes. A straightforward scientific style recedes and a more literary style evolves. Ensure that whatever categories you use as signposts earn their way into the narrative.

Categories don't work well when they are general or obvious. Why bother including them? By this time, you should be able to dispense with everything that strays from your purpose. Fewer, but novel, categories give you writing power and become concepts that readers will remember.

Consider including only those subcategories as explicit headings that explain new ideas. Keep the ideas but subjugate them to the main heading or purpose. At this point, think about whether including diagrams will clarify your analysis and argument for your reader. As we shift from analytic writing to communicating with an audience, what we need to do for ourselves as writers and analysts differs from what we need to write for our audience. You may collapse subcategories, condense descriptions, and dispense with obvious statements but add a diagram to pinpoint the conceptual relations that are abundantly clear to you but not to the reader.

> As we shift from analytic writing to communicating with an audience, what we need to do for ourselves as writers and analysts differs from what we need to write for our audience.

When we include all our subcategories, our voices grow ponderous and our writing, stilted. Yes, we may generate subcategory after subcategory to handle the work. But handling the work is not the same as writing to and for our readers. Think about what it would be like to read an analysis with every axial code carefully articulated.

A caveat. Making subcategories into explicit subheadings is useful when on unfamiliar terrain. Unconventional ideas and abstract conceptual schemes require more signposts. For example, we do not have a developed language to talk about experiencing time. Thus, I refused to let the copy editor automatically remove the subheadings (and the managing editor agreed). The following subheadings not only serve as signposts, but also show how chronically ill people relate to time. These subheadings serve as conceptual categories and ground the analysis in contexts and actions.

Illness as a Timemarker
Many people use illness to mark time and to divide periods of their lives (Roth, 1963). They celebrate certain markers as anniversaries to note a positive change. Markers can also be cast as comparative anchor points for measuring illness, health, and self ...

Creating a Chronology
Ill people note how the time within periods of their lives directly relates to self. Their illness chronologies render their experiences more comprehensible. They draw upon their chronologies to help them explain what had happened, why they got worse, or better, and what illness meant to them ...

Establishing Markers
What are the benchmarks of time? Why do some events stand out forever and others blur into the past ...?

Markers as Measures
When people mark time by illness, what do the markers mean? What lies between the marked events? By comparing views of self in illness with other views of self, one can measure the present self. Measures can be taken of how 'sick' or 'well' the person is. Similarly, marking time prospectively takes a different cast than finding retrospective markers ... (Charmaz, 1991a, pp. 198–206)

Use your major categories for headings of sections. Grounded theory gives you a decided advantage when developing a completed report. Your categories ground readers in your topic and direct them through your analysis. They foreshadow the content and emphasize the logic of the piece. Action categories involve readers much more than 'Findings' or 'Analysis of Data.' If you must adopt a traditional quantitative research format, then include standard sections early in the report: 'Introduction,' 'Review of the Literature,' 'Theoretical Framework' and 'Methods and Data.' When you have done admirable work in these areas, you have

> Use your major categories for headings of sections. Grounded theory gives you a decided advantage when developing a completed report. Your categories ground readers in your topic and direct them through your analysis. They foreshadow the content and emphasize the logic of the piece.

built a solid foundation for your analysis—and earned some latitude. Take full advantage of it. Showcase the analysis section with *your* categories and make it the most compelling—and lengthiest—section of your report.

Returning to the Library: Literature Reviews and Theoretical Frameworks

What happens when you return to the library to write your literature review and theoretical framework? Do you envision an objective scholar who labours over the materials to present an impartial analysis? Although scholars may don a cloak of objectivity, research and writing are inherently ideological activities. The literature review and theoretical frameworks are ideological sites in which you claim, locate, evaluate, and defend your position (see also Holliday, 2002). These two parts of your report should contain much more than summaries. Instead, show why you favor certain arguments, what evidence you accept and reject, and how you arrived at considered

> Although scholars may don a cloak of objectivity, research and writing are inherently ideological activities. The literature review and theoretical frameworks are ideological sites in which you claim, locate, evaluate, and defend your position (see also Holliday, 2002).

decisions. What do you need to take into account? How do you go about it?

Start with the formal requirements and informal traditions that shape your task. Lines often blur between a literature review and a theoretical framework. Whether you make sharp distinctions between them depends on the task at hand and its requirements. Student research projects at all levels typically require both a literature review and theoretical framework. Other tasks take varied forms. In most disciplines, a book differs from a dissertation. A research report for a funding agency diverges from books and dissertations. A journal article may draw on all the chapters in a thesis, but not replicate any one chapter. A chapter in a collection may take still another form.

Disciplines and genres also shape how, where, and to what extent you 'review' the literature and 'use' extant theories. Departments and advisors vary in their requirements for covering the literature and theoretical framework. One department's thesis requirements may demand lengthy separate chapters for each; another may ask students to weave the research literature and theoretical arguments throughout their analyses.

If you plan to submit your grounded theory for publication, first take note of where related studies appear. Next take a careful look at these journals and publishers. Their editorial policies can help you judge each editor's potential interest in your study. You can find these policies in journal editors' statements at the beginning of their editorial terms and in guidelines in the journal. Publishing houses often post them on their websites. It helps to study related articles or books for their substantive topics, analytic style and level, research approaches, and audiences. After assessing editorial policies and practices and evaluating authors' works, you can choose several potential outlets for your work. Examine how authors review the literature and write the theoretical framework in your targeted journals or publisher's lists. Study the rhetorical style of the best authors but develop your own style.

The best writers may not be the most well-known scholars. Once a scholar has an established reputation, an editor may accept his or her work despite less than stellar writing. That said, some senior scholars have honed their skills and write with clarity, grace, and style. Their work evinces none of the tortuous jargon and convoluted sentences of their junior colleagues (Derricourt, 1996). These authors merit close attention for their writing as well as for their ideas because the scale for writing has shifted upward over the past four decades and differentially affects newer authors. Choose your writing role models well.

When you plan to submit your work for external review, use the acceptable substantive conventions and manuscript style for your targeted journal, or publisher. Published works differ by disciplines in how authors treat topics and organize narratives. One discipline may valorize exhaustive coverage of preceding literatures; another may emphasize a succinct and limited survey. One publisher may ask you to acknowledge relevant works throughout a chapter; another may expect you to use notes at the end. Articles for many scholarly journals include citations with little discussion of most works. Some journal policies forbid endnotes but assume authors will have numerous citations. Coverage of the literature may appear in the introduction. Preceding chapters in a book may form the foundation for a discussion of extant theories that appears after the analysis rather than before it.

Do varied styles leave you with endless choices? No. Draft your literature review and theoretical framework *in relation to your grounded theory*. You can use it to direct how you critique earlier studies and theories and to make comparisons with these materials. Aim to get your ideas out in clear statements. Then revise the sections to fit your specific task. Write for your audience and professional standards *after* you have developed your analysis.

> Draft your literature review and theoretical framework *in relation to your grounded theory*. You can use it to direct how you critique earlier studies and theories and to make comparisons with these materials.

The constant comparative method in grounded theory does not end with completion of your data analysis. The literature review and theoretical framework can serve as valuable sources of comparison and analysis. Through comparing other scholars' evidence and ideas with your grounded theory, you may show where and how their ideas illuminate your theoretical categories and how your theory extends, transcends, or challenges dominant ideas in your field.

The Disputed Literature Review

When should you delve into the literature? How do you go about doing it? What do you need to cover? The place of the literature review in grounded theory research has long been both disputed and misunderstood. Recall that classic grounded theorists (Glaser & Strauss, 1967; Glaser, 1978) advocate delaying the literature review until after completing the analysis. They do not want you to see your data through the lens of earlier ideas, often known as 'received theory.'

Glaser and Strauss raise a valuable although problematic point. Not uncommonly, teachers judge students by how well they recite key theories in their fields. Some graduate departments expect students to produce dissertations that demonstrate their competence in working out applications of well-established theories and methods. Period. Novices may become enthralled with other people's ideas; established scholars may become enamored with their own. In either case, scholars old and new may force their data into pre-existing categories. The intended purpose of delaying the literature review is to avoid importing preconceived ideas and imposing them on your work. Delaying the review encourages you to articulate *your* ideas.

In their battle to free new scholars from the shackles of old ideas, Glaser and Strauss either overstated their position or differed on it. For Strauss, key points in the *Discovery* book were rhetorical.[3] Strauss and Corbin (1990) clarify their position by saying, 'We all bring to the inquiry a considerable background in professional and disciplinary literature' (p. 48). Glaser's (1992, 1998) position on prior knowledge is somewhat ambiguous. He continues to imply that grounded theorists can and should keep themselves uncontaminated by extant ideas. Yet in *Theoretical Sensitivity* (1978), Glaser speaks to possessing prior knowledge in his discussion of theoretical codes. He writes, 'It is necessary for the grounded theorist to know many theoretical codes in order to be sensitive to rendering explicitly the subtleties of the relationships in his data' (p. 72). How do we know these codes if they have not become part of our repertoire? And if they have, would we not know something of the major works from which they are derived?

Other scholars have rejected Glaser and Strauss's original pronouncement and continue to do so. For example, Bulmer (1979), Dey (1999), and Layder (1998) assume that Glaser and perhaps Strauss naively viewed the researcher as a *tabula rasa*. Despite the early works, not all grounded theorists share this view. Karen Henwood and Nick Pidgeon's (2003: 138) apt term 'theoretical agnosticism' provides a useful stance to take throughout the research process.

They argue that researchers should take a critical stance toward earlier theories. Their stance is congruent with Glaser's (1978) position of requiring extant concepts to earn their way into your narrative. Consider treating extant concepts as problematic and then look for the extent to which their characteristics are lived and understood, not as given in textbooks.

Requirements for a research or grant proposal probably led you to the library months before you conducted your study. The proposal demanded a sophisticated knowledge of leading studies and theories in your field. If so, you can let this material lie fallow until after you have developed your categories and the analytic relationships between them. Then begin locating your work within the relevant literatures. Since you began your study, you may have traveled to new substantive terrain and scaled unimagined theoretical heights. If need be, satisfy your teachers by outlining your path but first attend to writing your grounded theory.

Delaying the literature review differs from writing a scanty one. Nor does delaying it excuse careless coverage. Some grounded theorists' statements or inattention reflect a cavalier attitude toward earlier works. Certain scholars loathe acknowledging their colleagues' competing ideas—or any crucial ideas—that might undermine their stance. Still others cite competitors' lesser works instead of their most significant contributions. Lazy scholars fail to cite the most significant points of convergence and divergence. Give earlier works their due. Completing a thorough, sharply focused literature review strengthens your argument—and your credibility. For grounded theorists, writing a thorough but focused literature review often means going across fields and disciplines (for excellent examples see Baszanger, 1998; Casper, 1998; Clarke, 1998, 2005; Wiener, 2000).

Many research reports require a standard—rigid—format. The trick is to use it without letting it stifle your creativity or strangle your theory. The literature review can serve as an opportunity to set the stage for what *you* do in subsequent sections or chapters. Analyze the most significant works in relation to what you addressed in your now developed grounded theory. *Assess* and *critique* the literature from this vantage point. Your literature review can do more work for you than merely list, summarize, and synthesize major works.

Key points from the literature and earlier theories often appear in the introduction of an article or report. In the introduction to her article 'The other side of help: the negative effects of help-seeking processes of abused women,' Lora Bex Lempert addresses key studies in the literature, presents her argument, and juxtaposes it against earlier theories. The following excerpt illustrates her logic:

> In this article I offer an examination of some significant social actions that abused women take to access help from informal network resources, initially to preserve their relationships and later to leave them. Collective representations of 'wife abuse' reduce such relationships to acts of violence and hold that abused women should resolve the problem of their abuse by leaving their abusing mates (Loseke, 1992). Abused women, however, hold much more complex interpretations of their mates and their relationships.

They believe in their partners as their primary sources of love and affection and, simultaneously, as the most dangerous persons in their lives (Walker, 1979; Lempert, 1995). It is this simultaneity that must be grasped analytically to understand when, why, and how abused women seek help to cope with, change, and/or leave their relationships.

Theories developed to explain 'domestic violence' and/or 'wife abuse' have contributed to an understanding of the whole of the complex dynamic (see Walker, 1979, 1989 on psychosocial cycle of violence theory; Straus, Gelles & Steinmetz, 1980 for culture of violence theory; Pagelow, 1984 for social learning theory; Giles-Sims (1983) for general systems theory; Dobash & Dobash, 1979 and Martin, 1976 for conflict theory; Straus 1977 for intimate resource theory); MacKinnon, 1993 for eroticization of violence theory). Yet none is complete.

With few exceptions (Dobash & Dobash, 1981; Ferraro & Johnson, 1983; Mills, 1985; Loseke, 1987; Chang, 1989), researchers on wife abuse have focused on what women in violent relationships *do* rather than *how* abused women interpret the violent actions, or events, and *how* those meaning-making interpretations affect their help-seeking process. Most of the research on battered women's help-seeking has focused on formal agencies, primarily police and medical responses (or lack thereof) and community shelters (Berk et al., 1983, 1984; Berk & Loseke, 1980/81; Bowker & Maurer, 1987; Edwards, 1987; Ferraro, 1987, 1989; Schechter, 1982; Stark & Flitcraft, 1983, 1988; Loseke, 1992). My analysis has as its fundamental focus the informal help-seeking overtures of women in abusive relationships, that is, within the contradictory, but simultaneous contexts of love and violence, and it includes the unanticipated consequences of these overtures. By directing analytic attention to some negative effects of well-intentioned assistance efforts, this work extends the reports of previous researchers and highlights both help-seeking processes and their unanticipated consequences. It further calls attention to the ways that binary divisions of either/or logic impede both the help-seeking and the help-provision processes. (1997: 290–291)

Engaging the literature goes beyond a short section of a paper or a chapter of a thesis. Weave your discussion of it throughout the piece. A required section or chapter compels you to lay the foundation for this discussion. You might treat it as a challenge to do the following:

- Clarify your ideas
- Make intriguing comparisons
- Invite your reader to begin a theoretical discussion
- Show how and where your work fits or extends relevant literatures.

Subsequently, you create a dialog and enter the current conversations in your field (see also Silverman, 2000). Becoming part of a sophisticated conversation in a substantive area signifies that your readers can view you as a serious scholar.

BOX 7.3   WRITING THE LITERATURE REVIEW

A literature review provides a place to engage the ideas and research in the areas that your grounded theory addresses. It also serves as a way to evaluate your grasp of these areas. A literature review gives *you* the opportunity to fulfill the following objectives:

- To demonstrate your grasp of relevant works
- To show your skill in identifying and discussing the most significant ideas and findings in these works
- To prompt you to make explicit and compelling connections between your study and earlier studies
- To permit you to make claims from your grounded theory

Use the literature review to analyze relevant works in relation to your specific research problem and now developed grounded theory. Use the literature review to do the following tasks:

- Enlist your conceptual argument to frame, integrate, and assess the literature
- *Evaluate* earlier studies
- Specify who did what, when and why, and how they did it
- Reveal *gaps* in extant knowledge and state how your grounded theory answers them
- Position your study and clarify its contribution.

Instead of summarizing, argue why readers must examine the cited works—in relation to your objectives for the report. How exhaustive the literature review needs to be depends on the requirements of your task. In any case, engage the leading works—whether or not they support your grounded theory and show points of divergence as well as convergence. Think about showing how your work transcends specific works later in the conclusion. Craft a pertinent and focused literature review. An exhaustive literature review does not mean an endless list of summaries. Should your teacher or department expect an exhaustive literature review, focus and organize your remarks. Again, use your grounded theory to organize how you frame the review.

Think beyond the immediate substantive area to connections with other areas. Make the most of your innovative analytic contributions. Also take the opportunity to contribute a fresh topic, study a new group of research participants, or create new methods.

Writing the Theoretical Framework

How can a grounded theorist who conducted an inductive study write a required theoretical framework? Might not this framework clutter rather than clarify? Perhaps. Would not such a framework imply that you used deductive logic? Not necessarily. You might balk, then stumble over the theoretical framework. Rather than stumble, use it to provide an anchor for your reader and to demonstrate how your grounded theory *refines*, *extends*, *challenges* or *supercedes* extant concepts. Thus, a theoretical framework does more than announce and summarize the conceptual underpinnings of the manuscript.

Theoretical frameworks differ in grounded theory from traditional quantitative research. We do not use theories for deducing specific hypotheses before data-gathering. Symbolic interactionist concepts happen to inform my worldview. Thus, these concepts influence what I see and how I see it, similar to how other researchers' perspectives influence them. However, these concepts remain in the background until they become relevant for immediate analytic problems.

Your argument tells how you want readers to think about your analysis. The theoretical framework locates the specific argument that you make. Here, how you use and develop a theoretical framework takes a new twist: it emerges from your analysis and argument about it. In contrast, researchers who use a traditional quantitative design invoke an established theory and deduce hypotheses from it before conducting their studies. For them, the theory to use in their theoretical framework is already there.

> Your argument tells how you want readers to think about your analysis. The theoretical framework locates the specific argument that you make.

In contrast, in a grounded theory study you put your sensitizing concepts and theoretical codes to work in the theoretical framework. These concepts and codes locate your manuscript in relevant disciplines and discourses. Sensitizing concepts account for your starting point. Theoretical codes can help you explain how you conceptualize the arrangement of key ideas.

Write a sound theoretical framework that serves your grounded theory. How might you go about it? Think about using the theoretical framework to:

- Explicate your conceptual logic and direction(s)
- Engage leading ideas
- Acknowledge prior theoretical works
- Position your new grounded theory in relation to these theories
- Explain the significance of your original concepts
- Fit your immediate writing task and readers.

Theoretical frameworks are not all alike. They need to fit your intended audience and to fulfill the task at hand. What you need to write for one journal, for example, can differ from another. I wrote the theoretical framework below for an article for *The Sociological Quarterly*, a journal whose readers are well schooled in symbolic interactionist social psychology. This theoretical framework takes into account relationships between body, self, and identity for adapting to illness and disability.

Theoretical Framework

This article takes a symbolic interactionist perspective on identity (Blumer, 1969; Cooley, 1902; Lindesmith, Strauss, & Denzin, 1988; Mead, 1934; and Strauss, 1959) and builds upon the emerging literature on the body (DiGiacomo, 1992; Frank, 1990; 1991a; 1991b; Frankenberg, 1990; Freund,

1982; 1988; 1990; Gadow, 1982; Glassner, 1988; 1989; Kotarba, 1994; Olesen, 1994; Olesen, Schatzman, Droes, Hatton & Chico, 1990; Sanders, 1990; Scheper-Hughes & Lock, 1987; Zola, 1982; 1991). I draw upon the philosopher Sally Gadow's (1982) clarification of the relation between body and self and on my earlier work on the self in chronic illness (Charmaz, 1991[a]) and the effects of loss upon identity (Charmaz, 1987).

In keeping with symbolic interactionism, personal identity means the way an individual defines, locates, and differentiates self from others (see Hewitt, 1992). Following Peter Burke (1980), the concept of identity implicitly takes into account the ways people *wish* to define themselves. Wishes are founded on feelings as well as thoughts. If possible, ill people usually try to turn their wishes into intentions, purposes, and actions. Thus, they are motivated to realize future identities, and are sometimes forced to acknowledge present ones. However implicitly, they form identity goals. Here, I define identity goals as *preferred identities* that people assume, desire, hope, or plan for (Charmaz, 1987). The concept of identity goals assumes that human beings create meanings and act purposefully as they interpret their experience and interact within the world. Some people's identity goals are implicit, unstated, and understood; other people have explicit preferred identities. Like other categories of people, some individuals with chronic illnesses assume that they will realize their preferred identities; others keep a watchful eye on their future selves and emerging identities as they experience the present (see also, Radley & Green, 1987).

Gadow (1982) assumes that human existence essentially means embodiment and that the self is inseparable from the body. I agree. Mind and consciousness depend upon being in a body. In turn, bodily feelings affect mind and consciousness. Yet, as Gadow points out, body and self, although inseparable, are not identical. The relation between body and self becomes particularly problematic for those chronically ill people who realize that they have suffered lasting bodily losses. The problematic nature of such realizations intensifies for ill people who had previously pursued and preserved an endless youth through controlling and constructing their bodies (Turner, 1992). Thus, meanings of loss are embedded in assumptions and discourses about the body. Not only do individuals assume bodily control through rational practices, but they also assume their practices achieve and, quite literally, embody individualism (Shilling, 1993).

As Victor Kestenbaum (1982) observes, illness threatens a person's sense of integrity of self and the body and of self and the world. People who have serious chronic illnesses find progressive losses repeatedly threaten their body and self-integrity. They risk becoming socially identified and self-defined exclusively by their impaired bodies (Bury, 1988; Goffman, 1963; Locker, 1983; MacDonald, 1988). Thus, chronically ill people who move beyond loss and transcend stigmatizing negative labels define themselves as much more than their bodies and as much more than an illness (Charmaz, 1991[a]).

Gadow argues that illness and aging result in loss of the original unity of body and self and provide the means of recovering it at a new level. She assumes that an original unity existed and implies that loss and recovery of unity is a single process. However, what unity means can only be defined subjectively. Some people may not have defined themselves as having experienced such unity before illness, or as only having partially experienced it. Further, with each new and often unsuspected bodily impairment, people with chronic illnesses *repeatedly* experience loss of whatever unity between body and self they had previously defined or accepted. Thus, at each point when they suffer and define loss, identity questions and identity changes can emerge or reoccur. Throughout this article, I deal with the loss of body–self unity and its recovery through acknowledging bodily experience and opening oneself to the quest for harmony between body and self.

In order to understand how loss and recovery of body–self unity occurs, we must understand ill people's meanings of their bodily experiences and the social contexts in which they occur (Fabrega & Manning, 1972; Gerhardt, 1979; Radley & Green, 1987; Zola, 1991). Such meanings arise in dialectical relation to their biographies (Bury, 1982; 1988; 1991; Corbin & Strauss, 1987; 1988; Dingwall, 1976; Gerhardt, 1989; Radley, 1989; Radley & Green, 1987; Williams, 1984) and are mediated by their interpretations of ongoing experiences. Consistent with symbolic interactionist social psychology, present meanings of the ill body and self develop from, but are not determined by, past discourses of meaning and present social identifications (Blumer, 1969; Goffman, 1963; Mead, 1934).

As chronic illness encroaches upon life, people learn that it erodes their taken-for-granted preferred identities as well as their health. Further, they may discover that visible illness and disability can leave them with a master status and overriding stigmatized identity. Because of their physical losses, they reassess who they are and who they can become. Subsequently, they form identity goals as they try to reconstruct normal lives to whatever extent possible (Charmaz, 1987; 1991[a]). Frequently, people with chronic illnesses initially plan and expect to resume their lives unaffected by illness, or even to exceed their prior identity goals. As they test their bodies and themselves, ill people need to make identity trade-offs at certain points, or even to lower their identity goals systematically until they match their lessened capacities. At other times, they may gradually raise their hopes and progressively increase their identity goals when they meet with success. Therefore, both raised or lowered identity goals form an implicit identity hierarchy that ill people create as they adapt to bodily loss and change (Charmaz, 1987). (Charmaz, 1995a: 659–660)

Note that I engaged Sally Gadow's (1982) arguments directly. They are central to my argument and the analysis that follows. Gadow's philosophical argument provides one fundamental source for understanding what I try to do in the article; symbolic interactionist social psychology provides another. Because readers of *The Sociological Quarterly* already understand symbolic interactionist theories of the self, I acknowledge significant works but do not need to explain them. The amount and depth of explanation you give in a published article depends on the journal and its readers. A class project or thesis remains an entirely different matter. Rather than writing for a reader who shares your knowledge, you must prove that you can explain, critique, and use extant theories.

Think about using the theoretical framework to inform a specific argument in a particular piece of work—rather than your entire research project. You may have several papers with different arguments. For that matter, you may construct several grounded theories that begin with the same data. Sally Gadow's ideas became significant as I worked out ideas about 'adapting to impairment.' Gadow and I both take bodily experience as real and as tied to self. My argument extends Gadow by emphasizing personal meaning, repeated loss and regaining of body–self unity, and reconstruction of identity within an implicit identity hierarchy.

Rendering through Writing

Writing reflects the choices authors make. Grounded theorists' writing style typically relies on conventional reporting. Researchers record their grounded theories and recount 'facts' to support them. However, you can broaden the range of possibilities—and publishing venues—by attending to your writing. As Laurel Richardson (1990) declares, writing matters.[4] You can make use of those rhetorical devices and writing strategies that mirror how you constructed your grounded theory. Taking this tactic can help you advance your grounded theory and enhance the power of your writing. Several strategies and examples may help.

Go beyond an analysis of acts and facts. Think about what is relevant but lurks in the background of your analysis. Cultural context? Historical antecedents? Organizational climate? Emotional ambiance? See how rendering it explicitly in the text affects your writing—and moves your analysis beyond reporting. In my studies, the gamut of emotions shades scenes and statements. Thus, I evoke experiential feeling through rendering it in writing—*as part of the analysis and evidence.* This strategy includes taking the reader into a story and imparting its mood through linguistic style and narrative exposition. Such approaches set your writing apart from typical scientific format without transforming it into fiction, drama, or poetry. I framed key definitions and distinctions in words that reproduced the tempo and mood of the experience:

> *Existing* from day to day occurs when a person plummets into continued crises that rip life apart (Charmaz, 1991a: 185)

> Others wait to map a future. And wait. They monitor their bodies and their lives. They look for signs to indicate what steps to take next. They map a future or move to the next point on the map only when they feel assured that the worst of their illness is over. These people map a future or move to the next point when they feel distant enough from illness to release their emotions from it. (p. 191)

Analogies and metaphors can explicate tacit meanings and feelings subsumed within a category (see also Charmaz & Mitchell, 1996; Richardson, 1994). In the first excerpt below, I wanted the reader to sense the constraints that certain chronically ill people experience. In the second excerpt, I aimed to impart how the duration of time felt.

Such men and women feel coerced into living one day at a time. They force it upon themselves, almost with clenched teeth. Here, living one day at a time resembles learning an unfamiliar, disagreeable lesson in grammar school; it is an unwelcome prerequisite to staying alive. (1991a: 179)

Drifting time, in contrast [to dragging time], spreads out. Like a fan, drifting time unfolds and expands during a serious immersion in illness. (p. 91)

Simple language and straightforward ideas make theory readable. Again, the extent to which you use these devices depends on your writing task and audience. For a department that expects you to write books, not dissertations, adopting these strategies expedites your work. For a spare theoretical article, use fewer of them. Whether the theory remains embedded in the narrative or stands out in bold relief depends on your task and your rendering of it. A theory becomes more accessible but less identifiable as theory when woven into the narrative.

Several other strategies foster making your writing accessible. Catching experiential rhythm and timing allows reproducing it within the writing:

From embarrassment to mortification. From discomfort to pain. Endless uncertainty. What follows? Regimentation. (p. 134)

Days slip by. The same day keeps slipping by. Durations of time lengthen since few events break up the day, week, or month. Illness seems like one long, uninterrupted duration of time. (p. 88)

Unexpected definitions and assertions can catch readers' attention.

The language of habit is silent. (Charmaz, 2002b: 31S)

Grounded theory served at the front of the 'qualitative revolution' (Denzin & Lincoln, 1994, p. ix). (Charmaz, 2000a: 509)

Questions help tie main ideas together or redirect the reader. Rhetorical questions quicken the pace and focus subsequent points. You can also use questions in novel ways. Consider adopting the role or standpoint of your readers or research participants and ask questions as they would.

Is it cancer? Could it be angina? Pangs of uncertainty spring up when current, frequently undiagnosed, symptoms could mean a serious chronic illness. (Charmaz, 1991a: 32)

Try to balance the logic of exposition with the logic of the theorized experience. Writers use a linear logic to organize their analyses and to make experience understandable. Yet experience is neither necessarily linear, nor always conveniently demarcated with clear boundaries. For example, experiencing illness, much less all its spiraling consequences, does not always fit neatly into one linear progressive process. Earlier grounded theory works (Glaser & Strauss, 1967; Glaser, 1978) stress discovering and analyzing *a* basic process, which may not work for you.

Consider the pacing and tone of your piece. Think about how and when you need to alter them. Set the tone as you lead the reader into the topic. Provide evidence that fits your tone as well as your point. The following excerpt opens a chapter titled 'Intrusive Illness.' I aimed to show how symptoms and impairment encroach on daily life and could not be easily dismissed. Research participants like John Garston identified 'good' days and 'bad days' at this point. He said,

> What's a good day now? There is no good day … Well, a good day now is sort of a neutral day. That's you know, there are never days when I have … almost never when I have lots of energy and runaround! … I really don't pay that much attention [to my body], and never have. I do pay more attention now because I am limited [by severe emphysema]. … I don't know if you could say I monitor; I observe [*laughs*]. Yeah, I'm forced to observe it. (Charmaz, 1991a: 41)

For grounded theorists, a story does not stand on its own. Instead, we use stories in service of our analyses. The power of a piece rests on the scope, incisiveness, and usefulness of the analysis. My analytic statement about a 'good' day reads:

> A good day means minimal intrusiveness of illness, maximal control over mind, body, and actions, and greater choice of activities. Ill people concentrate minimally, if at all, on symptoms and regimen during a good day, or they handle them smoothly and efficiently. Illness remains in the background of their lives. Spatial and temporal horizons expand and may even become expansive during a good day. When illness abates, people have much better days. Like ex-convicts just released from jail, they may wish to make up for lost time all at once. (p. 50)

Note how John Garston's frank statement sets the tone for the analysis, complements the incisiveness of the analysis, and provides a counterpoint to the rhythm of my authorial voice. The category 'a "good" day' was embedded in the larger analysis of experiencing an intrusive illness and juxtaposed against 'a bad day.' The analytic positioning of 'a "good" day' allowed me to stretch the distance between John's statement and its theoretical explanation. Think about places where you have latitude in contrast with those in which you need the empirical evidence right there.

Now consider a note about the writer's voice. I have noted in previous chapters that the analytic emphasis in grounded theory can lead to silent authorship replete with assumed neutrality, objectivist pretensions, and an absent author (Charmaz & Mitchell, 1996). Yet, completed grounded theories need not be voiceless, objectified recordings. We can weave our points of view into the text and portray a sense of wonder, imagery, and drama.

My examples above suggest that even grounded theorists do not have to write as disembodied technicians. We can bring evocative writing into our narratives. In the excerpts above, my voice pervades the passages and persuades the reader although I remain in the background as an interpreter of scenes and situations (see also Charmaz & Mitchell, 1996). Writers' rendering of experience becomes their own through word choice, tone, and rhythm. Voice echoes the researcher's involvement with the studied phenomena; it does not reproduce the phenomena. Yet through struggling with representing our research participants' experience we may find the collective in the subjective.

Listen to the difference between the following two passages:

> *Identity levels* are implicit or explicit objectives for personal and/or social identity that chronically ill people aim to realize. These identity levels reflect the kind of selves they wish to shape or select, their preferred identities. Hence, realizing them negates or overrides identifications derived from illness. The efforts of these chronically ill people to construct preferred identities emerged out of their experience as *ill individuals.* Almost none of my respondents derived their identity objectives from any organized group of similar others (cf. Anspach [2]). These ill persons then constructed their identity levels in relationship to their hopes, desires, or dreams juxtaposed with their expectations and definitions of their specific circumstances. Hence, particular individuals aimed toward different preferred identities representing different identity levels during specific phases in their illnesses and at particular points in their biographies. (Charmaz, 1987: 286–287)

> Through struggle and surrender, ill people paradoxically grow more resolute in self as they adapt to impairment. They suffer bodily losses but gain themselves. Their odyssey leads them to a deeper level of awareness—of self, of situation, of their place with others. They believe in their inner strength as their bodies crumble. They transcend their bodies as they surrender control. The self is of the body yet beyond it. With this stance comes a sense of resolution and an awareness of timing. Ill people grasp when to struggle and when to flow into surrender. They grow impervious to social meanings, including being devalued. They can face the unknown without fear while remaining themselves. At this point, chronically ill people may find themselves in the ironic position of giving solace and comfort to the healthy. They gain pride in knowing that their selves have been put to test—a test of character, resourcefulness, and will. They know they gave themselves to their struggles and lived their loss with courage.
>
> Yet the odyssey seldom remains a single journey for these chronically ill people. Frequently, they repeat their journey on the same terrain over and over and, also, find themselves transported to unplanned side trips and held captives within hostile territories as they experience setbacks, flare-ups, complications, and secondary conditions. Still they may discover that each part of their odyssey not only poses barriers, but also brings possibilities for resolution and renewal. (Charmaz, 1995a: 675)

In which passage did you hear a human voice? Which one was loaded with disciplinary codes? Of which would you want to hear more? By taking the first quote out of context, I'm not being quite fair to me. This quote begins with introducing my grounded theory concepts and sets the stage for what follows. I next spell out identity levels in the identity hierarchy–supernormal social identity, restored self, contingent personal identity and a salvaged self. These categories arrest the reader's attention more than the larger theoretical frame from which I yanked the excerpt. Again the second passage is out of context. Rather than comparing the two theoretical sections that draw upon the same concepts, I took the second passage from the ending. Writers are not always fair to other writers, even themselves. But the point remains: the sound of a human voice makes for compelling reading.

Concluding Thoughts

Writing is a social process. Draw upon friends and colleagues but write for yourself and your grounded theory first. You are now the expert; the theory is yours. Let the voices of teachers and earlier researchers grow faint while you compose the manuscript. Once you have drafted your core ideas, bring these voices back. Ask your mentors and close colleagues for constructive critiques. Enlist their help before you submit your manuscript for review—whether it is your thesis or an article. Then be willing to rethink, revise, and rework the entire manuscript according to your critical appraisal of their comments. That means more than cosmetic tinkering. It may mean reframing central points. A mentor, for example, may raise a serious criticism with which you disagree. Think about what sparked this criticism as well as its content. Quite possibly, vague statements, over-generalizations, or logical gaps weakened your argument and flashed caution lights to your mentor who may not see beyond them. You can fix such problems and avert delays and later disappointments, particularly at the stage of publication submission. One common reason for rejection of studies with solid data and interesting ideas stands out: too early submission.

By entertaining early critiques and revising your manuscript, you can submit a polished piece of work that makes your grounded theory shine. Each revision can make your manuscript stronger, sharper, and more compelling. As you think about each draft, the criteria in the next chapter, 'Reflecting on the Process' may help you develop your manuscript and anticipate reviewers' concerns. In the meantime, enjoy the discoveries you make along the way.

NOTES

1 Any rendering of meaning is an interpretive one. We cannot know what goes on in people's heads, but we can offer our interpretations of what they say and do.

2 Adele Clarke observes that ten or more revisions are common (personal communication, December 22, 2004). A writing teacher once told me that she made it a practice not to share her unpublished work for informal comments until after the fourth draft.

3 I base this point on many conversations and interviews I had with Strauss, who assumed that grounded theorists had prior lives and knowledge before embarking on their research. See also (Charmaz, 1983).

4 Glaser (2001: 80) reminds readers that 'GT gets known and remembered on its conceptual ideas. No one remembers how it was written.' Speaking as a former editor, I see Glaser as correct on the first point and wrong on the second. The best—and worst— writers and writing become part of disciplinary lore.

8 Reflecting on the Research Process

We end our journey by looking back on the steps we have taken and by looking forward to assess the impact of our grounded theory. Questions arise as to what stands as grounded theory and when it is an evolving method and when it is something else. A definition of grounded theory that takes into account methodological developments over the past half century holds vast potential for advancing knowledge. Grounded theory gives us analytic tools and methodological strategies that we can adopt without endorsing a prescribed theory of knowledge or view of reality. To begin to broaden the scope of grounded theory, I call for returning to its pragmatist roots and for making committed inquiry our goal for future research journeys.

This chapter ends our journey through the research process. Along the way, we have gathered data, stopped, and categorized them through coding. Subsequently we cut new analytic paths through memo-writing. We widened our route by conducting theoretical sampling, and specified directions for our grounded theorizing through sorting and integrating our categories. Last, we explored ways of imparting what we have learned through writing. What sense do we make of our journey? How do we evaluate our completed grounded theory? Where does the grounded theory method take us? To place these questions into perspective, we need to look back at our journey through the preceding chapters.

The Core of Grounded Theory: Contested Versions and Revisions

While reflecting on your view of grounded theory, consider what constitutes grounded theory. Everyone 'knows' what grounded theory is all about; however, do they share definitions and basic assumptions? Over the year after its inception in 1967 the term grounded theory has been packed with multiple meanings, but also fraught by numerous misunderstandings, and complicated by competing versions. Discourse about grounded theory blurs distinctions between the method as process and the theory as product of that process. What stands as grounded theory? How do we define a finished work as a grounded theory? Which properties, objectives and strategies constitute the core of the method? What counts as an evolving grounded theory method and what irrevocably changes it?

Emerging Constructions of Grounded Theory Methods and Grounded Theories as Emergent Constructions

When we think about what defines the grounded theory method, we may consider a specific philosophical stance, a particular logic of inquiry, a set of procedures, or flexible guidelines. All these views imply that the defining properties of grounded theory reside in attributes external to the researcher and the research process. Yet finished grounded theories are emergent, the grounded theory method itself is open-ended and relies on emergent processes, and the researcher's emerging constructions of concepts shape both process and product.

I have argued throughout this book that the strength of grounded theory methods lies in their flexibility and that one must engage the method to make this flexibility real. Researchers can draw on the flexibility of grounded theory without transforming it into rigid prescriptions concerning data collection, analysis, theoretical leanings, and epistemological positions. Must grounded theory methods be tied to a single epistemology? I think not. Just as these grounded methods need not be tied to a single method of data collection, or emerge from a specific theoretical perspective, the methods need not be tied to a single epistemology.

We can use the tools of grounded theory methods without subscribing to a prescribed theory of knowledge or view of reality. We are not compelled to view grounded theory as discovering categories that inhere in data in an external world. Nor do we need to see grounded theory as an application of procedures. Rather, we can view grounded theories as products of emergent processes that occur through interaction. Researchers construct their respective products from the fabric of the interactions, both witnessed and lived. The following points summarize my constructivist stance:

- The grounded theory research process is fluid, interactive, and open-ended.
- The research problem informs initial methodological choices for data collection.
- Researchers are part of what they study, not separate from it.
- Grounded theory *analysis* shapes the conceptual content and direction of the study; the emerging analysis may lead to adopting multiple methods of data collection and to pursuing inquiry in several sites.
- Successive levels of abstraction through comparative analysis constitute the core of grounded theory analysis.
- Analytic directions arise from how researchers interact with and interpret their comparisons and emerging analyses rather than from external prescriptions.

The Union of Comparative Methods and Interaction in Grounded Theory

The grounded theory method depends on using constant comparative methods *and* your engagement. Both constitute the core of the method. Making comparisons between data, codes, and categories advances your conceptual understanding because you define analytic properties of your categories and then begin to treat these properties to rigorous scrutiny. Your analysis becomes more explicitly theoretical when you ask: Of what theoretical category are these data an instance? And to the extent that you interrogate relationships between your categories and fundamental aspects of human existence such as the nature of social bond or relationships between choice and constraint, individuals and institutions or actions and structures, your work becomes yet more theoretical.

Comparative methods lend you basic tools, yet myriad interactions occurring in multiple forms at various levels shape the content of your grounded theory. Ultimately, the emerging content shapes how you use the tools. Your grounded theory journey relies on *interaction*–emanating from your worldview, standpoints, and situations, arising in the research sites, developing between you and your data, emerging with your ideas, then returning back to the field– or another field, and moving on to conversations with your discipline and substantive fields. To interact at all, we make sense of our situations, appraise what occurs in them, and draw on language and culture to create meanings and frame actions. In short, interaction is interpretive.

True, some scholars have long worried about the interpretive nature of data collection in qualitative research. Quantitative researchers have raised questions about the reliability of qualitative data based on immediate interactions that lone, possibly biased, qualitative observers have recorded. Qualitative researchers who tried to meet these concerns scrambled to take a distanced stance toward their studies. Such concerns have spawned debates about the place of interpretation in the resulting analyses. Historically, qualitative researchers have paid less attention to the entire research process as interactive, perhaps because many were struggling to earn a rightful place in traditional quantitative scientific discourses and therefore aimed to be objective.

The cloak of objectivity enshrouding grounded theory of the past reduced visibility of its interactive strength. Enlisting grounded theory in a contemporary more reflexive mode, keeps you interacting with your data and emerging ideas. It does so in ways that foster making abstract interpretations. From your tentative interpretations in initial coding and memos to your finished project, grounded theory methods capture your fleeting thoughts and immediate questions and prompt you to give your ideas concrete form in analytic writing.

Certainly we can see continuities between these strengths and Glaser and Strauss's (1967) original statement of the logic of grounded theory. Their statement resonated with wide audiences that included diverse researchers of both social constructionist and objectivist allegiances. Glaser's (1978) version elaborated basic grounded theory strategies and expressed its positivistic, objectivist antecedents but spoke to fewer scholars. Strauss's (1987) and Strauss and Corbin's (1990, 1998) immensely successful and accessible version of grounded theory attracted wide audiences but made using it more technical and procedural.

The development of software programs presumably built on the method, simultaneously enhanced interest in it (see Fielding & Lee, 1998) and raised concerns about short-changing the analytic process, generating superficial analyses, and forcing qualitative research into a single method (Coffey, Holbrook, & Atkinson, 1996;

Lonkila, 1995). The comparative logic of earlier versions is less apparent in Strauss and Corbin's (1990, 1998) version of grounded theory, while their additional techniques make it more procedural and less clearly rooted in pragmatist philosophy than Glaser and Strauss's original statement or in Strauss's (1987) exegisis.

My emphasis on constructivism loosens grounded theory from its objectivist foundations. Critics may interpret either my or Strauss and Corbin's recent directions as advancing the method or diverging from it. Glaser views his current version as classic grounded theory; however, Glaser's approach has changed, too, as I noted in earlier chapters. Glaser has always advocated streamlining data collection through grounded theory guidelines. His defense of very small samples, however, appears to have stiffened despite the resulting tensions between limited data collection and comparing many cases, as he recommends. When thinking about what to study, however, Glaser (2001) made a significant shift in thinking from his earlier insistence (1992) that participants will inform the researcher about what is significant when he acknowledged that researchers may define a major concern that participants view as routine. This shift allows at least some interpretive possibilities and brings the grounded theorist into the research process. We stand *within* the research process rather than above, before, or outside it.

What Defines a Grounded Theory?

When we think about identifying defining properties of grounded theory, we enter ambiguous terrain. To what extent do the goal and focus of grounded theory analysis constitute its defining properties? From a constructivist view, researchers may use grounded theory methods to pursue varied *emergent* analytic goals and foci instead of pursuing a priori goals and foci such as a single basic social process.

If studying social processes once defined grounded theory methods but no longer necessarily does, what does that mean for the method itself? Does it constitute a fundamental change in the method itself? A constructivist approach can invoke grounded theory methods for diverse analytic and substantive problems. When Glaser argues grounded theory is a 'theory of resolving a main concern' that can be theoretically coded in many ways, he offers an excellent use of grounded theory, but not the only one. For that matter, what constitutes a main concern depends on one's point of view. Constructions matter. Who defines this main concern? With which criteria? Whose definitions stick? Note that addressing such questions treats the main concern as problematic, not as given, and brings power and control into the analysis. Grounded theory offers tools to get at varied constructions or competing definitions of the situation, as given in *action*, not merely stated in reconstructed accounts.

Must grounded theory aim for the general level abstracted from empirical realities? No. In sharp contrast, I argue that situating grounded theories in their social, historical, local, and interactional contexts strengthens them. Such situating permits making nuanced comparisons between studies. Subsequently these comparisons can result in more abstract–and, paradoxically–general theories. The generality arises here from scrutinizing numerous particulars and after developing a substantive theory may include analyzing and conceptualizing the results of multiple studies to construct a formal theory.

Generality emerges *from* the analytic process rather than as a prescribed goal *for* it. When you situate your study and let generality emerge from the analysis, you construct a safeguard against forcing data into your favorite analytic categories. As I have noted earlier, situating grounded theory studies also reduces possibilities of importing preconceived assumptions such as those about human intentions, actions, and meanings and minimizes letting ethnocentric, gender, class, or racial biases seep into the analysis.

Does the *form* of analysis separate researchers who do 'genuine' grounded theory from those who merely claim to use the method? Not always. Must a finished grounded theory always be a variable analysis? No. Should it be a conceptual analysis of patterned relationships? Yes. Does it ignore relationships outside the pattern? No. These relationships suggest paths to learn about variations in a process or category and alternative interpretations. Ironically, a traditional grounded theory emphasis can lead to researchers' minimizing the significance of data and details that do not fit their emerging categories and subsequently they force the data into them.

One of the few written reflections on a grounded theory study speaks to this point. Carolyn Ellis (1986) states that her grounded theory focus caused her to force details of her ethnography into her emerging categories with the result that her categories had explanatory value but 'presented life as lived much more categorically than actual day-to-day experiences warranted' (p. 91). You might think that this problem might be resolved by invoking the criterion of modifiability. But does that occur? How often do researchers conduct subsequent studies that alter a category or promote a different understanding? Ellis visited this community many times before and during her research. After a troubling revisit to the community three years following publication of her book, her subsequent reflections sparked new insights. Researchers with limited involvement in their respective fields probably would not have realized the limitations of their categories. Without such knowledge no one acts on the criterion of modifiability. Meanwhile, the usefulness of the theory diminishes, or worse, less than useful public or professional policies may result from it.

Grounded theory involves taking comparisons from data and reaching up to construct abstractions and simultaneously reaching down to tie these abstractions to data. It means learning about the specific and the general—and seeing what is new in them—then exploring their links to larger issues or creating larger unrecognized issues in entirety. An imaginative interpretation sparks new views and leads other scholars to new vistas. Grounded theory methods can provide a route to see beyond the obvious and a path to reach imaginative interpretations.

Evaluating Grounded Theory

As we evaluate where we have been and what we have gained, we look back into our journey and forward to imagining how our endpoint appears to our readers or viewers. The method of transporting us through our journey differs from what we gain from this journey. The sense we make of the journey takes form in our completed work. The endpoint that we portray makes sense to us because we have been immersed in the process. For our audiences, however, lines become blurred between process and product. Other scholars will likely judge the grounded theory process as an integral part of the product. I have argued throughout the book that grounded theory methods contain untapped versatility and potential. We need to consider our audiences, be they teachers or colleagues. They will judge the usefulness of our methods by the quality of our final product.

Criteria for evaluating research depend on who forms them and what purposes he or she invokes. Glaser's (1978: 4–5) criteria of fit, work, relevance, and modifiability are particularly useful for thinking about how your constructed theory renders the data.

Other important criteria take into account disciplinary, evidentiary, or aesthetic issues. Each is significant for your project. Different disciplines adhere to different standards for the conduct of research and for acceptability of evidence (see for example, Conrad, 1990; Thorne, 2001). Criteria for barely adequate research may differ from those studies accorded respect. Disciplines or departments may also require less their graduate students than of qualified professionals. Although expectations for grounded theory studies may vary, the following criteria may give you some ideas.

Criteria for Grounded Theory Studies[1]

Credibility

- Has your research achieved intimate familiarity with the setting or topic?
- Are the data sufficient to merit your claims? Consider the range, number, and depth of observations contained in the data.
- Have you made systematic comparisons between observations and between categories?
- Do the categories cover a wide range of empirical observations?
- Are there strong logical links between the gathered data and your argument and analysis?
- Has your research provided enough evidence for your claims to allow the reader to form an independent assessment—and *agree* with your claims?

Originality

- Are your categories fresh? Do they offer new insights?
- Does your analysis provide a new conceptual rendering of the data?
- What is the social and theoretical significance of this work?
- How does your grounded theory challenge, extend, or refine current ideas, concepts, and practices?

Resonance

- Do the categories portray the fullness of the studied experience?
- Have you revealed both liminal and unstable taken-for-granted meanings?

- Have you drawn links between larger collectivities or institutions and individual lives, when the data so indicate?
- Does your grounded theory make sense to your participants or people who share their circumstances? Does your analysis offer them deeper insights about their lives and worlds?

Usefulness

- Does your analysis offer interpretations that people can use in their everyday worlds?
- Do your analytic categories suggest any generic processes?
- If so, have you examined these generic processes for tacit implications?
- Can the analysis spark further research in other substantive areas?
- How does your work contribute to knowledge? How does it contribute to making a better world?

A strong combination of originality and credibility increases resonance, usefulness, and the subsequent value of the contribution. A claim to making a scholarly contribution requires a careful study of relevant literatures, including those that go beyond disciplinary boundaries, and a clear positioning of your grounded theory. These criteria address the implicit actions and meanings in the studied phenomenon and help you analyze how it is constructed. The above criteria account for the empirical study and development of the theory. They say little about how the researcher writes the narrative or what makes it compelling. Other criteria speak to the aesthetics of the writing. Our written works derive from aesthetic principles and rhetorical devices—in addition to theoretical statements and scientific rationales. The act of writing is intuitive, inventive, and interpretive, not merely a reporting of acts and facts, or in the case of grounded theory, causes, conditions, categories, and consequences—or an outline of processes that depict resolving a main concern.

When born from reasoned reflections and principled convictions, a grounded theory that conceptualizes and conveys what is meaningful about a substantive area can make a valuable contribution. Add aesthetic merit and analytic impact, and then its influence may spread to larger audiences.

Grounded Theory of the Past, Present, and Future

A Constructive Return to Classic Grounded Theory

My version of grounded theory looks back into its past, explores its present, and turns forward to the future. The dual roots of grounded theory in mid-century positivism and Chicago school sociology, with its foundation in pragmatist philosophy, have given grounded theory its rigor and its reliance on emergence. Throughout the preceding chapters, I have attempted to bring the Chicago school antecedents of grounded theory back into the foreground and to show they inform and enrich current discussions of grounded theory.

Our journey forward through the grounded theory process took into account its pragmatist antecedents. Now I call for other scholars—old and new—to journey back to the pragmatist heritage of grounded theory and to build on these antecedents while invoking twenty-first century constructivist sensibilities. A constructivist grounded theory retains the fluidity and open-ended character of pragmatism as evidenced in Strauss's works and those influenced by him (see for example, Baszanger, 1998; Bowker & Star, 1999; Clarke, 1998, 2005; Corbin & Strauss, 1988; Strauss, 1959, 1978a, 1978b, 1993, 1995). In typical grounded theory practice, you follow the leads in your data, as you see them—and constructivist grounded theory takes you one step further. With it, you try to make everyone's vantage points and their implications explicit— yours as well as those of your various participants. Not only does a constructivist approach help you to remain clear about the antecedents of your constructed theory, this approach helps other researchers and policy-makers to establish the boundaries of the usefulness of your grounded theory and, possibly, to ascertain how and where to modify it.

A pragmatist foundation can help you preserve an emphasis on language, meaning, and action in grounded theory. Subsequently you avoid reducing grounded theory research to studies of overt behavior or interview accounts taken at face value. If you hold constructivist sensibilities, you may learn and interpret nuances of meaning and action while becoming increasingly aware of the interactive and emergent nature of your data and analyses. In short, returning to the pragmatist foundations encourages us to construct an *interpretive rendering* of the worlds we study rather than an external reporting of events and statements.

Although constructivist grounded theory provides a methodological route to renewing and revitalizing the pragmatist foundations of classic grounded theory, constructivist grounded theory can also serve researchers from other traditions. Thus, constructivist sensibilities are congenial with other approaches such as feminist theory, narrative analysis, cultural studies, critical realism, and critical inquiry.

You may see connections between your work and the Chicago school that you had not realized before. If you were not familiar with the Chicago school earlier, you might wish to ponder how this tradition could reveal new vistas and transport you to new heights. In brief, several advantages of Chicago School traditions with their pragmatist underpinnings stand out. These traditions:

- Foster openness to the world and curiosity about it
- Encourage an empathetic understanding of research participants' meanings, actions, and worlds
- Take temporality into account
- Focus on meaning and process at the subjective and social levels.

Transforming Knowledge

Now that you have finished your grounded theory study, consider the purposes it serves. Your original purposes may have been immediate: to use the grounded theory method in practice to do the job before you. Other purposes may have remained under the surface while your pressing project and involvement in the process narrowed your attention. In a larger sense, what purpose does your grounded theory serve?

Taking the question to a wider level, what purposes *should* knowledge serve? Robert S. Lynd (1939) raised this question, *Knowledge for What?*, in his book of the same title almost seven decades ago. The question still persists; the answers still remain contested. Yet if we take the constructivist position to its logical extension, the questions become more specific and the answers clear. Should knowledge transform practice and social processes? Yes. Can grounded theory studies contribute to a better world? Yes. Should such questions influence what we study and how we study it? Yes.

Turning to researchers' actions, does the grounded theory research literature reflect efforts to transform knowledge, social processes—and grounded theory *as* practice? Grounded theorists in nursing and education have moved forward in these areas, and some sociologists have too. Yet career advancement may spawn more grounded theory studies than commitment to a subject area or emergent goals to transform knowledge. To the extent that researchers rely on claims of value neutrality, their explicit and implicit purposes may remain obscure. Claims of value neutrality may mask the implications of the knowledge we produce, whether significant or trivial. Objectivist grounded theorists may claim neutrality in producing knowledge and separation from public affairs. Knowledge is not neutral, nor are we separate from its production or the world.

The research journey can be an end in itself rather than a means to establishing a career. We can use grounded theory methods to do more than score career points. Through using grounded theory, you can realize impassioned goals.

Grounded theory methods enhance possibilities for you to transform knowledge. Topics that ignite your passions lead you to do research that can go beyond fulfilling academic requirements and professional credits. You'll enter the studied phenomenon with enthusiasm and open yourself to the research experience and follow where it takes you. The path may present inevitable ambiguities that hurl you into the existential dislocation of bewilderment. Still, when you bring passion, curiosity, openness, and care to your work, novel experiences will ensue and your ideas will emerge. Recall Margie Arlen at the beginning of this book, who avowed her chronic illness changed her as she learned to look outward to other people. Like Margie's journey with chronic illness, your journey through grounded theory may transform you.

NOTE

1 This section is expanded from Charmaz (2005a).

Glossary

Abduction   a type of reasoning that begins by examining data and after scrutiny of these data, entertains all possible explanations for the observed data, and then forms hypotheses to confirm or disconfirm until the researcher arrives at the most plausible interpretation of the observed data.

Axial coding   a type of coding that treats a category as an axis around which the analyst delineates relationships and specifies the dimensions of this category. A major purpose of axial coding is to bring the data back together again into a coherent whole after the researcher has fractured them through line-by-line coding.

Categorizing   the analytic step in grounded theory of selecting certain codes as having overriding significance or abstracting common themes and patterns in several codes into an analytic concept. As the researcher categorizes, he or she raises the conceptual level of the analysis from description to a more abstract, theoretical level. The researcher then tries to define the properties of the category, the conditions under which it is operative, the conditions under which it changes, and its relation to other categories. Grounded theorists make their most significant theoretical categories into the concepts of their theory.

Chicago school sociology   a tradition in sociology that arose at the University of Chicago during the early decades of the twentieth century. Pragmatist philosophy and ethnographic fieldwork formed the respective intellectual foundations and methodological principles of this tradition. Chicago school sociologists were not as homogeneous as textbooks portray them and not all members of the sociology department at the University of Chicago at that time had any affinity toward the Chicago school; however, this school spawned a rich tradition of symbolic interactionist social psychology and of ethnographic and qualitative research. Chicago school sociology assumes dynamic, reciprocal relationships between interpretation and action. Social life is interactive, emergent, and somewhat indeterminant. Chicago school ethnography fosters openness to the world and curiosity about it and symbolic interactionism fosters developing an empathetic understanding of research participants and their worlds.

Coding   the process of defining what the data are about. Unlike quantitative researchers, who apply *preconceived* categories or codes to the data, a grounded theorist creates qualitative codes by defining what he or she sees in the data. Thus, the codes are emergent—they develop as the researcher studies his or her data. The coding process may take the researcher to unforeseen areas and research questions. Grounded theory proponents follow such leads; they do not pursue previously designed research problems that lead to dead-ends.

Concept-indicator model   a method of theory construction in which the researcher constructs concepts that account for relationships defined in the empirical data and each concept rests on empirical indications. Thus, the concept is 'grounded' in data.

Conditional/consequential matrix   a coding device to show the intersections of micro and macro conditions/consequences on actions and to clarify the connections between them.

Constant comparative method   a method of analysis that generates successively more abstract concepts and theories through inductive processes of comparing data with data, data with category, category with category, and category with concept. Comparisons then constitute each stage of analytic development.

Constructivism   a social scientific perspective that addresses how realities are made. This perspective assumes that people, including researchers, construct the realities in which they participate. Constructivist inquiry starts with the experience and asks how members construct it. To the best of their ability, constructivists enter the phenomenon, gain multiple views of it, and locate it in its web of connections and constraints. Constructivists acknowledge that their interpretation of the studied phenomenon is itself a construction.

Deduction   a type of reasoning that starts with the general or abstract concept and reasons to specific instances.

Formal theory   a theoretical rendering of a generic issue or process that cuts across several substantive areas of study. The concepts in a formal theory are abstract and general and the theory specifies the links between these concepts. Theories that deal with identity formation or loss, the construction of culture, or the development of ideologies can help us understand behavior in diverse areas such as juvenile gangs, the socialization of professionals, and the experience of immigration.

Grounded theory   a method of conducting qualitative research that focuses on creating conceptual frameworks or theories through building inductive analysis from the data. Hence, the analytic categories are directly 'grounded' in the data. The method favors analysis over description, fresh categories over preconceived ideas and extant theories, and systematically focused sequential data collection over large initial samples. This method is distinguished from others since it involves the researcher in data analysis while collecting data—we use this data analysis to inform and shape further data collection. Thus, the sharp distinction between data collection and analysis phases of traditional research is intentionally blurred in grounded theory studies.

Induction   a type of reasoning that begins with study of a range of individual cases and extrapolates patterns from them to form a conceptual category.

Memo-writing   the pivotal intermediate step in grounded theory between data collection and writing drafts of papers. When grounded theorists write memos, they stop and analyze their ideas about their codes and emerging categories in whatever way that occurs to them (see also Glaser, 1998). Memo-writing is a crucial method in grounded theory because it prompts researchers to analyze their data and to develop their codes into categories early in the research process. Writing successive memos keeps researchers involved in the analysis and helps them to increase the level of abstraction of their ideas.

Objectivist grounded theory   a grounded theory approach in which the researcher takes the role of a dispassionate, neutral observer who remains separate from the research participants, analyzes their world as an outside expert, and treats research relationships and representation of participants as unproblematic. Objectivist grounded theory is a form of positivist qualitative research and thus subscribes to many of the assumptions and logic of the positivist tradition.

Positivism   an epistemology that subscribes to a unitary scientific method consisting of objective systematic observation and experimentation in an external world. The goal of positivistic inquiry is to discover and to establish general laws that explain the studied phenomena and from which predictions can be made. Subsequently, experimentation and prediction can lead to scientific control over the studied phenomena.

Postmodernism   a theoretical turn that challenges the foundational assumptions of the Enlightenment with its belief in human reason, belief in science, and belief in progress through science. Postmodernists range from those who wish to acknowledge intuitive forms of knowing to those who call for nihilistic rejection of modern ways of knowing and of being in the world and their foundation in Enlightenment values.

Pragmatism   an American philosophical tradition that views reality as characterized by indeterminacy and fluidity, and as open to multiple interpretations. Pragmatism assumes that people are active and creative. In pragmatist philosophy, meanings emerge through practical actions to solve problems, and through actions people come to know the world. Pragmatists see facts and values as linked rather than separate and truth as relativistic and provisional.

Reflexivity   the researcher's scrutiny of his or her research experience, decisions, and interpretations in ways that bring the researcher into the process and allow the reader to assess how and to what extent the researcher's interests, positions, and assumptions influenced inquiry. A reflexive stance

informs how the researcher conducts his or her research, relates to the
research participants, and represents them in written reports.

Social constructionism   a theoretical perspective that assumes that people
create social reality(ies) through individual and collective actions. Rather
than seeing the world as given, constructionists ask, how is it accomplished?
Thus, instead of assuming realities in an external world—including global
structures and local cultures—social constructionists study what people at a
particular time and place take as real, how they construct their views and
actions, when different constructions arise, whose constructions become taken
as definitive, and how that process ensues. Symbolic interactionism is a
constructionist perspective because it assumes that meanings and obdurate
realities are the product of collective processes.

Substantive theory   a theoretical interpretation or explanation of a delimited
problem in a particular area, such as family relationships, formal organizations,
or education.

Symbolic interactionism   a theoretical perspective derived from pragmatism
which assumes that people construct selves, society, and reality through
interaction. Because this perspective focuses on dynamic relationships between
meaning and actions, it addresses the active processes through which people
create and mediate meanings. Meanings arise out of actions, and in turn
influence actions. This perspective assumes that individuals are active, creative,
and reflective and that social life consists of processes.

Theoretical sampling   a type of grounded theory sampling in which the
researcher aims to develop the properties of his or her developing categories or
theory, not to sample randomly selected populations or to sample representative
distributions of a particular population. When engaging in theoretical sampling,
the researcher seeks people, events, or information to illuminate and define the
boundaries and relevance of the categories. Because the purpose of theoretical
sampling is to sample to develop the theoretical categories, conducting it can
take the researcher across substantive areas.

Theoretical saturation   refers to the point at which gathering more data about a
theoretical category reveals no new properties nor yields any further theoretical
insights about the emerging grounded theory.

References

Alasuutari, P. (1992). *Desire and craving: A cultural theory of alcoholism*. New York: State University of New York Press.

———. (1995). *Researching culture: Qualitative method and cultural studies*. London: Sage.

———. (1996). Theorizing in qualitative research: A cultural studies perspective. *Qualitative Inquiry, 2*, 371–384.

———. (2004). The globalization of qualitative research. In Clive Seale, Giampietro Gobo, Jaber F. Gubrium, & David Silverman (Eds.) *Qualitative research practice* (pp. 595–608). London: Sage.

Albas, C., & Albas, D. (1988). Emotion work and emotion rules: The case of exams. *Qualitative Sociology, 11*, 259–274.

Albas, D., & Albas, C. (1988). Aces and bombers: The post-exam impression management strategies of students. *Symbolic Interaction, 11*, 289–302.

———. (1993). Disclaimer mannerisms of students: How to avoid being labeled as cheaters. *Canadian Review of Sociology and Anthropology, 30*, 451–467.

Anderson, E. (1976). *A place on the corner*. Chicago: University of Chicago Press.

———. (2003). Jelly's place: An ethnographic memoir. *Symbolic Interaction, 26*, 217–237.

Anspach, R. (1979). From stigma to identity politics: Political activism among the physically disabled and former mental patients. *Social Science & Medicine, 13A*, 765–763.

Arendell, T. (1997). Reflections on the researcher–researched relationship: A woman interviewing men. *Qualitative Sociology, 20*, 341–368.

Ashworth, P. D. (1995). The meaning of 'participation' in participant observation. *Qualitative Health Research, 5*, 366–387.

Atkinson, P. (1990). *The ethnographic imagination: Textual constructions of reality*. London: Routledge.

Atkinson, P., Coffey, A., & Delamont, S. (2003). *Key themes in qualitative research: Continuities and changes*. New York: Rowan and Littlefield.

Baker, C., Wuest, J., & Stern, P. (1992). Methods slurring: The grounded theory, phenomenology example, *Journal of Advanced Nursing, 17*, 1355–1360.

Baszanger, I. (1998). *Inventing pain medicine: From the laboratory to the clinic*. New Brunswick, NJ: Rutgers University Press.

Becker, H. S. ([1967] 1970). Whose side are we on? Reprinted as pp. 123–134 in his *Sociological work: Method and substance*. New Brunswick, NJ: Transaction Books.

———. (2003). The politics of presentation: Goffman and total institutions. *Symbolic Interaction, 26*, 659–669.

Becker, P. H. (1998). Pearls, pith, and provocations: Common pitfalls in grounded theory research. *Qualitative Health Research, 3*(2), 254–260.

Bergson, H. ([1903] 1961). *An introduction to metaphysics*. (Mabelle L. Andison, translator). New York: Philosophical Library, Inc.

Berk, R. A., Berk, S. F., Loseke, D. R., & Rauma, D. (1983). Mutual combat and other family violence myths. In D. Finkelho, et al. (Eds.), *The dark side of families* (pp. 197–212). Beverly Hills, CA: Sage.

Berk, R. A., Berk, S. F., Newton, J., & Loseke, D. R. (1984). Cops on call: Summoning the police to the scene of spousal violence. *Law & Society Review, 18*(3), 480–498.

Berk, S. F., & Loseke, D. R. (1980–1981). Handling family violence: Situational determinants of police arrest in domestic disturbances. *Law & Society Review, 15*(2), 317–346.

Biernacki, P. (1986). *Pathways from heroin addiction: Recovery without treatment.* Philadelphia: Temple University Press.

Biernacki, P. and Davis, F. (1970). Turning off: A study of ex-marijuana users. Paper presented at the Conference on Drug Use and Subcultures, Asilomar, California.

Bigus, O. E., Hadden, S. C., & Glaser, B. G. (1994). The study of basic social processes. In B. G. Glaser (Ed.), *More grounded theory methodology: A reader* (pp. 38–64). Mill Valley, CA: Sociology Press.

Blumer, H. (1969). *Symbolic interactionism.* Englewood Cliffs, NJ: Prentice–Hall.

——. (1979). Comments on 'George Herbert Mead and the Chicago tradition of sociology'. *Symbolic Interaction, 2*(2), 21–22.

Bogard, C. (2001). Claimsmakers and contexts in early constructions of homelessness: A comparison of New York City and Washington, D.C. *Symbolic Interaction, 24*, 425–454.

Bowker, L. H., & Mauer, L. (1987). The medical treatment of battered wives. *Women & Health, 12*(1), 25–45.

Bowker, G., & Star, S. L. (1999). *Sorting things out: Classification and its consequences.* Cambridge, MA: MIT Press.

Bryant, A. (2002). Re-grounding grounded theory. *Journal of Information Technology Theory and Application, 4*(1), 25–42.

——. (2003). A constructive/ist response to Glaser. *FQS: Forum for Qualitative Social Research, 4*(1), www.qualitative-research.net/fqs/.

Blumer, M. (1984). *The Chicago school of sociology: Institutionalization, diversity, and the rise of sociology.* Chicago: University of Chicago Press.

Burawoy, M. (1991). The extended case method. In M., Burawoy, A. Burton, A. A. Ferguson, K. Fox, J. Gamson, N. Gartrell, L. Hurst, C. Kurzman, L. Salzinger, J. Schiffman, & S. Ui, *Ethnography unbound: Power and resistance in the modern metropolis* (pp. 271–290). Berkeley: University of California Press.

——. (2000). Grounding globalization. In M. Burawoy, J. A. Blum, S. George, G. Sheba, Z. Gille, T. Gowan, L. Haney, M. Klawiter, S. A. Lopez, S. O' Riain, & M. Thayer *Global ethnography: Forces, connections, and imaginations in a postmodern world* (pp. 337–373). Berkeley, CA: University of California Press.

Burke, P. J. (1980). The self: Measurements from an interactionist perspective. *Social Psychology Quarterly, 43*, 18–29.

Bury, M. (1982). Chronic illness as biographical disruption. *Sociology of Health & Illness, 4*, 167–182.

——. (1988). Meanings at risk: The experience of arthritis. In R. Anderson & M. Bury (Eds.), *Living with chronic illness* (pp. 89–116). London: Unwin Hyman.

——. (1991). The sociology of chronic illness: A review of research and prospects. *Sociology of Health & Illness, 13*, 452–468.

Calkins, K. (1970). Time perspectives, marking and styles of usage. *Social Problems, 17*, 487–501.

Casper, M. (1998). *The unborn patient.* New Brunswick, NJ: Rutgers University Press.

Chang, D. B. K. (1989). An abused spouse's self-saving process: A theory of identity transformation. *Sociological Perspectives, 32*, 535–550.

Chang, J. H.-L. (2000). Symbolic interaction and transformation of class structure: The case of China. *Symbolic Interaction, 23*, 223–251.

Charmaz, K. (1973). *Time and identity: The shaping of selves of the chronically ill.* PhD dissertation, University of California, San Francisco.

——. (1983a). The grounded theory method: An explication and interpretation. In R. M. Emerson (Ed.), *Contemporary field research* (pp. 109–126). Boston: Little Brown.

——. (1983b). Loss of self: A fundamental form of suffering in the chronically ill. *Sociology of Health & Illness*, *5*, 168–195.

——. (1987). Struggling for a self: Identity levels of the chronically ill. In J. A. Roth & P. Conrad (Eds.), *Research in the sociology of health care: Vol. 6. The experience and management of chronic illness* (pp. 283–321). Greenwich, CT: JAI Press.

——. (1990). Discovering chronic illness: Using grounded theory. *Social Science and Medicine*, *30*, 1161–1172.

——. (1991a). *Good days, bad days: The self in chronic illness and time*. New Brunswick, NJ: Rutgers University Press.

——. (1991b). Translating graduate qualitative methods into undergraduate teaching: Intensive interviewing as a case example. *Teaching Sociology*, *19*, 384–395.

——. (1995a). Body, identity, and self: Adapting to impairment. *The Sociological Quarterly*, *36*, 657–680.

——. (1995b). Grounded theory. In J. A. Smith, R. Harré, & L. Van Langenhove (Eds.), *Rethinking methods in psychology* (pp. 27–49). London: Sage.

——. (1998). Research standards and stories: Conflict and challenge. Plenary presentation, Qualitative Research Conference. University of Toronto, Toronto, Ontario. May 15.

——. (1999). Stories of suffering: Subjective tales and research narratives. *Qualitative Health Research*, *9*, 362–382.

——. (2000). Constructivist and objectivist grounded theory. In N. K. Denzin & Y. Lincoln (Eds.), *Handbook of Qualitative Research* (2nd ed., pp. 509–535). Thousand Oaks, CA: Sage.

——. (2001). Qualitative interviewing and grounded theory analysis. In J. F. Gubrium & J. A. Holstein (Eds.), *Handbook of interview research* (pp. 675–694). Thousand Oaks, CA: Sage.

——. (2002a). Grounded theory: Methodology and theory construction. In N. J. Smelser & P. B. Baltes (Eds.), *International encyclopedia of the social and behavioral sciences* (pp. 6396–6399). Amsterdam: Pergamon.

——. (2002b). The self as habit: The reconstruction of self in chronic illness. *The Occupational Therapy Journal of Research*, *22* (Supplement 1), 31s–42s.

——. (2002c). Stories and silences: Disclosures and self in chronic illness. *Qualitative Inquiry*, *8*(3), 302–328.

——. (2003). Grounded theory. In Jonathan A. Smith (Ed.), *Qualitative psychology: A practical guide to research methods* (pp. 81–110). London: Sage.

——. (2004). Premises, principles, and practices in qualitative research: Revisiting the foundation. *Qualitative Health Research*, *14*, 976–993.

——. (2005). Grounded theory in the 21st century: A qualitative method for advancing social justice research. In N. Denzin & Y. Lincoln (Eds.), *Handbook of qualitative research* (3rd ed., pp. 507–535). Thousand Oaks, CA: Sage.

——. (2006a). Grounded theory. In G. Ritzer (Ed.), *Encyclopedia of sociology*. Cambridge, MA: Blackwell.

——. (2006b). Stories, silences, and self: Dilemmas in disclosing chronic illness. In D. Brashers D. Goldstein (Eds.), *Health communication*. New York: Lawrence Erlbaum.

Charmaz, K., & Mitchell, R. G. (1996). The myth of silent authorship: Self, substance, and style in ethnographic writing. *Symbolic Interaction*, *19*(4), 285–302.

——. (2001). An invitation to grounded theory in ethnography. In P. Atkinson, A. Coffey, S. Delamonte, J. Lofland, & L. H. Lofland (Eds.), *Handbook of Ethnography* (pp. 160–174). London: Sage.

Charmaz, K., & Olesen, V. (1997). Ethnographic research in medical sociology. *Sociological Methods and Research, 25*(4), 452–494.

Chenitz, W. C., & Swanson, J. M. (Eds.) (1986). *From practice to grounded theory: qualitative research in nursing.* Reading, MA: Addison–Wesley.

Clark, C. (1997). *Misery and company: Sympathy in everyday life.* Chicago: University of Chicago Press.

Clarke, A. E. (1998). *Disciplining reproduction: Modernity, American life sciences, and the problems of sex.* Berkeley, CA: University of California Press.

——. (2003). Situational analyses: Grounded theory mapping after the postmodern turn. *Symbolic Interaction, 26,* 553–576.

——. (2005). *Situational Analysis: Grounded theory after the postmodern turn.* Thousand Oaks, CA: Sage.

Clifford, J., & Marcus, G. (1986). *Writing culture: The poetics and politics of ethnography.* Berkeley, CA: University of California Press.

Coffey, A., & Atkinson, P. (1996). *Making sense of qualitative data: Complementary research strategies.* Thousand Oaks, CA: Sage.

Coffey A., Holbrook, P., & Atkinson, P. (1996). Qualitative data analysis: Technologies and representations. *Sociological Research On-line,* 1.

Collins, P. H. (1990). *Black feminist thought: Knowledge, consciousness, and the politics of empowerment.* New York: Routledge, Chapman, Hall.

Collins, R. (2004a). Interaction ritual chains. Distinguished Lecture, sponsored by Alpha Kappa Delta, presented at the American Sociological Association. San Francisco, August 14.

——. (2004b). *Interaction ritual chains.* Princeton, NJ: Princeton University Press.

Cooley, C. H. (1902). *Human nature and social order.* New York: Charles Scribner's Sons.

Conrad, P. (1990). Qualitative research on chronic illness: A commentary on method and conceptual development. *Social Science & Medicine, 30,* 1257–1263.

Corbin, J. M. (1998). Alternative interpretations: Valid or not? *Theory & Psychology, 8,* 121–128.

Corbin, J., & Strauss, A. L. (1987). Accompaniments of chronic illness: Changes in body, self, biography, and biographical time. In J. A. Roth & P. Conrad (Eds.), *Research in the sociology of health care: Vol. 6. The experience and management of chronic illness* (pp. 249–281). Greenwich, CT: JAI Press.

——. (1990). Grounded theory research: Procedures, canons, and evaluative criteria. *Qualitative Sociology, 13*(1), 3–21.

——. (1988). *Unending Work and Care: Managing Chronic Illness at Home.* San Francisco: Jossey–Bass.

Creswell, J. (1998). *Qualitative inquiry and research design: Choosing among five traditions.* Thousand Oaks, CA: Sage.

Dahlberg, C. C., & Jaffe, J. (1977). *Stroke: A doctor's personal story of his recovery.* New York: Norton.

Dalton, M. (1959). *Men who manage.* New York: Wiley.

Daly, K. (2002). Time, gender, and the negotiation of family schedules. *Symbolic Interaction, 25,* 323–342.

Davis, F. (1963). *Passage through crisis: Polio victims and their families.* Indianapolis: Bobbs–Merrill.

Davis, M. S. (1971). 'That's interesting!' Towards a phenomenology of sociology and a sociology of phenomenology. *Philosophy of the Social Sciences, 1,* 309–344.

Deely, J. N. (1990). *Basics of semiotics.* Bloomington: Indiana University Press.

Denzin, N. K. (1984). *On understanding emotion.* San Francisco: Jossey–Bass.

——. (1994). The art and politics of interpretation. In N. K. Denzin & Y. S. Lincoln (Eds.), *Handbook of qualitative research* (pp. 500–515). Thousand Oaks, CA: Sage.

Denzin, N. K., & Lincoln, Y. S. (Eds.) (1994). *Handbook of qualitative research*. Thousand Oaks, CA: Sage.

Derricourt, R. (1996). *An author's guide to scholarly publishing*. Princeton, NJ: Princeton University.

Dey, I. (1999). *Grounding grounded theory*. San Diego: Academic Press.

——. (2004). Grounded theory. In C. Seale, G. Gobo, J. F. Gubrium, & D. Silverman (Eds.), *Qualitative research practice* (pp. 80–93). London: Sage.

Diamond, T. (1992). *Making gray gold*. Chicago: University of Chicago Press.

DiGiacomo, S. M. (1992). Metaphor as illness: Postmodern dilemmas in the representation of body, mind and disorder. *Medical Anthropology, 14*, 109–137.

Dingwall, R. (1976). *Aspects of Illness*. Oxford: Martin Robertson.

Dobash, R. E., & Dobash, R. P. (1979). *Violence against wives*. New York: Free Press.

——. (1981). Community response to violence against wives: Charivari, abstract justice and patriarchy. *Social Problems, 28*, 563–581.

Durkheim, E. (1902/1960). *The division of labor in society*. Glencoe, IL: Free Press.

——. (1915/1965). *Elementary forms of religious life*. New York: Free Press.

——. (1925/1961). *Moral education: A study in the theory and application of the sociology of education*. New York: Free Press.

——. (1951). *Suicide*. Glencoe, IL: Free Press.

Edwards, S. (1987). Provoking her own demise: From common assault to homicide. In J. Hanmer and M. Maynard (Eds.), *Women, violence and social control* (pp. 152–168). Atlantic Highlands: Humanities press International, Inc.

Eide, L. (1995). *Work in progress: A guide to writing and revising* (3rd ed.). New York: St Martins.

Elbow, P. (1981). *Writing with power*. New York: Oxford University Press.

Ellis, C. (1986). *Fisher Folk: Two communities on Chesapeake Bay*. Lexington, KY: The University of Kentucky.

——. (1995). Emotional and ethical quagmires of returning to the field. *Journal of Contemporary Ethnography, 24*(1), 68–98.

Emerson, R. M. (1983). Introduction to Part II: Theory and evidence and representation. In R. M. Emerson (Ed.), *Contemporary field research: A collection of readings* (pp. 93–107). Boston: Little Brown.

——. (2001). Introduction to Part III: producing ethnographies: Theory, evidence and representation. In R. M. Emerson (Ed.), *Contemporary field research: Perspectives and formulations* (2nd ed., pp. 281–316). Prospect Heights, IL: Waveland Press.

——. (2004). Working with 'Key Incidents.' In Clive Seale, Giampietro Gobo, Jaber F. Gubrium, & David Silverman (Eds.), *Qualitative Research Practice* (pp. 457–472). London: Sage.

Fabrega, H. Jr., & Manning, P. K. (1972). Disease, illness and deviant careers. In R. A. Scott & J. D. Douglas (Eds.), *Theoretical perspectives on deviance* (pp. 93–116). New York: Basic Books.

Fann, K. T. (1970). *Peirce's theory of abduction*. The Hague: Martinus Nijhoff.

Ferraro, K. J. (1987). Negotiating trouble in a battered women's shelter. In M. J. Deegan, & M. R. Hill (Eds.), *Women and symbolic interaction* (pp. 379–394). Boston: Allen & Unwin.

——. (1989). Policing woman battering. *Social Problems, 30*(3), 61–74.

Ferraro, K. J., & Johnson, J. M. (1983). How women experience battering: The process of victimization. *Social Problems, 30*, 325–339.

Fielding, N. G., & Lee, R. M. (1998). *Computer analysis and qualitative data*. London: Sage.

Finch, J. and Mason, J. (1990). Decision taking in the fieldwork process: Theoretical sampling and collaborative working. In R. G. Burgess (Ed.), *Studies in qualitative methodology: Reflections on field experience* (pp. 25–50). Greenwich, CT: JAI Press.

Fine, G. A. (1986). *With the boys: Little league baseball and preadolescent culture*. Chicago: University of Chicago Press.

——. (1998). *Morel tales: The culture of mushrooming*. Cambridge, MA: Harvard University Press.

Flick, U. (1998). *An introduction to qualitative research*. Thousand Oaks, CA: Sage.

Flowers, L. (1993). *Problem-solving strategies for writing* (4th ed.). Fort Worth, TX: Harcourt Brace, Jovanovich.

Frank, A. W. (1990). Bringing bodies back in: A decade review. *Theory, Culture & Society*, 7, 131–162.

——. (1991a). *At the will of the body*. Boston: Houghton Mifflin.

——. (1991b). For a sociology of the body: An analytical review. In M. Featherstone, M. Hepworth, & B. S. Turner (Eds.), *The body: Social process and cultural theory* (pp. 36–102). London: Sage.

Frankenberg, R. (1990). Disease, literature and the body in the era of AIDS – A preliminary exploration. *Sociology of Health & Illness*, 12, 351–360.

Freund, P. E. S. (1982). *The civilized body: Social domination, control, and health*. Philadelphia, PA: Temple University Press.

——. (1988). Bringing society into the body: Understanding socialized human nature. *Theory and Society*, 17, 839–864.

——. (1990). The expressive body: A common ground for the sociology of emotions and health and illness. *Sociology of Health & Illness*, 12, 452–477.

Gadow, S. (1982). Body and self: A dialectic. In V. Kestenbaum (Ed.), *The humanity of the ill: Phenomenological perspectives* (pp. 86–100). Knoxville, TN: University of Tennessee Press.

Geertz, C. (1973). *The interpretation of cultures*. New York: Basic Books.

Gerhardt, U. (1979). Coping and social action: Theoretical reconstruction of the life-event approach. *Sociology of Health & Illness*, 1, 195–225.

——. 1989. *Ideas about illness: An intellectual and political history of medical sociology*. New York: New York University Press.

Giles-Sims, J. (1983). *Wife battering: A systems theory approach*. New York: The Guilford Press.

Glaser, B. G. (1978). *Theoretical sensitivity*. Mill Valley, CA: The Sociology Press.

——. (1992). *Basics of grounded theory analysis*. Mill Valley, CA: The Sociology Press.

——. (Ed.) (1994). *More grounded theory*. Mill Valley, CA: The Sociology Press.

——. (1998). *Doing grounded theory: Issues and discussions*. Mill Valley, CA: The Sociology Press.

——. (2001) *The grounded theory perspective: Conceptualization contrasted with description*. Mill Valley, CA: The Sociology Press.

——. (2002). Constructivist grounded theory? Forum qualitative Sozialforschung/ Forum: *Qualitative Social Research* [*On-line Journal*], 3. Available at: http://www. qualitative-research.net/fqs-texte/3-02/3-02glaser-e-htm.

——. (2003). *Conceptualization contrasted with description*. Mill Valley, CA: The Sociology Press.

Glaser, B. G., & Strauss, A. L. (1965). *Awareness of dying*. Chicago: Aldine.

——. (1967). *The discovery of grounded theory*. Chicago: Aldine.

——. (1968). *Time for dying*. Chicago: Aldine.

——. (1971). *Status passage*. Chicago: Aldine.

Glassner, B. (1988). *Bodies*. New York: Putnam.

——. (1989). Fitness and the postmodern self. *Journal of Health and Social Behavior*, *30*, 180–191.

Goffman, E. (1959). *The presentation of self in everyday life*. Garden City, NY: Doubleday Anchor Books.

——. (1961). *Asylums*. Garden City, NY: Doubleday Anchor Books.

——. (1963). *Stigma*. Englewood Cliffs, NJ: Prentice–Hall.

——. (1967). *Interaction ritual*. Garden City, NY: Doubleday Anchor Books.

——. (1969). *Strategic interaction*. Philadelphia: University of Pennsylvania Press.

Gorden, R. (1987). *Interviewing: strategies, techniques, and tactics*. Homewood, IL: Dorsey.

Goulding, C. (2002). *Grounded theory: A practical guide for management, business, and market researchers*. London: Sage.

Guba, E. G., & Lincoln, Y. S. (1994). Competing paradigms in qualitative research. In N. K. Denzin, & Y. S. Lincoln (Eds.), *Handbook of qualitative research* (pp. 105–118). Thousand Oaks, CA: Sage.

Gubrium, J. F. (1993). *Speaking of life: Horizons of meaning for nursing home residents*. Hawthorne, NY: Aldine de Gruyter.

Gubrium, J. F., & Holstein, J. A. (1997). *The new language of qualitative research*. New York: Oxford University Press.

Gubrium, Jaber F. and Holstein, James A. (Eds.) (2001). *Handbook of interview research: Context and method*. Thousand Oaks, CA: Sage.

Hall, W. A., & Callery, P. (2001). Enhancing the rigor of grounded theory: Incorporating reflexivity and relationality. *Qualitative Health Research*, *11*, 257–272.

Hartsock, N. C. M. (1998). *The feminist standpoint revisited and other essays*. Boulder, CO: Westview.

Henwood, K., & Pidgeon, N. (2003). Grounded theory in psychological research. In P. M. Camic, J. E. Rhodes, & L. Yardley (Eds.), *Qualitative research in psychology: Expanding perspectives in methodology and design* (pp. 131–155). Washington, DC: American Psychological Association.

Hermes, J. (1995). *Reading women's magazines*. Cambridge, UK: Polity Press.

Hertz, R. (2003). Paying forward and paying back. *Symbolic Interaction*, *26*, 473–486.

Hewitt, J. P. (1992). *Self and society*. New York: Simon and Schuster.

Hogan, N., Morse, J. M., & Tasón, M. C. (1996). Toward an experiential theory of bereavement. *Omega*, *33*, 43–65.

Holliday, A. (2002). *Doing and writing qualitative research*. London: Sage.

Holstein, J. A., & Gubrium, J. F. (1995). *The active interview*. Thousand Oaks, CA: Sage.

Hood, J. C. (1983). *Becoming a two-job family*. New York: Praeger.

Jankowski, M. S. (1991). *Islands in the street: Gangs and American urban society*. Berkeley, CA: University of California Press.

Kearney, Margaret H. (1998). Ready to wear: Discovering grounded formal theory. *Research in Nursing & Health*, *21*, 179–186.

Kelle, U. (2005, May). Emergence vs. forcing of empirical data? A crucial problem of 'grounded theory' reconsidered [52 paragraphs]. *Forum Qualitative Sozialforschung/ Forum: Qualitative Social Research* [On-line Journal] 6(2), Art. 27. Available at http//www.qualitative-research.net/fqs-texte/2-05/05-2-27-e.htm [Date of Access: 05-30-05].

Kestenbaum, V. (1982). Introduction: The Experience of Illness. In V. Kestenbaum (Ed.), *The humanity of the ill: Phenomenological perspectives* (pp. 3–38). Knoxville: University of Tennessee Press.

Kleinman, A., Brodwin, D., Good, B. J., & Good, M. D. (1991). Introduction. In M. D. Good. P. E. Brodwin, B. J. Good, & A. Kleinman (Eds.), *Pain as human experience: An anthropological perspective* (pp. 1–28). Berkeley: University of California Press.

Kotarba, J. A. (1994). Thoughts on the body: Past, present, and future. *Symbolic Interaction*, 17, 225–230.

Kuhn, T. S. (1962). *The structure of scientific revolutions*. Chicago: University of Chicago Press.

Kusow, A. (2003) Beyond indigenous authenticity: Reflections on the inside/outsider debate in immigration research. *Symbolic Interaction*, 26, 591–599.

Latour, B., & Woolgar, S. ([1979] 1986). *Laboratory life: The social construction of scientific facts* (2nd ed.). Princeton, NJ: Princeton University Press.

Layder, D. (1998). *Sociological practice: Linking theory and social research*. London: Sage.

Lazarsfeld, P. and Rosenberg, M. (Eds.) (1955). *The language of social research; a reader in the methodology of social research*. Glencoe, IL: Free Press.

Lempert, L. B. (1996). The line in the sand: Definitional dialogues in abusive relationships. N. K. Denzin (Ed.), *Studies in Symbolic Interaction*, 18 (pp. 171–195). Greenwich, CT: JAI Press.

———. (1997). The other side of help: the negative effects of help-seeking processes of abused women. *Qualitative Research*, 20, 289–309.

Lewis, K. (1985). *Successful living with chronic illness*. Wayne, NJ: Avery.

Lindesmith, A., Strauss, A. L., & Denzin, N. K. (1988). *Social psychology*. Englewood Cliffs, NJ: Prentice–Hall.

Locke, K. (2001). *Grounded theory in management research*. Thousand Oaks, CA: Sage.

Locker, D. (1983). *Disability and disadvantage: The consequences of chronic illness*. London: Tavistock.

Lofland, J. (1970). Interactionist imagery and analytic interruptus. In T. Shibutani (Ed.), *Human nature and collective behavior*. Englewood Cliffs, NJ: Prentice–Hall.

Lofland, J., & Lofland, L. H. (1984). *Analyzing social settings* (2nd ed.). Belmont, CA: Wadsworth.

———. (1995). *Analyzing social settings* (3rd ed.). Belmont, CA: Wadsworth.

Lonkila, M. (1995). Grounded theory as an emerging paradigm for computer-assisted qualitative data analysis. In K. Udo (Ed.), *Computer-aided qualitative data analysis: Theory, methods and practice* (pp. 41–51). London: Sage.

Loseke, D. R. (1987). Lived realities and the construction of social problems: The case of wife abuse. *Symbolic Interaction*, 10, 229–243.

———. (1992). *The battered woman and shelters: The social construction of wife abuse*. Albany, NY: State University of New York Press.

Luker, K. (1984). *Abortion and the politics of motherhood*. Berkeley, CA: University of California Press.

Lynd, R. S. (1939). *Knowledge for what?: The place of social science in American culture*. Princeton, NJ: Princeton University Press.

MacDonald, L. (1988). The experience of stigma: Living with rectal cancer. In R. Anderson & M. Bury (Eds.), *Living with chronic illness* (pp. 177–202). London: Unwin Hyman.

MacKinnon, C. A. (1993). Feminism, marxism, method and the state: Toward a feminist jurisprudence. In P. B. Bart and E. G. Moran (Eds.), *Violence against women* (pp. 201–208). Newbury Park, CA: Sage.

Maines, D. R. (2001). *The faultline of consciousness: A view of interactionism in sociology*. New York: Aldine de Gruyter.

Markovsky, B. (2004). Theory construction. In G. Ritzer (Ed.), *Encyclopedia of social theory, volume II* (pp. 830–834). Thousand Oaks, CA: Sage.

Martin, D. (1976). *Battered wives*. New York: Pocket Books.

Maynard, D. (2003). *Good news, bad news: Conversational order in everyday talk and clinical settings*. Chicago: University of Chicago Press.

Mead, G. H. (1932). *Philosophy of the present*. LaSalle, IL: Open Court Press.

———. (1934). *Mind, self and society*. Chicago: University of Chicago Press.

Melia, K. M. (1987). *Learning and working: The occupational socialization of nurses*. London: Tavistock.

———. (1996). Rediscovering Glaser. *Qualitative Health Research, 6*, 368–378.

Merton, R. K. (1957). *Social theory and social structure*. Glencoe, IL: Free Press.

Miller, D. E. (2000). Mathematical dimensions of qualitative research. *Symbolic Interaction, 23*, 399–402.

Miller, G. (1997). Contextualizing texts: Studying organizational texts. In G. Miller & R. Dingwall (Eds.), *Context and method in qualitative research* (pp. 77–91). London: Sage.

Mills, T. (1985). The assault on the self: Stages in coping with battering husbands. *Qualitative Sociology, 8*, 103–123.

Mitchell, R. G. (1991). Field notes. Unpublished manuscript, Oregon State University, Corvallis, OR.

———. (2002). *Dancing to armageddon: Survivalism and chaos in modern times*. Chicago: University of Chicago Press.

Morrill, C. (1995). *The executive way: Conflict management in corporations*. Chicago: University of Chicago Press.

Morse, J. M. (1995). The significance of saturation. *Qualitative Health Research, 5*, 147–149.

Murphy, E., & Dingwall, R. (2003). *Qualitative methods and health policy research*. New York: Aldine de Gruyter.

Murphy, R. F. (1987). *The body silent*. New York: Henry Holt.

Olesen, V. (1994). Problematic bodies: Past, present, and future. *Symbolic Interaction, 17*, 231–237.

Olesen, V., Schatzman, L., Droes, N., Hatton, D., & Chico, N. (1990). The mundane ailment and the physical self: Analysis of the social psychology of health and illness. *Social Science & Medicine, 30*, 449–455.

Pagelow, M. D. (1984). *Family Violence*. Praeger: New York.

Park, R. E., & Burgess, E. W. (Eds.) (1921). *The city*. Chicago: University of Chicago Press.

Parsons, T. (1953). *The social system*. Glencoe, IL: Free Press.

Peirce, C. S. (1958). *Collected Papers*. Cambridge, MA: Harvard University Press.

Pollner, M., & Emerson, R. M. (2001). Ethnomethodology and ethnography. In P. Atkinson, A. Coffey, S. Delamont, J. Lofland, & L. H. Lofland (Eds.), *Handbook of ethnography* (pp. 118–135). London: Sage.

Prior, L. F. (2003). *Using documents in social research*. London: Sage.

Prus, R. C. (1987). Generic social processes: Maximizing conceptual development in ethnographic research. *Journal of Contemporary Ethnography, 16*, 250–293.

———. (1996). *Symbolic interaction and ethnographic research: Intersubjectivity and the study of human lived experience*. Albany, NY: State University of New York Press.

Radley, A. (1989). Style, discourse and constraint in adjustment to chronic illness. *Sociology of Health & Illness, 11*, 230–252.

Radley, A., & Green, R. (1987). Illness as adjustment: A methodology and conceptual framework. *Sociology of Health & Illness, 9*, 179–206.

Reinharz, S. (1992). *Feminist methods in social research*. New York: Oxford University Press.

Reinharz, S., & Chase, S. E. (2001). Interviewing women. In J. F. Gubrium & J. A. Holstein (Eds.), *Handbook of interview research* (pp. 221–238). Thousand Oaks, CA: Sage.

Richardson, L. (1990). *Writing strategies: Researching diverse audiences*. Newbury Park, CA: Sage.

———. (1994). Writing: A method of inquiry. In N. K. Denzin & Y. S. Lincoln (Eds.), *Handbook of qualitative research* (pp. 516–529). Thousand Oaks, CA: Sage.

Rico, G. L. (1983). *Writing the natural way: Using right-brain techniques to release your expressive powers*. Los Angeles: J. P. Tarcher.

Ritzer, G., & Goodman, D. J. (2004). *Classical sociological theory* (4th ed.). Boston: McGraw Hill.

Robrecht, L. C. (1995). Grounded theory: Evolving methods. *Qualitative Health Research*, *5*, 169–177.

Rock, P. (1979). *The making of symbolic interactionism*. London: Macmillan.

Rosenthal, G. (2004). Biographical research. In C. Seale, G. Gobo, J. F. Gubrium, & D. Silverman (Eds.), *Qualitative research practice* (pp. 48–64). London: Sage.

Roth, J. (1963). *Timetables*. New York: Bobbs–Merrill.

Rubin, H. J., & Rubin, I. S. (1995). *Qualitative interviewing: The art of hearing*. Thousand Oaks, CA: Sage.

Sanders, C. R. (1990). *Customizing the body*. Philadelphia, PA: Temple University Press.

Sarton, M. (1988). *After the stroke: A journal*. New York: W. W. Norton.

Schechter, S. (1982). *Women and male violence*. Boston: South End Press.

Scheper-Hughes, N., & Lock, M. M. (1987). The mindful body: A prolegomenon to future work in medical anthropology. *Medical Anthropology Quarterly*, *1*, 6–41.

Schneider, M. A. (1997). Social dimensions of epistemological disputes: The case of literary theory. *Sociological Perspectives*, *40*, 243–264.

Schreiber, R. S. & Stern, P. N. (Eds.)(2001). *Using Grounded Theory in Nursing*. New York: Springer.

Shostak, S. (2004). Environmental justice and genomics: Acting on the futures of environmental health. *Science as Culture*, *13*, 539–562.

Schutz, A. (1967 [1932]). *The phenomenology of the social world*. Evanston, IL: Northwestern University Press.

Schwalbe, M., & Wolkomir, M. (2002). Interviewing men. In J. F. Gubrium & J. A. Holstein (Eds.), *Handbook of interview research* (pp. 203–219). Thousand Oaks, CA: Sage.

Schwandt, T. A. (1994). Constructivist, interpretivist approaches to human inquiry. In N. K. Denzin & Y. S. Lincoln (Eds.), *Handbook of qualitative research* (pp. 118–137). Thousand Oaks, CA: Sage.

Seale, C. (1999). *The quality of qualitative research*. London: Sage.

Seidman, I. E. (1998). *Interviewing as qualitative research: A guide for researchers in education and the social sciences* (2nd ed.). New York: Teachers College Press.

Shilling, C. (1993). *The body and social theory*. London: Sage.

Silverman, D. (1997). *Discourses of counselling: HIV counselling as social interaction*. London: Sage.

——. (2000). *Doing qualitative research: A practical handbook*. London: Sage.

——. (2001). *Interpreting qualitative data: Methods for analysing talk, text, and interaction.* (2nd ed.). London: Sage.

——. (2004). *Instances or sequences?: Improving the state of the art of qualitative research.* Paper presented at the Qualitative Research Section of the European Sociological Association, Berlin, September.

Smith, D. E. (1987). *The everyday world as problematic: A feminist sociology*. Boston, MA: Northeastern University Press.

——. (1999). *Writing the social: Critique, theory and investigations.* Toronto: University of Toronto Press.

Soulliere, D., Britt, D. W., & Maines, D. R. (2001). Conceptual modeling as a toolbox for grounded theorists. *Sociological Quarterly*, *42*(2), 253–269.

Speedling, E. (1982). *Heart attack: The family response at home and in the hospital*. New York: Tavistock.

Star, S. L. (1989). *Regions of the mind: Brain research and the quest for scientific certainty*. Palo Alto, CA: Stanford University Press.

——. (1999). The ethnography of infrastructure. *American Behavioral Scientist*, *43*, 377–391.

Stark, E. and Filcraft, A. (1983). Social knowledge, social policy, and the abuse of women. In D. Finkelhor, et al. (Eds.), *The dark side of families* (pp. 330–348). Beverly Hills, CA: Sage.

——. (1988). Violence among intimates—An epidemiological review. In V. B. VanHasselt, et al. (Eds.), *Handbook of Family Violence* (pp. 293–317). New York: Plenum Press.

Stephenson, J. S. (1985). *Death, grief, and mourning: Individual and social realities.* New York: Free Press.

Stern, P. N. (1994a). Eroding grounded theory. In J. Morse (Ed.), *Critical issues in qualitative research methods* (pp. 212–223). Thousand Oaks, CA: Sage.

——. (1994b). The grounded theory method: Its uses and processes. In B. G. Glaser (Ed.), *More grounded theory: A reader* (pp. 116–126). Mill Valley, CA: The Sociology Press.

Straus, M. A. (1977). A sociological perspective on the prevention and treatment of wife-beating. In M. Roy (Ed.), *Battered women* (pp. 194–238). New York: Van Nostrand Reinhold.

Straus, M. A., Gelles, R. J., & Steinmetz, S. (1980). *Behind closed doors.* Garden City, NY: Doubleday.

Strauss, A. L. (1959). *Mirrors and masks.* Mill Valley, CA: The Sociology Press.

——. (1978a). A social worlds perspective. *Studies in Symbolic Interaction, 1,* 119–128.

——. (1978b). *Negotiations: Varieties, contexts, processes and social order.* San Francisco: Jossey Bass.

——. (1987). *Qualitative analysis for social scientists.* New York: Cambridge University Press.

——. (1993). *Continual permutations of action.* New York: Aldine de Gruyter.

——. (1995). Notes on the nature and development of general theories. *Qualitative Inquiry, 1,* 7–18.

Strauss, A., & Corbin, J. (1990). *Basics of qualitative research: Grounded theory procedures and techniques.* Newbury Park, CA: Sage.

——. (1994). Grounded theory methodology: An overview. In N. K. Denzin & Y. S. Lincoln (Eds.), *Handbook of qualitative research* (pp. 273–285). Thousand Oaks, CA: Sage.

——. (1998). Basics of qualitative research: *Grounded theory procedures and techniques* (2nd ed.). Thousand Oaks, CA: Sage.

Strauss, A. L., & Glaser, B. G. (1970). *Anguish.* Mill Valley, CA: The Sociology Press.

Strauss, A. L., Schatzman, L., Bucher, R., Ehrlich, D., & Sabshin, M. (1963). The hospital and its negotiated order. In E. Friedson (Ed.), *The hospital in modern society* (pp. 147–168). Glencoe, IL: Free Press.

Thomas, J. (1993). *Doing critical ethnography.* Newbury Park, CA: Sage.

Thorne, S. E. (2001). The implications of disciplinary agenda on quality criteria for qualitative research. In J. M. Morse, J. M. Swanson, & A. Kuzel (Eds.), *The nature of qualitative evidence* (pp. 141–159). Thousand Oaks, CA: Sage.

Thorne, S., Jensen, L., Kearney, M.H., Noblit, G., & Sandelowski, M. (2004). Qualitative metasynthesis: Reflections on methodological orientation and ideological agenda. *Qualitative Health Research, 14,* 1342–1365.

Thulesius, H., Håkansson, A., & Petersson, K. (2003). Balancing: A basic process in the end-of-life care. *Qualitative Health Research, 13,* 1357–1377.

Timmermans, S. (1999). *Sudden death and the myth of CPR.* Philadelphia, PA: Temple University Press.

Turner, B. S. (1992). *Regulating bodies: Essays in medical sociology.* London: Routledge.

Tweed, A. E., & Salter, D. P. (2000). A conflict of responsibilities: A grounded theory study of clinical psychologists' experiences of client non-attendance within the British National Health Service. *British Journal of Medical Psychology, 73,* 465–481.

Urquhart, C. (1998) Exploring analyst-client communication: Using grounded theory techniques to investigate interaction in informal requirements. In A. S., Lee, J., Liebenau, & J. I. DeGross (Eds.), *Information systems and qualitative research* (149–181). London: Chapman & Hall.

——. (2003). Re-grounding grounded theory-or reinforcing old prejudices?: A brief response to Bryant. *Journal of Information Technology Theory and Application, 4*, 43–54.

van den Hoonaard, W. C. (1997). *Working with sensitizing concepts: Analytical field research.* Thousand Oaks, CA: Sage.

Van Maanen, J. (1988). *Tales of the field.* Chicago: University of Chicago Press.

Walker, L. E. (1979). *The battered woman.* New York: Harper & Row.

——. (1989). *Terrifying love.* New York: Harper & Row.

Wiener, C. L. (2000). *The elusive quest: Accountability in hospitals.* New York: Aldine de Gruyter.

Williams, G. (1984). The genesis of chronic illness: Narrative reconstruction. *Sociology of Health & Illness, 6*, 175–200.

Wilson, H. S., & Hutchinson, S. (1991). Triangulation of qualitative methods: Heideggerian hermeneutics and grounded theory. *Qualitative Health Research, 1*, 263–276.

——. (1996). Methodologic mistakes in grounded theory. *Nursing Research, 4*(2), 122–124.

Wuest, J. (2000). Negotiating with helping systems: An example of grounded theory evolving through emergent fit. *Qualitative Health Research, 10*, 51–70.

Zola, I. K. (1982). *Missing pieces: A chronicle of living with a disability.* Philadelphia, PA: Temple University Press.

——. (1991). Bringing our bodies and ourselves back in: Reflections on a past, present, and future 'Medical Sociology.' *Journal of Health and Social Behavior, 32*, 1–16.

Index

Indexed by Caroline Eley